H. (Hezekiah) Harvey

The Church

Its Polity ans Ordinances

H. (Hezekiah) Harvey

The Church
Its Polity ans Ordinances

ISBN/EAN: 9783744660624

Printed in Europe, USA, Canada, Australia, Japan

Cover: Foto ©Lupo / pixelio.de

More available books at **www.hansebooks.com**

THE CHURCH:

ITS POLITY AND ORDINANCES.

BY

H. HARVEY, D.D.,

PROFESSOR IN HAMILTON THEOLOGICAL SEMINARY.

PHILADELPHIA:
AMERICAN BAPTIST PUBLICATION SOCIETY
1420 CHESTNUT STREET.

Entered according to Act of Congress, in the year 1879, by the
AMERICAN BAPTIST PUBLICATION SOCIETY,
In the Office of the Librarian of Congress, at Washington.

WESTCOTT & THOMSON,
Stereotypers and Electrotypers, Philada.

PREFACE.

This volume contains the substance of lectures delivered, through a series of years, to the classes in the Hamilton Theological Seminary. The object of the writer was to place before his pupils the best results of investigation which recent scholarship and thought have reached on these subjects; and for this purpose, in addition to original researches, he has gathered materials from all available sources. In the departments of philology and archæology especially, the progress, as bearing upon the subjects here treated, has of late been marked and important, and of itself justifies a rediscussion of them. Many of the works consulted will be found indicated either in the text or in the foot-notes.

In the discussion of controverted subjects the writer has intended to state with candor and respect the views of Christian brethren who may differ from him; if, in any instance, he has failed in this, it will be to him a matter of sincere regret.

Trusting that the work may aid in elucidating God's word, especially in its teachings relating to the outward institutions of Christianity, it is now sent forth on its mission. H. H.

THEOLOGICAL SEMINARY, HAMILTON, N. Y., Oct. 30, 1879.

CONTENTS.

INTRODUCTION.

THE EXTERNAL INSTITUTIONS OF CHRISTIANITY DIVINELY CONSTITUTED 13

Fundamental Position: The Scriptures the only authority on the constitution and form of the church and the ordinances. Opposing theories stated and examined:

I. Theory of patristic authority stated; argument against: 1. No hint in Scripture of defect in apostles' organization of the church; 2. Diverse forms of the church in Patristic period; 3. This theory less reasonable than that of continued inspiration in the church held by Romanists.

II. Theory of expediency stated; argument against: 1. The Mosaic institutions unchangeable by man; 2. The vital influence of external institutions on doctrine and life; 3. Necessity of a divine form in order to certain obedience; 4. The Christian institutions actually ordained by Christ; 5. The apostles expressly inspired to complete the organization of Christianity; 6. The organization thus completed final, because no subsequent authority competent to alter or abolish it.

PART I.

CHURCH POLITY.

SECTION I.

RELATION OF THE CHURCH TO THE KINGDOM OF CHRIST 21

I. Kingdom of Christ future in Old Testament period, but established at his ascension.

II. Extent of his reign: (1.) Over the universe; (2.) Within each redeemed soul; (3.) Over each individual church.

III. Subjects of his kingdom distinguished: (1.) By a regenerate character and life; (2.) By vow of allegiance in baptism.

IV. The church the visible form of this kingdom and the divine organization for its establishment.

CONTENTS.

SECTION II.

MEANING OF THE WORD CHURCH.. 25

I. Usage of *ecclesia* in the classics.
II. Its usage in the Septuagint.
III. Its usage in New Testament: 1. The local church; 2. The invisible church.

SECTION III.

MEMBERSHIP OF THE CHURCH... 29

I. It is composed only of those who give credible evidence of faith in Christ, or experimental religion. Objections stated and considered.
II. It is composed only of those baptized on personal profession of faith.
III. Membership involves personal obligation to promote the objects of the church as expressed in the covenant. These objects three: 1. Social united worship; 2. Perpetuation and diffusion of the gospel; 3. Sanctification of its own members.

SECTION IV.

ORGANIZATION OF THE CHURCH....................................... 38

Three forms, Episcopal, Presbyterian, and Congregational: Proof that the Congregational is scriptural from following vital powers committed in Scripture to the congregation:
I. The power of receiving, disciplining, and excluding its own members.
II. The power of electing its own officers.
III. The power of deciding all other matters not already determined by Scripture.

SECTION V.

RELATION OF THE CHURCH TO ITS MEMBERS..................... 43

I. Rights and duties of a church.
II. Rights and duties of a member.

SECTION VI.

EXTERNAL RELATIONS OF THE CHURCH............................. 47

I. Each church is complete in itself; its decisions are subject to revisal by no ecclesiastical tribunal on earth. Objections stated and examined.
II. Each church, though independent of all ecclesiastical authority on earth, is accountable to Christ as its sovereign Head.

CONTENTS. 7

III. Churches are interdependent; every church, therefore, has relations and duties to other churches.
IV. The community of churches, so far as the character and acts of any individual church affect their common name and welfare, have certain rights and duties in relation to such church.
V. The external relations of churches are maintained through Associations, Councils, and Benevolent Societies; nature and constitution of these bodies examined.
VI. The church is in things temporal subject to the state, but in things spiritual independent of it, and subject only to Christ.

SECTION VII.

OFFICERS OF THE CHURCH.. 66

FIRST: *Extraordinary Officers.*
I. Temporary officers belonging only to the Apostolic period: 1. The apostles; 2. The prophets.
II. Officers permanently existing, but not essential to the full organization of a church: 1. Evangelists; 2. Teachers and preachers.

SECOND: *Ordinary Officers.*
I. *Pastors.*—1. The terms bishop, presbyter, pastor, designations of one office; 2. The duties of pastors, preaching of the gospel, administration of ordinances, and spiritual oversight of the church; 3. Pastors not a mediating priesthood with sacrificial and absolving powers; 4. The number of pastors in each church not fixed by Scripture; 5. A ruling eldership, as it exists under Presbyterianism, has neither precept nor example in Scripture.
II. *Deacons.*—1. The office permanent in the church; 2. Deacons chosen by the congregation and ordained by the ministry; 3. Their duty is to administer the temporal affairs of the church; 4. Importance of the office indicated by qualifications required; 5. Deacons not, as under episcopacy, a third order of spiritual officers.

SECTION VIII.

ORDINATION OF CHURCH OFFICERS.................................... 82

The scriptural form simple: 1. The ministry alone confer ordination; 2. The co-operation of other churches to be sought; 3. The form is prayer and the laying on of hands; 4. It confers no new internal grace or power.
The theory of apostolic succession stated; arguments against: 1. The sacerdotal powers supposed to be transmitted were not possessed by the apostles; 2. The Scriptures are silent as to the necessity of such a succession; 3. Ordination in Scripture did not, in fact, confer a new grace or power; 4. If such a succession is essential, there is no evidence of a valid ministry on earth; 5. It is incredible that salvation is made dependent on a succession so impossible to prove.

SECTION IX.

CHURCH DISCIPLINE.. 87

  I. The mutual watch-care of the members by encouragement, counsel, admonition, and rebuke.
 II. The adjustment of private personal grievances.
III. The adjustment of differences affecting worldly affairs.
 IV. Procedure in case of public offences, embracing all offences against the faith and life required in a church member. Nature and effect of exclusion. Discipline of a minister; peculiar, in that, 1. An accusation to be received with unusual caution; 2. As a council was had to invest with the ministerial office, it should also be had to divest of it.

SECTION X.

A CHURCH VALID ONLY AS CONFORMED TO GOD'S WORD........ 94

  Summary of principles thus far considered. What constitutes a body of Christians a church?
  I. Not mere historic succession from the apostles.
 II. A church valid only by virtue of conformity, in character, doctrine, and organization, to the constitution given in God's word.

SECTION XI.

HISTORICAL CONFIRMATION.. 97

  The constitution of the church, as here explained, confirmed by highest historical authority; citations from Mosheim, Neander, Gibbon, Archbishop Whately. Testimony of the apostolic and Christian Fathers to this organization of the church; to the popular election of officers; to the authority of the congregation as ultimate in matters of discipline; and to the primitive bishop as a simple pastor of one congregation.

PART II.

THE CHRISTIAN ORDINANCES.

SECTION I.

GENERAL VIEW OF THE ORDINANCES.. 105

  I. The number of the ordinances.
 II. The administration of ordinances.
III. Obligation of the ordinances.
 IV. Efficacy of the ordinances: 1. Symbols, or sensible representations of the vital, essential truths of the gospel; 2. Symbolic acts, in which a profession is made of personal faith in these truths.
  V. Ordinances, in their form and order, not to be changed by man.

CONTENTS.

SECTION II.

THE FORM OF BAPTISM... 118

I. THE CLASSIC USAGE OF BAPTIZO: Definitions of Conant, Anthon, Stuart, Liddell and Scott.
II. SEPTUAGINT USAGE OF BAPTIZO: Examination of Judith xii. 7; Sirach xxxiv. 25.
III. NEW TESTAMENT USAGE OF BAPTIZO: Always used with the fundamental idea of immersion, either literal or figurative. 1. The classic and Septuagint usage requires this sense in the New Testament, unless plain indications show a departure from it. 2. The lexicons of the New Testament, both earlier and later, almost without exception, restrict the meaning of *baptizo* to immersion. 3. The construction in which *baptizo* is found implies the sense of immersion. 4. The passages usually adduced as admitting a different sense do, in fact, require the sense of immersion. Passages examined, Mark vii. 3, 4; Luke xi. 37, 38; Acts ii. 41; Heb. ix. 10. 5. The baptisms of the New Testament, in the circumstances attending them, prove that the ordinance was an immersion. Instances examined: baptisms of John in the Jordan and at Enon; the baptism of Christ; of the eunuch; of the jailer. 6. The figurative usage of *baptizo* requires immersion as the fundamental idea. Passages examined, Luke xii. 50; Matt. xx. 22, 23; Acts i. 5; Rom. vi. 3, 4; 1 Cor. x. 1, 2; 1 Pet. iii. 21. 7. The design of baptism, as an ordinance, indicates immersion as the only form of administration.
IV. THE PATRISTIC USAGE OF BAPTIZO: The form of the act shown by the following: 1. The words and circumstances found in connection with the rite; 2. Those passages in which the force of a comparison or argument depends on an immersion; 3. The general opposition to clinic baptism; 4. The testimony of all reputable historians.
V. SUBSEQUENT USAGE OF CHRISTENDOM: 1. The Greek churches; 2. The Roman Catholic Church; 3. The German and Swiss Reformers; 4. The churches of Great Britain. Result of investigation: Immersion, as the primitive form, the doctrine of a vast majority of Christendom.
VI. BAPTISM AS REPRESENTED IN ANCIENT MONUMENTS AND ART: 1. Baptistories; 2. Mosaics and frescoes; 3. Representations and baptisteries in the catacombs.
VII. OBJECTIONS CONSIDERED: 1. Immersion always inconvenient, often dangerous, and sometimes impossible; 2. Immersion, though the scriptural form, is not essential.
VIII. DR. DALE'S THEORY: BAPTISM NEVER AN IMMERSION: 1. Statement of the theory; 2. Examination of his fundamental positions; 3. Examination of the theory as applied to the New Testament; 4. Examination of the theory as applied to patristic literature.

SECTION III.

THE SUBJECTS OF BAPTISM... 181

Presumption against infant baptism stated: 1. The contradictory grounds on which it is maintained: 2. The absence of precept or certain example in Scripture.

CONTENTS.

FIRST: ARGUMENTS FOR INFANT BAPTISM.

I. *From the covenant of circumcision:* Statement of the argument Reply: 1. The conclusion not contained in the premises; 2. The conclusion disproved by an analysis of the Abrahamic covenant; 3. Baptism not the substitute of circumcision in any such sense as to render the terms of admission to the one also the terms of admission to the other; and this is the only point in question; 4. The Scripture passages commonly adduced for the Abrahamic covenant as a ground of infant baptism furnish a decisive argument against it. Examination of Col. ii. 11, 12; Rom. xi. 16–24.

II. FROM SCRIPTURE PASSAGES: Examination of Matt. xix. 13–15; Acts ii. 38, 39; 1 Cor. vii. 14; Acts xvi. 15, 32–34; 1 Cor. i. 16.

SECOND: ARGUMENTS AGAINST INFANT BAPTISM.

I. *The Scriptures invariably require a personal faith in Christ as a prerequisite to baptism:* 1. The ministerial commission; 2. Apostolic example and teaching.

II. *The character and spirit of the new dispensation requires a spiritual church membership:* The new covenant as contrasted with the Mosaic. Jer. 31: 31–34.

III. *Infant baptism is useless to those who receive it:* Utility conceivable only when regarded as of saving efficacy; but this now rejected by evangelical Christians.

IV. *Infant baptism in itself wrong, and its ultimate results evil:* 1. It is will-worship; 2. It is the perversion of a divine ordinance; 3. Its practical tendency is to a false and fatal dependence on a mere ceremony; 4. Its results, as seen in history, are disastrous to the purity and power of the church of God.

V. *Infant baptism unknown in the first two Christian centuries:* 1. Passages cited (1) from the apostolic Fathers; (2) from the early Christian Fathers. Results: No trace of infant baptism in first two centuries: tendencies to it appearing in North Africa during first half of third century; no evidence of it elsewhere until later period. 2. It was founded on its supposed necessity and efficacy; proof of this. 3. It only slowly spread through the Roman Empire in third, fourth, and fifth centuries. Proofs: (1) From catechumenical system; (2) from the baptism of many Fathers in adult age, though of Christian parentage; (3) from the highest historical testimony.

SECTION IV.

THE DOCTRINE OF THE LORD'S SUPPER.................................... 213

Question of the mode of Christ's presence in the Supper a centre of conflict. Four Theories:

I. *Transubstantiation.* Formulated in ninth century; proclaimed a dogma of Romish Church 1215; the doctrine stated; based on John vi. 53; Matt. xxvi.: 26, 28; shown to be contrary to Scripture and reason.

II. *Consubstantiation.* Zwingle opposes it; formulated by Luther; statement of it.

CONTENTS. 11

III. *The Mystical Presence:* Doctrine as formulated by Calvin; objections to it stated.
IV. The Lord's Supper Symbolic: Statement of doctrine; significance of the ordinance: 1. Symbolizes Christ's death for us; 2. A personal profession of faith; 3. An act of grateful commemoration; 4. A symbol of church-fellowship; 5. Prophetic, as a type of the marriage-supper of the Lamb in heaven.

SECTION V.

QUALIFICATIONS FOR THE LORD'S SUPPER.......................... 222

General recognition, through the Christian ages, of regeneration, baptism, and a consistent life in the church as prerequisites to the Lord's Supper; the presumption, therefore, against unrestricted communion.

I. *The scriptural law of qualification: In the New Testament a credible profession of faith in baptism and a consistent membership in the church are made, both by precept and example, precedent to participation in the Lord's Supper.* This shown, 1. From the baptized position of the first participants and their union as a community with Christ; 2. From the great commission; 3. From the order uniformly observed by the apostles; 4. From the relation of the two ordinances.
II. *This law obligatory on the churches:* 1. The administration of ordinances committed to the churches and ministry; 2. The Supper a symbol of church-fellowship, and, as the church decides in regard to admission to actual fellowship, it ought to decide on admission to the symbol of fellowship: 3. If the candidate is to judge of qualification, then all who choose may come, and the Supper cease to be a symbol of truth.
III. *Restriction at the Lord's Table almost universal:* Christians differ as to what is the church and what is baptism, but not generally as to this restriction of the Supper to the baptized; citations in proof. The difference, therefore, relates to baptism, not to the Supper.
IV. *Objections Considered:* 1. The claim of members in Pædobaptist churches who have been immersed on profession of faith; 2. The sincerity of Pædobaptists as giving right to come to the Table; 3. All Christians expect to commune together in heaven, and therefore should do so on earth; 4. The narrowness and exclusiveness of restriction at the Lord's Table.

V. *Unrestricted Participation of the Supper inexpedient:* Union among different denominations at the Lord's Table has no real advantages, and is attended with manifold evils and inconsistencies: 1. It supplies no widefelt need; 2. It neither secures nor promotes Christian union; 3. It tends to destroy church authority and discipline; 4. It destroys the significance and value of both ordinances; 5. If practised, it is impossible to fix a consistent limit.

INTRODUCTION.

THE EXTERNAL INSTITUTIONS OF CHRISTIANITY DIVINELY CONSTITUTED.

IN the following discussion it is assumed that the outward institutions of the Christian religion are of God, and that, therefore, their form and order as delineated in the New Testament, are of divine obligation. The Bible presents a definite and final constitution of the church, the ordinances, and the ministry, and is on these subjects the sufficient guide and the only authority; no man may set aside, alter, or supplement the divine model there given.

Two classes of objectors, however, assail this position, one affirming the authority of the Fathers, the other the doctrine of expediency.

I. PATRISTIC AUTHORITY.

The first class regard the Christian institutions as existing only in the germ during the Apostolic age, and as receiving complete development in the Patristic period; they accept, therefore, the teachings of the Fathers as on this subject supplementing the teachings of Scripture. The church of the first six centuries, and not the church of the New Testament, is to them the true Church of Christ.

To these we reply: 1. The Scriptures give no intimation of imperfection in the apostolic organization of Christianity; on the contrary, they expressly require conformity to the apostolic model. Thus, Paul, addressing Titus, says (Tit. i. 5): "For this cause left I thee in Crete, that thou shouldst set in order the things that are wanting, and ordain elders in every city, as I had appointed thee." Explicit directions are given respecting the membership, officers, and discipline of the churches, and the ordinances to be administered, with no hint that these are to be supplemented by clearer instructions in after-ages. A gradual development of the Christian institutions is, indeed, apparent during the earlier ministry of the apostles, but there is all evidence that they attained their final constitution before these inspired men passed from earth. 2. The Christian institutions, as represented in the Fathers, were radically different at different periods. The simple parochial churches of the second century, for example, each complete in itself, and organized with its chosen bishop, presbyters, and deacons, were utterly unlike the great world-organization called the Church in the fifth century, with its hierarchy of metropolitan, diocesan bishops, and multitudinous priestly officials modelled in constitution after the Roman Empire; and the difference was so fundamental, in principle and form, that the former cannot be conceived as the divine germ from which the latter was normally developed. An appeal to the Fathers, therefore, would leave us in utter uncertainty as to what is the true church. 3. Besides, if the authority of men later than the apostles is to decide the form of the Christian institutions, we cannot logically stop with the Patristic period, but must, in that case, accept the Romish doctrine of a continued inspiration in the church, which through all ages supplements the Bible by defining and perfecting its statements of doctrine and duty. For the restriction of the alleged process of development to that earlier period rests upon no adequate reason; on the contrary, if such a development were designed, it would be far more natural to think that it would continue to the end of the world.

Plainly, this theory of development, by its denial of the sufficiency of Scripture, subverts the fundamental principle of Protestantism, and, while logically less coherent than Romanism, involves, by necessary sequence, all the pernicious results of the papal departure from the infallible authority of God's word to the fallible authority of man. Indeed, Patristic Ecclesiasticism, has no logical place among Protestants. It gravitates by natural and necessary laws to Roman Catholicism, and not a few of the ablest minds in the Episcopal body, especially in the Anglican communion, are therefore passing into the older and more consistent church.

II. The Doctrine of Expediency.

The other class insists that there is no divinely-required form of the Christian institutions, this being a matter of expediency, to be determined by men according to the ever-changing conditions and needs of human society. Neander, speaking of the New Testament church, says: The apostles "gave the church this particular organization, which, while it was best adapted to the circumstances and relations of the church at that time, was also best suited to the extension of the churches in their peculiar condition, and for the development of the inward principles of their communion. But forms may change with every change of circumstances. Whenever, at a later period, any form of church government has arisen out of a series of events according to the direction of divine providence, and is organized and governed with regard to the Lord's will, he may be said himself to have established it and to operate through it by his Spirit." Thus, in substance, Stillingfleet and Whately, and, in the present day, many popular leaders of religious thought. According to these, all the different forms of the church and of the ordinances are equally valid, provided they are adapted to the age and circumstances in which they exist. Expediency is the only criterion of validity.

The following considerations, however, seem to me conclusive against this doctrine:

1. The Mosaic institutions were established after a divine model, and might not be changed by the fallible judgment of man. The reason of this is found in their character as symbols of divine truth. The whole ancient ritual was a visible revelation of God's thoughts, and he only could direct the form of their expression. Men, ignorant of the truths to be expressed, could not originate these symbols nor could they change them without also changing the ideas symbolized. Hence, God himself instituted the forms, and made them unchangeable by man. Now, the Christian institutions, like the Mosaic, are a visible expression of divine truth; and a change in their form by man must needs impair or pervert their power as symbols of God's thought. All the reasons which forbade man to change the form of the ancient institutions also exist to forbid a change in the Christian. Indeed, the higher significance of Christianity would imply that the forms in which it finds expression are of higher importance and "obligation," and should be held even more sacred from human mutilation or change.

2. Reason and history alike show that the outward institutions of the gospel exert a vital influence on doctrine and life; it is not credible, therefore, that their constitution and form are left to the fallible wisdom

of man. The influence which the form of civil government exerts on the sentiments and life of a nation is one of the plainest teachings of history; it is a silent, everywhere-present power, moulding the opinions and character of a people. It is a significant fact that in the primitive churches the earliest departure from the gospel was not in the false statement of doctrine, but in the perversion of church government and ordinances. Sacerdotalism and sacramentalism led the way to the later corruption of Christianity in its doctrinal form.

3. These institutions must needs have in the New Testament some distinguishing characteristics clearly defining them; otherwise, the duties enjoined in connection with them can never be certainly performed. If the Scriptures do not define what a church is, how can a believer know whether he is a member of a church? If they do not make plain what baptism is, how can he be certain that he has been baptized? The duties required necessarily imply a divinely-revealed form of the church and the ordinances; otherwise, God would have imposed solemn obligations on men, but left them no means of knowing how to perform them. Indeed, the common sense of Christendom recognizes here the necessity of divine direction and the authority of apostolic example; for all parties, in the last resort, seek to maintain the validity of their organizations and ordinances by an appeal to the New Testament.

4. It is plain that Christ himself instituted the church and the ordinances and gave them a definite form; for, in giving directions respecting the discipline of an offending brother, he requires as the final step: "Tell it unto the church: but if he neglect to hear the church, let him be unto thee as an heathen man and a publican" (Matt. xviii. 17). Here the church is spoken of as an insti-

tution well understood by the apostles, which necessarily presupposes that it had been either already established by Christ or clearly defined by him. The ordinances of Baptism and the Lord's Supper were both expressly appointed by him, the form of the one being distinctly defined alike by the term employed and by his own example, and of the other by his personal administration of it. There is every reason for believing that the institutions of the gospel, thus appointed by its Founder, were established by the apostles according to the constitution and order which he prescribed; and the example of the apostles, therefore, carries with it the authority of Christ.

5. The apostles were expressly inspired for the full establishment of the Christian institutions. Christ said to them, "Verily I say unto you, Whatsoever ye shall bind on earth shall be bound in heaven, and whatsoever ye shall loose on earth shall be loosed in heaven" (Matt. xviii. 18), where, as is evident from the context, he refers to the order and government of the church. This promise, with others scarcely less explicit, assured to them divine guidance and sanction in their official acts in the outward organization of Christianity; and their example, therefore, in these acts has for us all the binding authority of divine law. The apostles did in fact establish these institutions with a definite form. They everywhere required, as a condition of church membership, the same spiritual character and the same general duties. They ordained the same officers in every church (Acts xiv. 23; Phil. i. 1; 1 Tim. iii. 1–15). They instituted in all places the same ordinances (Rom. vi. 3; 1 Cor. xi. 2, 20–34). Their assistants also were directed to constitute churches and establish ordinances in accordance with the apostolic form. The Epistles to Timothy and Titus are filled with direc-

tions in regard to the constitution and order of "the house of God, which is the church of the living God, the pillar and ground of the truth" (1 Tim. iii. 1–15; Tit. i. 5). Indeed, the large space which is given in the New Testament to instruction in regard to these outward institutions, while it emphasizes their importance, also demonstrates the permanence of their form; for, while in a few instances these directions refer to usages purely local and transient, the main body of them are manifestly permanent as Christianity, and are given for all time and all the world. The whole tenor of Scripture makes it plain that the church and the ordinances had in the Apostolic age a well-defined form and order, for everywhere they are referred to as definite and well understood and as established by apostolic authority.

True, there is in the Bible no formulated statement of the ecclesiastical constitution, but so also there is no formal scientific statement of a system of Christian doctrines; yet, as the latter fact does not prove that the Bible contains no system of divine truth; so neither does the former, that it has no definite ecclesiastical constitution. Plainly, in revelation as in nature God has set forth manifold facts and principles, and as a means of mental and spiritual development has made it obligatory on men, by careful investigation and comparison of these, to evolve from them the system of truth and the ecclesiastical constitution he has ordained. And if, as has been shown, the apostles, in establishing these institutions, acted under the guidance of the infallible Spirit, it necessarily follows that their example, when clearly ascertained, has all the force of a divine precept and is obligatory as a divine law. It follows also that the ecclesiastical constitution of the New Testament, being divinely established, remains through all ages as alone valid, there being no inspired authority, subsequent to the apostles, competent to alter or abolish it.

The Bible, therefore, is the all-sufficient guide and the only authority in respect to the outward institutions of Christianity. Whatever principles it inculcates, whatever forms it establishes, as pertaining to these institutions, are of solemn obligation. No man has the right to disregard or alter or abolish them; every such assumption is an invasion of the prerogatives of God.

THE CHURCH.

PART I.
CHURCH POLITY.

SECTION I.
THE CHURCH: ITS RELATION TO THE KINGDOM OF CHRIST.

MAN was excluded from the kingdom of God at his expulsion from Paradise: his restoration to that kingdom has been the grand end of all God's subsequent dispensations. This restoration, according to the divine plan, was to be accomplished through a mediatorial kingdom, of which the God-man Jesus Christ should be King. Under this kingdom of the Mediator the universe should no longer be governed immediately by God, but mediately through the God-man, all power in heaven and in earth being given unto him. The special end of his reign should be the accomplishment of human redemption, for which, under his sway, all the resources of the universe will be employed. When this end shall have been attained the mediatorial reign will cease and the sovereignty of the universe will revert to God; when the Son, having "put all enemies under his feet," " shall have delivered up the kingdom to God, even the Father," that thenceforth "God may be all in all."

I. In the Old Testament period this kingdom appears as future, the grand hope of the world, toward which the longing desire of all true souls is directed; and its outlines are adumbrated in type and prophecy. In type, it found clearest expression in the ancient theocracy especially in the kingdom of David, of which the invisible Jehovah was the true and ever-living King; and hence, in the later language of the Old Testament, the throne and sceptre of David often designate the reign of the Messianic King; and the triumphs of David, the triumphs of this coming and mightier Monarch. In prophecy, this kingdom is more clearly revealed. Its king shall be the God-man. He is the child of the race; yet "his name shall be called Wonderful, Counsellor, The mighty God, The everlasting Father, The Prince of Peace" (Isa. ix. 6, 7). "All people, nations, and languages shall serve him: his dominion is an everlasting dominion, which shall not pass away, and his kingdom that which shall not be destroyed" (Dan. vii. 13, 14). His reign shall fill the world with righteousness and peace and happiness (Isa. xi. 1-9). Bethlehem is indicated as the place of his birth (Micah v. 2), and the time of his coming shall be at the end of seventy weeks of years from the rebuilding of the walls of Jerusalem after the Captivity (Dan. ix. 23-27). And as the ages advance, all the lines of history, alike in Israel and in the heathen world, are seen converging toward this predicted period as the epoch of deliverance for the race.

In the fulness of time Christ the King appeared; and his kingdom, after his earthly humiliation and suffering, was fully inaugurated at his ascension, when he was enthroned in heaven. God "set him at his own right hand in the heavenly places, far above all principality and might and dominion, and every name that is named, not only in this world, but also in that which is to come: and put all things under his feet, and gave him to be head over all things to the church, which is his body, the fulness of him that filleth all in all" (Eph. i. 20-23).

II. The kingdom of Christ "is not of this world:" it has no visible, earthly throne, no great outward earthly organization; yet it is absolutely universal and all-comprehending, since to him is given "*all* power in heaven and in earth." Hence the dominion of the God-man appears in Scripture under several aspects: 1. He reigns as mediatorial King on the throne of the universe, swaying the sceptre of universal dominion. All the powers of the spiritual world, "thrones and dominions, principalities and powers," are under him and execute his behests. All the forces of the material universe, throughout immensity, are subject to his control. He is "King of kings and Lord of lords," "the Prince of the kings of the earth," ruling with absolute power among the nations of the world. And over this mighty realm he reigns as "Head over all things to the church," controlling the infinite resources of the universe for the accomplishment of the work of redemption. 2. He reigns in the invisible, spiritual church, enthroned, as the supreme object of love and homage, within all redeemed souls in heaven and on earth. A free and joyous submission of the will to this invisible Sovereign and faith in him are the initial acts in every Christian life, and loyalty to him becomes the mightiest principle in the soul—a bond binding each believer in eternal allegiance to Christ. The throne of Christ is the spiritual magnet of the universe, toward which all true souls, in every power of their being, are drawn with irresistible attraction. And the effect of his reign within their hearts is "righteousness, and peace, and joy in the Holy Ghost" (Rom. xiv. 17). 3. He reigns in each visible, earthly church as its sole Lawgiver and Head. All its powers are derived from him. "When he ascended up on high, he gave some, apostles; and some, prophets; and some, evangelists; and some, pastors and teachers, for the perfecting of the saints, for the work of the ministry, for the edifying of the body of Christ" (Eph. iv. 8–13). And as of old the revelator saw him, in glorious form, "walking amidst the seven golden candlesticks," so, through all the ages, Christ rules among the churches on earth, their Head and sovereign Lord, his word their only guide, his will their only law.

III. The subjects of Christ's kingdom are visibly distinguished: 1. *By their character.* They possess a new spiritual life; for "except a man be born again he cannot see the kingdom of God." They have "passed from death unto life," and "have been translated from the kingdom of darkness into the kingdom of God's dear Son." They exercise the holy affections which flow from this new life—"love, joy, peace, long-suffering, gentleness, goodness, faith, meekness, temperance." In heart and life they are loyal to the will of Christ. 2. *By their baptism,* the formal, outward symbol in which they avow their allegiance to Christ. Jesus said, "Except a man be born of water, and of the Spirit, he cannot enter into the kingdom of God" (John iii. 5); "He that believeth and is baptized shall be saved" (Mark xvi. 16). Baptism is the initial, public act of submission to him, the *sacramentum,* or oath of fealty to his kingdom; and hence this ordinance, which is commonly initiatory to the church, was administered to a believer, even where there was no local church, as the symbol of submission to the heavenly King (Acts viii. 26–40).

The church is the visible, earthly form of the kingdom

of Christ, and is the divine organization appointed for its advancement and triumph. Organized and governed by the laws of the invisible King, and composed of the subjects of the heavenly kingdom, who, by the symbol of fealty, have publicly professed allegiance to him, the church fitly represents that kingdom. Hence the apostles, in receiving authority to establish, under divine inspiration, the form and order of the church, received "the keys of the kingdom of heaven." Wherever they gathered disciples they organized a church; and at their death they left this as the distinctive and only visible form of the kingdom of Christ on earth. Thus divinely constituted and inspired, the church is God's organization, in which the Holy Spirit dwells, and from which divine, spiritual forces go forth to transform the world from sin to holiness and subject it to the sway of Christ. "The gates of hell shall not prevail against it;" but through it, as the medium of God's power, the grand visions of ancient prophecy, predicting the triumphs of the Messianic kingdom, shall find realization in human history.

SECTION II.

THE CHURCH: MEANING OF THE WORD.

Ekklesia, translated *church*, is derived from *ek-kaleo*, a verb signifying *to call forth;* hence it denotes an assembly summoned or called out, a select body separated from the mass of the people. Its usage may be traced as follows:

I. THE CLASSIC USAGE.

It is defined by Liddell and Scott "An assembly of the citizens summoned by the crier; the legislative assembly."

Cremer says it is "The common term for a meeting of the *eklectoi*, assembled to discuss the affairs of a free state." According to Trench, "*Ekklesia*, as all know, was the lawful assembly in a free Greek city of all those possessed of the right of citizenship for the transaction of public affairs. That they were *summoned* is expressed in the latter part of the word; that they were summoned *out of* the whole population, a select portion of it, neither the populace, nor yet strangers, nor those who had forfeited their civil rights,—this is expressed in the first. Both the *calling* and the calling *out* are moments to be remembered when the word is assumed into a higher Christian sense; for in them the chief part of its adaptation to its more august use lies." The word does not denote, except in rare figurative usage, a miscellaneous, unofficial assembly.

11. Usage of the Septuagint.

In the Greek version of the Old Testament *ekklesia* is the usual rendering of *kahal*, which, according to Vitringa, denotes "The entire multitude of any people united by the bonds of a society, and constituting a certain republic or state." Gesenius defines, as its ordinary meaning, "An assembly, a convocation of the people of Israel." Thus, Moses said, "An Ammonite or Moabite shall not enter into the *ekklesia* of the Lord;" and David declares, "My praise shall be of thee in the great *ekklesia*, my vows will I pay in the presence of all them that fear him,". where the word designates "the congregation of the Lord," composed only of Israelites qualified to act as the Lord's people, and to participate in the worship of his sanctuary. It excluded the uncircumcised, the unclean, and "the mixed multitude." The same restriction is evident in the use of *ekklesia* in the New Testament when it refers to ancient Israel as "the congregation of the Lord" (Acts vii. 38; Heb. ii. 12).

III. THE CHRISTIAN USAGE.

Ekklesia is used in the New Testament one hundred and fifteen times. Of these instances, two relate to the Hebrew "congregation of the Lord," three to the Greek assembly, and one hundred and ten to the Christian church.

1. Its ordinary use in the New Testament is to designate a specific, local assembly of Christians, organized for the maintenance of the worship, the doctrines, the ordinances, and the discipline of the gospel, and united, under special covenant, with Christ and with one another; as, "the church at Jerusalem," "the churches of Galatia." The word occurs in this local sense in ninety-two instances.

2. It denotes the entire body of the elect in heaven and on earth—all who are embraced in the covenant of grace and who shall be gathered into the everlasting kingdom of Christ. Here the word is used figuratively, the name of a part designating the whole; and all redeemed souls are conceived as forming one grand assembly. Thus, Paul said, "Husbands, love your wives, even as Christ loved the church and gave himself for it, that he might sanctify and cleanse it with the washing of water by the word, that he might present it to himself a glorious church, not having spot or wrinkle or any such thing, but that it should be holy and without blemish" (Eph. v. 25–27). Here the church is conceived as the bride of Christ, the Lamb's wife, but not as the local church, for in this case innumerable brides will be presented to Christ at last— an image wholly incongruous. Plainly, the whole body of Christ's redeemed is meant, conceived as when at last,

fully perfected, they shall be gathered in one glorious assembly and presented to him—an image eminently natural and beautiful. Thus, also, where Christ is declared to be "Head over all things to the church, which is his body, the fulness of him that filleth all in all," the language can hardly be applied to any one local church; but when spoken of the whole multitude of the redeemed, conceived as one body, it conveys a natural and adequate sense. Probably it is to be interpreted in this way also in Eph. iii. 10, 21; Col. i. 18, 24; Heb. xii. 23, and kindred passages. In Acts ix. 31, *ekklesia*, according to the best manuscripts, is to be read in the singular: "Then had the *church* rest throughout all Judea and Galilee and Samaria," where it would seem to designate the whole body of Christians in these regions, considered as forming a part of this universal church of Christ, "the whole family in heaven and earth."

Ekklesia, therefore, as used in this second sense, designates the invisible church, so called because it has no visible, earthly organization. Its predicates, as indicated in Scripture, are unity, sanctity, catholicity, and perpetuity—unity, because all its members are united by a living faith to its one Head, and thus constitute his body; sanctity, because all are renewed, sanctified, and inhabited by the one Holy Spirit; catholicity, because all, though separated in time and space, are embraced within the one fold; and perpetuity, because the existence and glory of this church shall continue, world without end.

The following uses of the word *church*, though now common, are not found in the New Testament *ekklesia:*
1. *As the designation of a universal visible church.* No officers of such a church are designated, for the apostles' office was plainly temporary, and expired with them. No provision is made for the assembling of such a church,

either actual or representative. No laws, ordinances, or discipline are given for such a church. All the elements, therefore, of such a body are wanting, nor is there any intimation of its existence. 2. *As the designation of a national or denominational church.* Different churches are expressly mentioned as existing in the same nation or district; as, "the churches of Judea," "the churches of Macedonia," "the churches of Galatia," "the seven churches of Asia." We read nothing respecting a "diocese," a "synod," a "conference," where many separate congregations compose one church; yet, had such been the apostolic organization of Christianity, we must have read of "the church of Judea," "the church of Macedonia," "the church of Galatia." Plainly, *ekklesia* has nothing corresponding to "the Protestant Episcopal Church," "the Methodist Episcopal Church," "the Presbyterian Church," when these titles designate a great national or district organization including in itself many distinct local congregations. Everywhere in Scripture a visible church is a local body.

SECTION III.

THE CHURCH: ITS MEMBERSHIP.

A CHURCH IS A CONGREGATION OF BELIEVERS IN CHRIST, BAPTIZED ON A CREDIBLE PROFESSION OF FAITH, AND VOLUNTARILY ASSOCIATED UNDER SPECIAL COVENANT FOR THE MAINTENANCE OF THE WORSHIP, THE TRUTHS, THE ORDINANCES, AND THE DISCIPLINE OF THE GOSPEL. This proposition involves three points:

I. IT IS COMPOSED ONLY OF THOSE WHO GIVE CREDIBLE EVIDENCE OF FAITH IN CHRIST, OR EXPERIMENTAL RELIGION. The unit in the church is a regenerate soul in living union with Christ, and the church itself is an assemblage of such souls, attracted to each other by the spiritual affinities of the new life each has received, and by the common bond which binds them to the Lord. Jesus said, "Except a man be born again, he cannot see the kingdom of God;" and a new spiritual birth was thus made for all ages the fundamental condition of membership in the Christian church. This is also shown by the following proofs: 1. The first church was composed only of such persons. The "one hundred and twenty" who "continued with one accord in prayer and supplication," awaiting the descent of the Holy Spirit, were "disciples." At the Pentecost only those "who gladly received the word," "such as should be saved," were "added to the church," and the body is described as "the multitude of them that believed." 2. The churches are always addressed as thus composed. The members of the church in Rome were "beloved of God, called to be saints," and their "faith was spoken of throughout the whole world." The Ephesian church was addressed as "the saints which are at Ephesus and the faithful in Christ Jesus." This is the habitual language of the apostles in addressing churches. No passage occurs in which members of a church are otherwise characterized, except when unfitness for membership is implied. 3. A marked contrast in spiritual character is everywhere drawn between the church and the world. Paul says of the Roman church, "God be thanked that ye were the servants of sin, but ye have obeyed from the heart that form of doctrine which was delivered unto you. Being, then, made free from sin, ye became the servants of righteousness" (Rom. vi. 17, 18). To the Ephesian church he says, "You hath he quickened who were dead in trespasses and sins" (Eph. ii. 1). And John, whose Epistles everywhere emphasize this distinction between the church and the world, says, "We know that we are of God, and the whole world lieth in wickedness" (1 John v. 19). 4. The churches are expressly required to withdraw themselves from those whose character furnishes no evidence of vital religion; it cannot, therefore, be right to admit them. The apostolic injunction is: "Withdraw yourselves from every brother that walketh disorderly." 5. The spiritual duties and exercises everywhere required of church members, such as faith, love, joy, hope, presuppose that they are regenerated persons, as also do the relations they sustain as "the children of God," "heirs of God and joint-heirs with Jesus Christ," "the light of the world," and "the salt of the earth." Clearly, such duties and relations imply experimental religion as the basis of church membership.

This position, however, is widely denied. The papal church, modelled after the Mosaic commonwealth, insists that all who are born within her pale are members, and this as a birthright, wholly irrespective of character. In state-churches, where, as in Prussia, civil privileges depend on membership in the Establishment, all citizens are entitled to the privileges of the church. The Presbyterian standards define the visible church as consisting of "all those who profess the true religion, with their children;" and on the reception of adults, though requiring "a credible profession of faith," they deny the right of the church to require evidence of regeneration. If the applicant possesses competent knowledge and good moral character, his profession of faith is to be deemed "credible;" and as to the fact of his regeneration, Dr. Hodge says, "No judgment is expressed or implied in receiving any one into the church." He affirms that "the church is not called upon to express a judgment as to the real piety of applicants for membership," and argues that all attempts to judge of the spiritual state of such are an invasion of the divine prerogatives.* The Episcopal Church, in like manner, receives to membership without an examination as to spiritual character, requiring only a profession of faith rendered credible by adequate knowledge and a moral life.

The principal objections against requiring evidence of regeneration as a condition of church membership are the following: 1. It is said the church is represented in Scripture as composed of saints and sinners intermingled. Thus the kingdom of heaven is compared to a field in which good seed was sown, but tares also sprang up; and to a net which gathered of every sort. The separation was not to be made till the last day. To this we reply: It is evident that in these parables the Lord is describing, not the terms of admission to his church, but the inevitably mixed character of his professed people on earth. Bad men would creep in among them, notwithstanding all precautions. The devil would sow tares among the wheat. But, surely, satanic example in this ought not to be adduced as a divine warrant for introducing unconverted men into the church of Christ. 2. It is also said: Man, being incompetent to read the heart, cannot discriminate between the true and the false Christian. This is the prerogative only of Omniscience. A simple assent, therefore, to the doctrines and rules of the gospel is to be accepted as sufficient, unless the life is openly scandalous. We answer: All admit that certain criteria of regeneration are clearly given in Scripture—characteristics and dispositions in which the new birth manifests itself. The church is, indeed, not infallible, and often mistakes in judging spiritual character; but, these criteria having been recorded,

* *Theology*, vol. iii. pp. 545-548, 576-579.

fidelity to Christ, to her own purity, and to the souls of men evidently requires her to apply these divinely-given tests to those who seek admission. 3. It is further objected: In all the recorded instances in the New Testament, admission to the church was without examination, on a simple profession of faith. This objection, however, if valid, would equally prove the duty to admit without inquiry as to moral character, for no example of this is given. Plainly, the churches of the New Testament ascertained in some way the faith and character of those who applied, though it may not always have been, as now in our churches, by a full and extended examination of the experience and life. It was the age of the miraculous manifestation of the Holy Spirit, who attested the new spiritual life of the believer by the bestowal of *charisms*, or miraculous gifts. It was on this ground Peter justified his recognition of the spiritual character of Cornelius and those in his house; and these *charisms* were evidently the common attestations of the Spirit's work in the Apostolic period (Acts xi. 15–17; xix. 6; Gal. iii. 2; Eph. i. 13, 14). Then, also, a profession of Christ often imperilled social position, property, and even life itself, and the act of profession, under such circumstances, might ordinarily be in itself strong proof of spiritual character. But in the reversed circumstances of our age, the church, having no such means of ascertaining character, must needs adopt such method as may seem best fitted for that end. Probably no one method would everywhere be alike effectual; but the relation of the experience before the whole body of disciples, coupled with other inquiries carefully conducted, would certainly seem a reasonable course. 4. The objection is also made " that all attempts to make a church consisting exclusively of the regenerate have failed. So far as known, no such church has ever existed. This of itself is proof that its existence did not enter into the purpose of God."* But we reply: In like manner, there is no perfectly holy Christian on earth, for "there is no man that sinneth not;" and "if we say we have no sin, we deceive ourselves." But would any reasonable person argue from this universal failure to attain perfect holiness that God has not required holiness, and that the Christian need not seek it? Plainly, the church on earth is fallible: it sometimes errs in judging character. In spite of all precautions unworthy men will find admission, and possibly no church exists which, as seen by the omniscient Eye, does not contain unregenerate souls. But, surely, this fact does not argue that the church is to use no precaution, and to admit to its bosom all comers with no examination in respect to regeneration—that vital spiritual change which constitutes the chief point and fontal source of distinction between the church and the world. And however imperfect the realization of a purely regenerate church has been, and must be, on earth, it remains true that those churches in which evidence of regeneration has been required, have, as a rule, approximated most nearly to purity in faith and life.

II. A CHURCH IS COMPOSED ONLY OF THOSE WHO HAVE BEEN BAPTIZED ON A PERSONAL PROFESSION OF FAITH. The following considerations make this evident: 1. The apostolic commission requires the ministry first to disciple, and then to baptize (Matt. xxviii. 19). This order—discipleship, and then baptism—is here definitely prescribed, and is of divine authority. 2. In the Scriptures baptism is the first public act of a believer, and is ordinarily initiatory to the church. At the Pentecost they first "gladly received the word," and were then baptized and added to the church (Acts ii. 41). In Samaria," when they believed

* Hodge's *Theology*, vol. iii., p. 548.

ITS POLITY. 35

Philip preaching the things concerning the kingdom of God and the name of Jesus Christ, they were baptized, both men and women" (Acts viii. 12). This was the uniform practice in admitting to the church. 3. The churches are addressed as composed only of baptized persons. Thus, Paul bases one of the main arguments in his Epistle to the Roman church on the fact of their symbolic burial and resurrection with Christ in baptism; and Peter, in writing to the churches, in like manner indicates the universality of baptism (Rom. vi. 1–14; 1 Pet. iii. 21).

It being thus evident that baptism is a ceremonial qualification for admission to the church, the question arises, Who shall judge of the fact of baptism, whether in any particular case the ordinance has been truly administered? We answer: The church must judge, and not the candidate only; for the responsibility of admission is clearly devolved on the church, and it is held accountable for the due observance of the ordinances. Were the decision left with the applicant, some totally different rite might be substituted and the ordinance of Christ be set aside. Besides, it is evidently among the fundamental rights of a church, as of any organization, to judge of the qualifications of those desiring admission.

III. A CHURCH IS COMPOSED ONLY OF THOSE WHO ARE VOLUNTARILY ASSOCIATED, UNDER SPECIAL COVENANT, TO MAINTAIN THE WORSHIP, THE TRUTHS, THE ORDINANCES, AND THE DISCIPLINE OF THE GOSPEL: MEMBERSHIP, THEREFORE, INVOLVES A PERSONAL OBLIGATION TO PROMOTE THE OBJECTS OF THE BODY AS EXPRESSED IN THE COVENANT. These objects are three:

1. *The social, united worship of God.* Hence, adoration, praise, thanksgiving, and prayer constitute a leading feature in its assemblies, as described in Scripture. In-

struction is subservient to worship; its end in the Christian assembly is to inspire devotion. The Puritan conception of the church tends to exalt the sermon at the expense of devotion; the sermon consequently is apt to degenerate into a lecture, and the congregation becomes a mere audience. The Episcopal conception, on the other hand, tends to exalt worship at the expense of the sermon, and to make the service a mere formal ritualism. Undoubtedly, the fundamental idea of the New Testament church service is social, united worship, as inspired by instruction in the truths of the gospel.

2. *The perpetuation and diffusion of the gospel* by the public proclamation of its truths, the observance of its ordinances, and the illustration of its divine purity and power in the holy lives of its confessors. The church is "the pillar and ground of the truth," as divinely appointed to support and proclaim the gospel. For this its ministry are called and qualified by Christ, and its spiritual forces are quickened and developed by the Spirit. It is the divine institution for the conversion of the world.

3. *The sanctification of its own members.* It is a school of instruction and discipline, in which souls are prepared for heaven. The church, thus comprehensive in its scope, looks upward to God, outward upon the needs of a lost world, and inward to the processes of sanctification in the souls of its own members; and the neglect of any one of these grand objects of its organization imperils its whole design.

A church, therefore, is a permanent organization with a definite design and a mutually obligatory compact; and it differs from an ordinary assembly of Christians in that it is organized under a divine constitution and according to a divine model. Otherwise, any Christian organization—as a missionary society—would be a church. The compact naturally consists of a covenant or pledge to maintain together the duties of a church, and of a statement of the fundamental truths of the gospel as received by them.

The covenant and articles of faith should be distinctly expressed in written or printed form, and be accessible to the church and the community. For, 1. Church creeds, while claiming no inherent authority, are a definite statement or interpretation of those truths of the gospel which the church deems fundamental; and in the present conflict of opinion as to the import of Scriptures, it seems the part of frankness and honesty for each church to define its views on fundamental principles. 2. The discipline of a church must be seriously embarrassed without such a statement, as the offender might plead that when he entered the church he had no means of knowing that the views or practices with which he is charged were condemned. 3. The want of a definite creed, in almost all instances, results in an actual departure from the gospel, while it imperils the security of church property. Edifices and endowments, given for the advancement of evangelical religion, have often been perverted to the use of heresy because the intention of the original donors was not clearly defined. 4. A creed is often necessary to vindicate a church from the misconstructions and perversions of its enemies and place its real principles in their true light before the community.

SECTION IV.

THE CHURCH: ITS ORGANIZATION.

Three distinct forms of the church exist, differing from each other in the fundamental principles of their organization: 1. *The Episcopal*, in which the hierarchical idea is dominant, ecclesiastical power belonging to the priesthood in three orders, bishops, priests, and deacons, who constitute a hierarchy or priestly government. To this form belongs the Roman Catholic Church—in which the pope is supreme bishop—the Church of England and the Protestant Episcopal Church of the United States, and the Methodist Episcopal Church; in which last, however, the bishops differ from presbyters, not as a distinct order, but only in function. With all these the chief power resides in the clergy, who constitute a self-perpetuating body, distinct from and virtually independent of the individual local congregation. 2. *The Presbyterian*, in which the reception of members and the discipline are committed to the session, composed of the pastor and elders elected by the congregation; but all ecclesiastical acts are subject to revision before higher church courts, composed of pastors and elders from many other congregations. The church, according to the Presbyterian conception, consists of many distinct congregations assembled representatively, by pastors and elders, in one body, with which body resides all ecclesiastical power. Hence, there is a gradation of courts—the session, elected by the individual congregation; the presbytery, composed of delegates from the several sessions; the synod, a local body composed of delegates from several presbyteries; and the general assembly, composed of delegates from all the presbyteries, and constituting the court of last appeal.

All officers appointed and all acts performed by the individual congregation may be set aside by these higher church authorities. 3. *The Congregational*, in which all ecclesiastical power is exercised by each local church, assembled as a congregation; and the decisions thus made in the individual church are subject to no reversal by any other ecclesiastical body. To this class belong, with slight difference in details of organization, the Independents of England, the Congregational churches of America, and the Baptist churches throughout the world.

THE DIVINE CONSTITUTION OF THE CHURCH CONGREGATIONAL.

The position is here maintained that the constitution of the church, as delineated in the New Testament, is congregational, since the following vital powers of the organization are plainly given to the entire assembly of the church.

I. THE POWER OF RECEIVING, DISCIPLINING, AND EXCLUDING ITS MEMBERS. Christ, in prescribing the treatment of private grievances, directs, as the ultimate step (Matt. xviii. 17): "Tell it unto the church; but if he neglect to hear the church, let him be unto thee as an heathen man and a publican;" and as the term *church* is always elsewhere used to denote the whole assembly of disciples, and not merely the officers, such must be its meaning here. The final appeal, therefore, of the aggrieved party is to the church as a congregation. Paul, in the case of the incestuous man, referred both the exclusion and the restoration to the whole church (1 Cor. v. 1-5; 2 Cor. ii. 4, 5). He directs the Corinthian church, when "gathered together," to "put away from among themselves that wicked person;" and afterward this punishment, "which was inflicted of many," was to be remitted by the same when the offender had repented. Thus, also, he directs the Roman church to "mark them which cause divisions and offences" and "avoid them," and the church at Thessalonica to "withdraw themselves from every brother that walketh disorderly" (Rom. xvi. 17; 2 Thess. iii. 6). The Lord, in the epistles to the seven churches of Asia, clearly holds each church as a whole responsible for its doctrine and discipline; but had these churches been organized Episcopally or Presbyterially, the rebukes for unsound doctrine and life would have been directed to the session or the presbytery or the bench of bishops, and not, as they are, to the congregation. But it is evident that the right of discipline, exclusion, and restoration, thus clearly given to the whole assembly of the church, involves also the right of admission. For no church could rightfully be held responsible for its own character and acts if it did not control the door of entrance.

II. THE POWER OF ELECTING ITS OWN OFFICERS. Several examples of the choice of officers are given in the New Testament, in all of which the election was by the people. 1. The election of the apostle Matthias (Acts i. 15–26). This, whether the choice was by vote or lot, was by the action of the whole body, not by the eleven only; for Luke, when saying "they appointed two," "they prayed," "they gave forth their lots," is clearly speaking of the one hundred and twenty disciples. Indeed, the "lots" may have been ballots, as the verb employed is not the one usually denoting the act of casting lots. 2. The election of the seven (Acts vi. 1–6). The apostles, in directing the appointment of these men, said to "the multitude of the disciples," "Look ye out among you seven men of honest report, full of the Holy Ghost and of wisdom, whom we may appoint over this business." "The whole multitude" then made the election of the seven, and the apostles "prayed and laid their hands on them." The principle of election by the whole body for church officers was thus distinctly fixed in these two earliest and most marked examples, and all the subsequent allusions to the subject are in harmony with this principle. 3. The election of delegates to accompany the apostles (1 Cor. xvi. 3). Thus, the men who should carry the collection for the poor to Jerusalem were to be those "whomsoever the churches shall approve by letters;" and Paul, when afterward alluding to one of them, speaks of him as "chosen of the churches to travel with us with this grace," where the word translated "chosen" in its primary sense signifies to choose by outstretched hands—a sense which, it is probable, was in the New Testament period its usual one. 4. The election of bishops, or elders (Acts xiv. 23). Paul and Barnabas, when retracing their way to Antioch on the first missionary journey, "ordained them elders in every church." Here the word rendered "ordained" is the same as that rendered "chosen" above, denoting primarily to vote with uplifted hands. Alford comments on this: There is "no reason for departing from the usual meaning of electing by show of hands. The apostles may have admitted to ordination those presbyters whom the churches elected." Lange says, "The expression suggests the thought that the apostles may have appointed and superintended a congregational election. And this view is supported by the circumstances related (ch. vi. 2), where the twelve directed that the election of the seven should be held." Thus also Alexander and Barnes, with whom concur nearly all the best commentators. Hackett in dissenting overlooks the fact that the Greek participle has here the causative sense: "Caused them to elect elders in every church." All the early English translations previous to King James's, which was prepared under the influence of prelacy, translate, "Ordained them elders by election in every congregation."

It seems clear, therefore, that the selection of officers by the congregation was the established principle of procedure; in those instances, therefore, where apostles or evangelists are said to ordain elders, the presumption is that, as in the more fully related cases, they ordained men previously selected by the people. Indeed, in a voluntary body, the right to choose its own officers is inherent; unless, therefore, it is expressly ordained otherwise, this right remains in the church; but there is in Scripture neither record nor intimation of a different principle of selection. The idea of a clerical order, as of a self-perpetuating body of ministers outside of and independent of the congregation, is wholly foreign to the New Testament, and belongs to the later Patristic period. The right of the congregation to elect its own ministers, either spontaneously or by nomination of the eldership, was long retained. This is clearly indicated not only in the apostolic and early Fathers, but Cyprian, speaking of the election of Cornelius as Bishop of Rome (A. D. 251), says that he was chosen by the judgment of God and of his Christ through the suffrages of the people who were there present, and the college of pastors or ancient bishops, all good men.* Many of the most prominent bishops, as is well known, were selected by spontaneous choice of the people, such as Athanasius (A. D. 328), Ambrose (374), and Chrysostom (398).

III. THE POWER OF DECIDING ALL OTHER MATTERS NOT ALREADY DETERMINED BY SCRIPTURE. Thus the place and time of its meetings, the order of its worship and business, the frequency and place of celebrating the ordinances, and

* *Ep.* lii. 2, 8.

ITS POLITY. 43

many other necessary things not divinely ordered, are to be determined by the congregation under the general direction (1 Cor. xiv. 40), "Let all things be done decently and in order." This right is inherent in them as a voluntary body, and its exercise is recognized as a duty by the reproofs administered to the whole congregation at Corinth for disorderly conduct at the Lord's Supper (1 Cor. xi.). Indeed, the apostles direct their epistles, not to officers nor to church judicatories, but to the churches as congregations, and thus plainly recognize the right as well as the responsibility of each church as a congregation in regard to the conduct of its affairs.

Now, as the powers thus committed to the church as a congregation constitute the vital functions of a church, it follows that church power resides neither in a hierarchy, nor in an ecclesiastical judicatory, but in the whole assembly of the membership. The organization, therefore, is neither prelatical nor presbyterial, but congregational. It follows, also, that since a church is entrusted with power so grave and responsible, no body of believers should be constituted a church unless it possesses the intellectual capacity, knowledge, and gifts adapted to the wise exercise of such powers; and in the absence of these, the body should not take on it a church organization, but should remain a mission station under the care of some well-organized church.

SECTION V.

THE CHURCH: RELATIONS TO ITS OWN MEMBERS.

The relations between a church and its members are peculiarly solemn, tender, and vital, involving on the part of each the most serious responsibility.

I. Rights and Duties of a Church.

1. Every believer in Christ is under obligation, if Providence permits, to unite with a church, since it is an institution ordained by him and neglect of it is dishonor put on him. As each church has ordinarily its own special field, it is entitled to the membership of all believers who live within its natural boundaries, unless either providential disability prevents a public profession or special reasons exist for membership elsewhere. This right a church may not enforce by discipline or penalties, but it is evidently one which the believer is under obligations to respect. 2. Every member is required to fulfil, to the extent of his ability, the covenant obligations assumed on becoming a member. The church, therefore, is entitled to the duties thus promised, together with his good will, his sympathy, his influence, and such time and means as Providence may enable him to use for its advancement. 3. Each member is a soul entrusted by Christ to the church to protect and develop and prepare for heaven. The church, therefore, is bound to furnish the best possible public instruction in the gospel, to exercise a tender, loving, patient, watch-care over the member, and to use the utmost diligence and effort for his enlightenment, sanctification, and usefulness, with the view to present him at last "perfect in Christ Jesus." 4. When a member falls into immorality or departs from the faith of the church, or otherwise violates or neglects covenant obligations, it is the right as well as the duty of the church to place him under discipline and deal with him according to the laws Christ has given in the New Testament. Upon sufficient proof of guilt, it may admonish him, may for a reasonable time suspend him from church privileges, or may exclude him from the church.

II. Rights and Duties of Members.

1. Every member, while in good standing, is entitled to all the privileges of the church, including attendance on its meetings, the sympathy and watch-care of the members, participation in the Lord's Supper when administered, elegibility, if qualified, to all offices of the church, and an equal voice on all questions before the body, limited only by the biblical law, which restricts the ministerial office to males, and the natural law, which restricts the right of voting to persons of suitable age. Many churches, however, have no rule restricting the right of voting. 2. Any member in good standing is entitled, on application, to a certificate of his church standing or to a letter of dismission, unless it appear that he seeks it for an improper purpose. No letter of dismission, however, can be granted, unless it is, *bona fide*, the intention of the applicant to use such letter in uniting with another church. The letter of dismission is simply a permission given to unite elsewhere, and does not dissolve, or in any respect alter, the relation of the member to the church until he is actually received into another church. It gives him permission to join elsewhere; but he remains in full standing a member, with all rights and duties undiminished and unchanged, until he has actually united with another church. 3. Every member has the right of private judgment. Each church has, indeed, certain clearly-defined principles, either written or implied, which constitute its articles of faith and practice, and a professed belief of which is necessary to membership; and if any member materially dissents from these, it is evident he ought not to retain his membership. But outside of these fundamental principles, on which membership is necessarily conditioned, there is a wide range of subjects which belong exclusively to the individual judgment

and conscience, and in respect to which the church may indeed, and should, have an influence by sound teaching, but may not exercise an authoritative control. Thus, the dress he wears, the books he reads, the social relations he forms, the business he pursues, the politics he adopts,—these and other kindred subjects, so long as in them he contravenes neither sound doctrine nor good morals, are questions to be determined by himself, as lying between the individual conscience and God. In all these the church will exert a potential influence, and by instructing and enlightening the conscience, will elevate and ennoble the individual character and life; but it may not interpose by the exercise of authority. Dr. Francis Wayland remarks: "A church has no right to command, as a duty, a *particular mode* of showing our attachment to Christ, unless he has himself commanded it. . . . They have no right to resolve themselves into a temperance, or an abolition, or a missionary, or a peace, or any other society." Nor can it pledge any member to anything but what he has pledged himself to. "He has united himself to a particular church by promising to obey it in all that Christ has commanded, and in nothing more. In everything else he is perfectly unpledged and uncommitted."[*]

4. A member, when charged with wrong, is to be presumed innocent until by due investigation he has been proved guilty, and is entitled to a full and fair trial, with every opportunity for defence. The only exception to this is in cases of flagrant crime or immorality in which the offence is public and unmistakable, when an immediate exclusion may follow without formal trial.

[*] *Limitations of Human Responsibility*, pp. 134, 144.

SECTION VI.

THE CHURCH: ITS EXTERNAL RELATIONS.

I. EACH CHURCH IS COMPLETE IN ITSELF: ITS DECISIONS ARE SUBJECT TO REVISAL BY NO ECCLESIASTICAL TRIBUNAL ON EARTH.

This position is in itself reasonable. For the word of God, the completed revelation from heaven, is entrusted to each church; and, as a special promise of the Spirit is given to it, none could be better fitted to interpret the will of Christ than the church itself. Jesus said to his church (Matt. xviii. 20), "Where two or three are gathered together in my name, there am I in the midst of them." Besides, each church in the New Testament does in fact appear thus independent. No example or intimation is found of the subordination of a church to organizations outside of itself; but in all the counsels, rebukes, and warnings addressed to churches, each is represented as directly accountable to Christ. The church is required to obey civil magistrates in things not inconsistent with God's word, and is to be in subjection to the spiritual teachers and guides whom by her own election to office she has recognized as called of God to official position. But she is subject to no ecclesiastical control from without: diocesan bishops and higher church judicatories are nowhere found in Scripture.

OBJECTIONS TO INDEPENDENCY CONSIDERED.

1. It is objected that the church at Jerusalem (and other large cities), from the number of Christians there, must have embraced several separate organized congregations, which, however, were under one general organization, and were collectively called "the church at

Jerusalem;" such an organization must have been a presbytery or a diocese. To this we answer: (*a.*) The existence of several organized congregations in these cities, under a common presbyterial or prelatic government, is a mere assumption, there being no intimation of it in Scripture; on the contrary, repeated instances occur in which the whole body of believers met together. It is said of the church at Jerusalem, "all that believed were together," "continuing daily with one accord in the temple," "they were all with one accord in Solomon's porch." No less than six occasions are recorded in which the entire body of disciples at Jerusalem met as a church in one place; and in some of these cases the form of statement indicates it as an ordinary occurrence (Acts ii. 44, 46; iv. 31, 32; v. 12, 13; vi. 2–5; xv. 22; xxi. 22). (*b.*) This assumption ignores the circumstances of Christians in those cities. Of the multitude converted at Jerusalem, as also at Ephesus, many were strangers and soon dispersed, while many others were scattered abroad by persecution. They had as yet no church edifices, and met only occasionally in one place as they had opportunity; and, with their plural eldership, instruction was doubtless given, not only "publicly" in the occasional united gathering of the disciples, but also "from house to house" in smaller and local gatherings. There is, however, no proof that these latter were organized churches; the reverse is plainly apparent. (*c.*) Besides, if such a union of several organized congregations in one city, under a common prelatic or presbyterial government, were shown, it would not prove enough for those advancing it; for, confessedly, there was no such union under one government of all the churches in a district or country; yet this last is essential to the Presbyterian or Episcopal theory. "The seven churches of Asia" would have formed a convenient diocese or presbytery; yet we read, not of "the church of Asia," but of "the churches of Asia." The truth is, when the facts are carefully considered, there is not even a shadow of evidence that either in city or country the churches were under a common government, either diocesan or presbyterial.

2. It is objected that the body assembled at Jerusalem to consider the question of Gentile circumcision was a legislative and judicial council, with authority higher than that of individual churches, and was a divine model of Episcopal or Presbyterial judicatories (Acts xv.). Let us, then, examine the character of this assembly. (*a.*) It was constituted of "the church, the apostles and elders at Jerusalem;" no others acted on the question. The churches of Judea, of Samaria, and of Galilee were not represented. So far as appears from the record, it was a simple church-meeting, convened to consider a disputed article of belief on a request for advice from the church at Antioch; there is not the most distant resemblance to a modern "council," "synod," or "general assembly," in all which *many* local churches are represented, and not, as here, only a *single* church. (*b.*) In the decision of the question, the apostles proposed; the elders and the whole congregation approved. It was so far a simple church act declaring the opinion of the church at Jerusalem on the point presented. (*c.*) The authority of the decision, as binding other churches, was derived from the apostles. These inspired men announced it as the divine will; hence the decree went forth thus: "It seemed good to the Holy Ghost and to us." Plainly, in the absence of inspired apostles, no similar decree can ever issue from a church. The association of the elders and church with the apostles in the

decree, while the binding authority of it sprang from the apostles alone, may be compared with the association of Timothy, Silas, and others with Paul in his Epistles, while yet the divine authority of these Epistles is all derived from Paul alone as an inspired apostle.

This case, therefore, furnishes no authority for church judicatories as authoritative tribunals of appeal in matters of doctrine and discipline. It simply teaches the propriety of consulting another church, or other churches, in subjects of difficulty; but the decision thus obtained can now be only advisory, as no inspired men are present to give it divine sanction.

3. It is objected that independency destroys the visible unity of the kingdom of Christ on earth by breaking up Christendom into a multitude of isolated units; it presents to the world no grand, organized unity. This objection, however, is founded on a misconception of church unity. A great ecclesiasticism, with its gradations of officers and courts, may have external uniformity; but this is not necessarily unity. If centralization and uniformity were the marks of a true church, the Romish, with its vast and elaborate organization, would be the truest church on earth. But unity consists in oneness of spirit, doctrine, and life, developing itself under the one church constitution of the New Testament. This true, spiritual unity exists in a far higher degree under independency than under opposing systems. Of this the Baptists are an eminent illustration. Tenacious as they are of independency, they present throughout the vast extent of their churches—now numbering in the United States more than two million members—a unity of doctrine, spirit, and life seen among no other body of Christians of equal extent on earth.

4. It is objected that doctrine and discipline cannot

safely be entrusted to the people, who are liable to be swayed by ignorance, prejudice, and passion; whereas a judicatory of educated ecclesiastics would act intelligently and dispassionately. We answer: If God has left these subjects in the hands of the people, it is safe to trust his arrangement, and unsafe to depart from it. But this charge of incompetency, so often made against the people, is utterly disproved by history. Truth and justice, whether in state or church, have nowhere proved so safe as in the keeping of the masses. The popular judgment and conscience of the church are, and must be, subject to occasional aberration, but, *in the long run*, the verdict they pronounce is faithful to the truth and the right. The errors and wrongs which have oppressed Christendom through the ages did not spring from the people, but from hierarchies and synods. The Sanhedrin condemned the Lord Jesus, but "the common people heard him gladly." History in all succeeding ages has shown the same result.

II. EACH CHURCH, THOUGH INDEPENDENT OF ALL ECCLESIASTICAL AUTHORITY ON EARTH, IS ACCOUNTABLE TO CHRIST AS ITS SOVEREIGN HEAD.

Christ is the sovereign Head and only Lawgiver of his church. He constantly asserts this in his word as his rightful position. Hence, a church has no power to legislate or to act contrary to or beyond the New Testament, but is simply an executive body to interpret and execute the will of Christ. Thus subject to the supreme, sovereign headship of Christ, the church is not authorized to establish as articles of faith doctrines not taught in Scripture; to make judicial decisions on other than scriptural principles; to alter the constitution of the church as divinely given; or to establish new ordinances or alter or abrogate those established in the New Testament. In all things on which the Scriptures reveal the will of Christ, the church is simply the interpreter and executive; if it pass beyond these functions, it invades the sphere of the divine prerogatives. And when in these things a church departs from the faith and practice of Scripture, it is clearly the right and duty of other churches to withhold their fellowship from it as a true church, because in so doing it has rejected Christ as Head.

III. CHURCHES ARE INTERDEPENDENT; EACH CHURCH, THEREFORE, HAS RELATIONS AND DUTIES TO OTHER CHURCHES.

Independency is not isolation; there is also an interdependence among churches which is equally recognized in Scripture, and the observance of which is equally obligatory. A church may not stand in solitary isolation; it is a unit, indeed, but a unit among a multitude forming a great whole. It is one in a great community of churches bound to each other in the mightiest bonds. They have all a common relation to Christ as their one Head, and to the kingdom of Christ as each the representative of it. They have a common life and experience, as regenerated, illumined, and inhabited by the one Spirit. They have a common constitution, derived from the one word of God; a common responsibility, as entrusted with the one gospel; and a common mission, as alike charged to give this gospel to the world. Each church thus forms one in the grand fellowship of churches, all of which are affected in their good name and welfare by its character and acts; and to all of which, therefore, it has imperative duties. Thus, 1. Each church is bound to promote, to the extent of its power, the welfare of other churches. The mutual sympathy and co-operation of the apostolic churches are plainly indicated, while yet in no instance was there interference with the self-government of any church. They ministered to each other's need in seasons of destitution, the Gentile churches sending large contributions to the impoverished church at Jerusalem. They sought from each other and gave to each other advice in matters of difficulty, as when the church at Antioch applied for advice to that in Jerusalem. They sent ministerial aid to each other when special laborers were needed (Acts xi. 22). The evidence of warm and generous sympathy among churches, in prayer and labor and sacrifice for each other, appears in all the apostolic history. 2. Each church also is bound to respect the ecclesiastical character and acts of other churches, and avoid the weakening of their just authority and influence. It should recognize the validity of their ministry and ordinances, and give and receive letters of commendation and dismission. It may not disregard the discipline of another church by encouraging offenders, or receiving excluded persons, except in case of manifest injustice. Even then the consent of the excluding church or the advice of a council should be obtained before admission; otherwise, all disciplinary power is destroyed, and the laws of Christ are set at naught. No church may intrude into the natural territory of another so as unduly to narrow its field and weaken its power, nor may it by any other act impair its efficiency or injure its welfare. 3. Each church is bound also, in combination with other churches, to aid, according to its ability, in sending the gospel to the world. A church is in its essential idea a missionary body. Entrusted with the gospel, it is the divine organization for the conversion of the world, and it fails in its highest end so far as it fails to bear its part among the sisterhood of churches in securing the triumph of Christ's kingdom on earth. Evidently, the missionary enterprise in the Apostolic period was not left to fortuitous organizations formed by individuals, but was regarded as the proper work of the church, as God's own organization, and was carried on by the combined efforts of churches. Paul was sent forth, not by a society, but by the church at Antioch, and so far as his own hands did not support him he was sustained by many different churches; for, in reasoning with the church at Corinth, he says, "I preached to you the gospel of God freely, I robbed other churches, taking wages of them, to do you service." His Epistles abound, especially that to the Philippians, with grateful recognitions of kindness done to him by the churches. We have all reason for supposing that such was the fact in the case of other evangelical laborers: each church bore its part in sustaining them in their work.

IV. THE COMMUNITY OF CHURCHES, SO FAR AS THE CHARACTER AND ACTS OF AN INDIVIDUAL CHURCH AFFECT THEIR COMMON NAME AND WELFARE, HAVE CERTAIN RIGHTS AND DUTIES IN RELATION TO EACH CHURCH.

1. If any church has departed from the faith and practice of the gospel, it is clearly the duty of sister churches to seek, with all tenderness and fidelity, its recovery from the error, and, failing in this, it is their duty publicly to withdraw fellowship from that church. Such withdrawal of fellowship has, indeed, no compulsory power to compel the erring church to renounce either its error or the common name which its error injures and misrepresents, for it is an independent body, and its own decisions are final within itself; but the vindication of the truth and of their common name before the world evidently requires this action on the part of the churches. 2. When a church is organized and takes the common name of a community of churches, thereby claiming public recognition as one of them, the plain duty of such church, if circumstances admit, is to seek the counsel of those churches, submitting to them

a statement of its reasons for organizing, its material for membership, and its articles of faith and practice, and inviting their approval. Failing in this, it has no right to assume the common name, nor can it *claim* a recognition from other churches. Thus, also, when a pastor is ordained, since such pastor is expected to be recognized as a minister in other churches, it is evidently proper to invite the community of churches to share in the examination of his qualifications for the ministry, and to concur in setting him apart to the office; and a church which should refuse to recognize in this way the comity of the churches could not complain if they declined to recognize its pastor by inviting him to ministerial functions among them. In both the cases supposed, however, the withholding of recognition would affect only the external relations. It would not render the church less a church, nor its church acts less valid; nor would it invalidate the ordination of the pastor, or impair his right to exercise the pastoral function in that church. Non-recognition would simply leave the church and the pastor outside of, isolated from, the fellowship of the community of churches, and unentitled to bear their common name.

3. When a church has excluded a member under circumstances which suggest that the exclusion was the result of prejudice or passion, it may be the duty of some other church, on an application from the excluded person, presenting reasonable evidence that the proceeding was irregular and unjustifiable, to invite an investigation of the case by the community of churches. This might be required alike to secure justice to an injured brother, who by unjust exclusion was separated from the fellowship not only of that church, but of all the churches, and to vindicate the common name from the charge of ecclesiastical injustice. If such an investigation resulted in

favor of the excluded party, this would not reinstate him in the church which excluded him—for no outside body can reverse the act of a church—but it would leave any other church at liberty to admit him.

The independence of the individual church in all such cases must needs be held inviolable: no action of outside ecclesiastical bodies can impair the validity and authority of its acts, as binding on its own membership. But when its acts affect, not itself only, but also the common name and welfare of the whole community of churches, it is obvious they have the right of self-vindication and protection, and may refuse to recognize such acts as binding on themselves, or to be held responsible for them before the world.

V. THE EXTERNAL RELATIONS OF CHURCHES ARE MAINTAINED THROUGH ASSOCIATIONS, COUNCILS, AND BENEVOLENT SOCIETIES.

The constitution of these bodies has not been divinely prescribed, but is evidently left to the wisdom of the churches, as, in their varying circumstances, they shall be guided from age to age by the Spirit and providence of God. The duty, however, of combining for evangelical and benevolent work is not only the dictate of reason, but is also plainly recognized in Scripture; as in the united movement of the Gentile churches for the relief of the Judean Christians, and the common support of Paul and other missionary laborers by different churches. These organizations have no ecclesiastical power; they are simply agencies through which the churches put forth efforts for the advancement of the kingdom of Christ.

ASSOCIATIONS.

An Association is composed of pastors and delegates from churches occupying a particular district. Its purpose is twofold—the promotion of the welfare of the churches connected with it, and the spread of the gospel, especially through the region occupied by them. It has a constitution defining its objects, organization, and duties, and usually containing an outline of the leading articles of faith and practice as held in common by the churches connected with the body. This last is not always formally stated, but is in all cases distinctly implied. At its annual session officers are elected for the year, letters are read from the several churches giving a statement of their condition, and subjects of common interest to the churches are considered. The proceedings are afterward published, with the statistics of the churches, for the information of the churches and the general public.

The Association is a purely voluntary body; no church is compelled to join it. Churches are admitted on application, if found to conform in character, doctrine, and practice to the principles stated in the constitution; and they are at liberty to withdraw from it whenever, in their judgment, their welfare requires it. It has no ecclesiastical authority, but its official acts are strictly limited to the objects and methods prescribed in the constitution. If any church belonging to it has departed from the common faith and practice of the churches in the body, the Association may seek fraternally to recover it from the error; and, failing in this, it may dissolve the relation of the Association to the erring church. But it has no power to discipline or to dissolve the church, or in any way to act as a court of review, to put on trial the character and acts of a church, except as its character and acts affect its relation to the Association. No church can delegate to another body the rights and functions Christ has committed to it; hence, an Association is not a representative body in any such sense that it can perform any properly ecclesiastical act, such as admitting, disciplining, or excluding members of a church, electing or displacing the officers of a church, or administering church ordinances.

Councils.

A Council is composed of delegates from several churches, usually the pastor and one or more laymen from each, called, ordinarily, by some church to give advice on a subject proposed. The letters by which it is called specify the time and place of meeting, the subject to be considered, and the churches invited to participate; and the Council is, in all cases, strictly limited in its scope to the subject thus named and to the churches thus invited. It has no power to enlarge its scope, nor to increase or diminish or alter its membership. It elects its own officers, usually a moderator and clerk, determines its own mode of procedure, gives its opinion or advice on the subject proposed, and is then dissolved. Councils are of four kinds:

1. *Council for the recognition of a church.* When a number of persons propose to organize as a church, it is customary to seek the advice and co-operation of neighboring churches by means of a Council. Before this body they present their reasons for organizing a church, the letters and Christian standing of those who propose to form it, the means they possess for the support of public worship, and the articles of faith and the covenant they propose to adopt. The Council then gives its advice in regard to the desirableness of the step proposed; and, if it approves, the church is then constituted by the public adoption, on the part of those entering it, of the articles of faith and covenant, and by public services of recog-

nition on the part of the Council, consisting usually of a sermon, a prayer, a charge, and the giving of the hand of fellowship. Sometimes the organization of the church is consummated previous to the call of the Council; in such cases, the Council is not called to give advice as to the propriety of organization, but only to give a public recognition of the body as a regularly-organized church. In all cases the essential act of organization is the adoption of the articles of faith and covenant by those forming the body: the Council only advises and gives public admission to the fellowship of other churches. A church self-organized, without a Council, would be a church, and its church acts would rightfully claim validity among its own members; but it would stand isolated, with no rightful *claim* to recognition as a church by other churches, and with no moral right to assume the common name of the churches. For the distinctive name of a Christian denomination is the symbol of a certain character and of certain ideas, perhaps the inheritance of ages of heroic conflict and suffering; it is, therefore, as truly the exclusive right of that denomination as a trade-mark is the exclusive right of the man of business using it. No church has a right to use it without the consent of the churches to whom it belongs; and to attach it to a body having a different character and holding different ideas from those churches would be a gross act of fraud. In constituting a church, therefore, a Council of recognition, whenever possible, should always be called, that the newly-formed body may have an ascertained standing in the fellowship of the churches.

2. *Council for the ordination of a minister.* An ordaining Council is called to examine a candidate for the ministry, and to give advice in regard to his public ordination. After organizing, the Council receives a report from the

church as to the steps taken in regard to the proposed ordination. The candidate then submits a statement of his Christian experience, his call to the ministry, and his views of Christian doctrine and practice. Full opportunity is given for questions on all these. The Council then decides whether to recommend his ordination; but as, according to Scripture example, none but ordained persons confer ordination, a majority of the ordained ministry present ought to concur in a vote to ordain, and only ordained ministers may perform the proper ordaining acts—the laying on of hands and prayer. The functions of the Council consist, therefore, in two really distinct acts—the examination of the candidate and the public recognition of his divine call to the ministerial office by the whole Council, and the act of ordination by the laying on of hands and prayer of the presbyters. In the former, he is publicly recognized as called of God to the sacred office; in the latter, he is publicly set apart to that office, under divine authority, by the presbytery.

3. *Council for the trial of a minister.* As a Council is called to induct a minister into his office, it is evidently proper that one should be had to depose him from it. When, therefore, grave charges have been preferred against a minister, and the church, on examination of them, has found the evidence such as either to create a presumption of his guilt, or to render a public investigation and vindication essential to his further usefulness, a Council is called to investigate the case. Great care is to be taken that it be composed of men recognized by the public as reliable and impartial. A committee of the church lays before the Council the charges and evidence, aided sometimes by a minister acting as counsel. The accused has the right to similar assistance. The rules of evidence are necessarily the same as in a court of justice, except that

evidence is not given under oath. The whole Council decides by vote on all questions of law or procedure, as also on the final question of acquittal or conviction. If the charge, or charges, involve several specifications, a distinct vote is taken on each specification, as well as on the general charge. If the case require deposition from the ministry, the Council, by vote, first withdraws from the offender that which the ordaining Council conferred—viz., the public recognition of his divine call to the ministerial office, and of his authority to exercise among the churches the functions of that office—and then advises the church to divest him of that which he received from it—viz., his pastoral office, his license, and his membership. A church which should depose its pastor without the concurring act of a Council would, indeed, silence him in that church, but it could not withdraw from him that which the ordaining Council had conferred; and the church so deposing him would have no right to complain if other churches continued to recognize him as a minister and permitted his exercise of the functions of the office among them.

4. *Council for the settlement of difficulties in a church.* This has two forms—the *mutual* and the *ex-parte*. A Council is *mutual* when both parties to the controversy unite in calling it; it is *ex-parte* when one of the parties refuses to unite in its call, or to submit the case to its consideration. An *ex-parte* Council should never be called if it is possible to secure a mutual one, nor should such a Council consent to act until it has used all proper means to induce both parties to present their case; for this is evidently desirable, in order to a just decision on the matter in controversy. But if, after due effort and patience, one of the parties still refuses to unite in the submission of the case, the vindication of character or the cause of

public justice may justify an *ex-parte* procedure. The decision of such a Council will have such moral weight as its character and the fulness and fairness of its investigation of the case may give it. The power of a Council, whether *mutual* or *ex-parte*, is wholly advisory: it investigates and gives advice. Usually that advice is, and ought to be, accepted by the parties calling it, since, in matters of difference, no Council ought ordinarily to be called unless the parties are prepared to abide by its decision. But such decision is in no sense an ecclesiastical decree to be enforced: it cannot set aside or modify the act of a church. It is advice voluntarily sought and accepted.

BENEVOLENT OR MISSIONARY SOCIETIES.

When Christ ascended he left the command, *Go ye into all the world and preach the gospel to every creature;* but, apart from the local church and its simple agencies, he instituted no general organizations through which this command should be fulfilled. These, therefore, have been left to the wisdom of the churches, as they may be guided by the indications of Providence and the general principles of the gospel. Hence, organizations have arisen, in different departments of Christian work, through which the churches are sending the gospel to the world. Such are the societies for home and foreign missions, for ministerial and general Christian education, for Bible and religious book and tract publication and circulation, and for Sunday-school and charitable work. The constitutions of these societies differ. Some are composed only of delegates from' churches; others, only of members made such by the payment of a specified sum; and others combine both these forms of membership. The officers are a president, one or more vice-presidents. a treasurer, a corresponding and a recording secretary, and a board of directors, to whom, in the intervals between the meetings of the body, the management of its work is committed.

These organizations are plainly a legitimate development of the beneficent spirit of Christianity, seeking the evangelization of the world; for only through comprehensive combination of effort can the gospel be carried throughout the world. The Christian spirit, therefore, will prompt to their hearty, generous support. But they are not, like the church, of divine constitution. Hence,
1. They are purely voluntary: no church may require its members to belong to them, or to contribute to the spread of the gospel through them. It may, and should, discipline a member for covetousness if he in *no* way gives for the work of evangelization, but it may not prescribe the channel through which he shall give for this object.
2. They possess no ecclesiastical power: they are simply agencies through which the voluntary activities of the churches are put forth and combined for the evangelization of the world.

VI. THE CHURCH IS IN THINGS TEMPORAL SUBJECT TO THE STATE, BUT IN THINGS SPIRITUAL INDEPENDENT OF IT AND SUBJECT ONLY TO CHRIST.

Christ declared, *My kingdom is not of this world*, and commanded, *Render, therefore, unto Cæsar the things that are Cæsar's, and unto God the things that are God's.* He thus for ever separated the church from the state, and assigned to each its own distinct and independent sphere. The relations of the church to the state may be thus expressed:
1. The church is in things temporal subject to the state, under obligation to seek its welfare, to pray for its rulers, and to obey its laws, except when these contravene the requirements of God; in this case the church is bound to

obey the higher authority of God, and to submit, if need be, to the penalties of human law (Matt. xvii. 24-27; xxii. 21; Acts iv. 19, 20; xiii. 1-3; xvi. 13-17; 1 Tim. ii. 1, 2; Tit. iii. 1; 1 Pet. ii. 13-17). 2. The church is in things spiritual independent of the state. It is formed under authority from Christ, and owes supreme allegiance to him Its doctrines, ordinances, officers, discipline, and worship are under the authority of God's word, and for these it is accountable only to God. 3. Every man has the natural right to worship God according to the dictates of his own conscience, unrestricted by human law, provided that in so doing he does not interfere with the similar right of every other man nor work injury to society. This right of worship, like every other natural right, the state is under obligation to protect, but may not restrict; hence, it can enjoin no prescribed form of worship or doctrine, nor can it rightfully impose taxes for the support of such form. The conscience is absolutely free as it respects coercion from human law, and is subject only to the law of God. This principle of soul-liberty, maintained alone by Baptist churches through ages of persecution, has at last found full recognition in the United States, and is steadily advancing to similar recognition in all the nations of the world. 4. The church, in the management of its secular affairs, conforms to the laws of the government under which it exists. These laws differ in different States, and even in the same State there are optional forms of civil relation which a church may adopt. The best legal advice, therefore, should be sought when organizing a church, so as to ensure its proper legal status, and thus fully secure its property. The civil relation of the church has three forms in this country: (*a.*) The church, as a church, acts in a civil capacity, managing its own temporal affairs, and is recognized in law as a body corporate with all legal powers. Such recognition is in some States granted by general laws; in others, it is a privilege conceded by special charter. The Episcopal, the Reformed, and other churches have in New York such charters. (*b.*) The male members of a church, of legal age, organize themselves as a religious society, and thus become a body corporate, legally capable of holding property and of transacting all the business of such a society. This also is done in some places under general law of the State, in others under special charter obtained. (*c.*) A body is organized under a general law of incorporation and known as the Society, composed of such persons of legal age as are pew-holders, or regular attendants on the worship of the church and contributors to its support. The executive power of this body is lodged in a board of trustees. The Society has the legal control of the property, the power to fix the salary of the pastor, and to determine all other expenses of worship. Ordinarily, a majority of the Society, as well as of the board of trustees, are members of the church, and the affairs of the church are thus practically in its own hands. This, however, has not always been the case, and the result has sometimes proved disastrous. A special law for Baptist churches has lately been enacted in New York which is supposed to guard against this danger.*

---

* See this law, called the "Centennial Trustee Law," published by New York *Examiner;* also, "A Digest of Ecclesiastical Laws of New York," in *Manual of Plymouth Church*, Brooklyn; an article of Dr. H. M. Storrs on "The Relation of Church and Parish," in *Congregational Quarterly*, 1860, vol. ii.; and Dexter's *Congregationalism*, pp. 206-213.

SECTION VII.

THE CHURCH: ITS OFFICERS.

Offices in the church are of divine constitution They can, therefore, be neither changed nor multiplied nor abrogated by human authority. Nor can the power belonging to a church office by divine appointment be increased or lessened by man. This is evident from the pledge Christ gave of his perpetual presence with the ministry to the end of the world, from his perpetuation of the ministry after his ascension by bestowing special gifts for it, and from the institution of the ministry by the apostles in every congregation. Church officers, being thus divinely established, are to be received as appointed by God, and are to be perpetuated unchanged to the end of time; and in exercising the power God has given to their office, they are to be recognized as acting by his authority. Other officers, though proper and useful, are only of human authority, and may be changed with the varying exigences of the church.

The officers of the new dispensation are thus indicated: "When he ascended on high, he gave some, apostles; and some, prophets; and some, evangelists; and some, pastors and teachers, for the perfecting of the saints for the work of the ministry, for the edifying of the body of Christ" (Eph. iv. 8–13). And Paul, when addressing the church, speaks of it as organized with "bishops and deacons" (Phil. i. 1; 1 Tim. iii. 1–13). These officers may be divided into two classes:

FIRST: EXTRAORDINARY OFFICERS.

This class consists of those who either belonged exclusively to the first age of Christianity or are not essential to the full organization of a church.

I. THE TEMPORARY OFFICERS, BELONGING ONLY TO THE APOSTOLIC PERIOD. In this division we place:

1. *The apostles.* Twelve were originally appointed, that being the number of the tribes of Israel to whom was their special mission. The thirteenth, afterward added, was specially sent to the Gentiles (Matt. xix. 27, 28; Gal. ii. 7-9; Acts xxii. 17-21). The qualifications of an apostle were—a commission from Christ in person (Acts i. 24; Gal. i. 1); an actual sight of him in the body after he had risen, so as to attest, in the character of a witness, the fact of his resurrection (Acts i. 22, 23; 1 Cor. ix. 1); a reception of the gospel, without human intervention, by the direct personal instruction of Christ (Gal. i. 11-20); and finally, the power to impart the Holy Spirit or confer ability to exercise supernatural gifts (Acts viii. 14-17). All these qualifications are either expressly stated as necessary to an apostle, or, in Paul's defence of his apostleship, are urged as evidences of his apostolic authority. The apostleship, like the office of Moses and Joshua at the introduction to the old dispensation, had a special design. Its purpose was the introduction of Christianity and the full organization of the church. When this was accomplished the office ceased. Hence, there is neither command nor suggestion in regard to its perpetuation, and the papal and ritualistic assumption that prelatical bishops are the successors of the apostles does not rest on even the semblance of divine authority.

2. *Prophets.*—These had a twofold function—to foretell future events, and thus confirm the divine origin of the gospel, as in the case of Agabus; and to unfold by special inspiration the truths of the gospel, and thus supply the lack of the completed revelation now contained in the books of the New Testament (Acts xxi. 10, 11; 1 Cor. 14). These books were at that time either unwritten, or,

if written, in very limited circulation, and the gospel was known only as revealed in the Old Testament, or as expounded in the oral discourses of the apostles and their assistants. Hence, there was need of the gift of special inspiration in each church, through which these truths might be unfolded to the people. This office was also temporary. Its necessity ceased with the completion of the New Testament canon.

II. OFFICERS PERMANENTLY EXISTING, BUT NOT ESSENTIAL TO THE FULL ORGANIZATION OF A CHURCH. Here belong:

1. *Evangelists.* This term occurs only three times. It seems to designate the itinerant ministry, or missionaries. Such were Apollos, Timothy, Titus, Silas, and Philip—men who, without a permanent local charge, were ordained to preach the gospel, administer ordinances, and constitute and strengthen churches, either in regions unevangelized or among feeble churches. Thus, Barnabas is sent from Jerusalem to Antioch to guide and assist in the great awakening in that heathen city. Silas and Timothy remain at Berea to organize and strengthen the infant church when Paul is driven away by persecution. Titus is left in Crete to "set in order the things that are wanting and ordain elders in every city" (Acts xi. 22-24; xvii. 14; Tit. i. 5).

2. *Teachers and preachers*—terms which designate, in a general way, all those who were gifted for public instruction and were set apart to it. The simple worship of the church of the New Testament naturally called forth all the gifts of the body; it is probable, therefore, that many were thus recognized as public instructors.

It is evident that these officers, though not essential to the full organization of a church, are, from the nature of their work, permanent as Christianity itself; for the work of evangelization and instruction belongs to all ages. But they have no official authority in the church as church officers. They are members of it, entitled to its privileges and amenable to its discipline; and in their relation to the church they differ from other members only in the fact that they are invested with authority to preach the gospel and administer ordinances as God may call them

SECOND: ORDINARY OFFICERS.

Of these, the church, as divinely constituted, has only two classes—pastors and deacons. For in Scripture these are the only officers mentioned as ordinary, and the qualifications and duties of these only are stated in connection with the usual officers of a church. This is confirmed, also, by the fact that, in the Post-apostolic age, these officers alone are found in the churches. This position is opposed: 1. By the Papal Church, in which three orders of clergy exist—bishops, priests, and deacons, all subordinate to the universal bishop, the Pope of Rome. 2. By the Episcopal Church, which has these three orders of clergy, but denies papal supremacy. 3. By the Presbyterian Church, which makes a distinction of order between the presbyter and the ruling elder, the latter being not a clerical but a lay officer. In all these, also, the clergy exist as a self-perpetuating and self-regulative body, distinct from, and for the most part independent of, the congregation.

I. PASTORS.

On this class we submit the following propositions:

1. *The terms presbyter, bishop, pastor, are designations of one office.*

For, (*a.*) These terms are used interchangeably in Scripture. The elders of Ephesus are called also overseers or bishops. Paul, in giving charge to Titus respecting the ordination of this class, terms them, interchangeably, elders and bishops. And Peter exhorts elders to take the oversight, or act as bishops, of the flock (Acts xx. 17–28; Tit. i. 5–7; 1 Pet. v. 1, 2). (*b.*) The qualifications and duties required of these are identical (1 Tim. iii. 1–7; Tit. i. 5). (*c.*) Ordination, which Episcopacy claims as a prerogative of bishops, was plainly conferred by elders; for Timothy was set apart to his work by the presbytery, or eldership (1 Tim. iv. 14). The New Testament gives no intimation of a distinction between bishops and elders, the term *bishop* being simply the Greek word for designating the person whom the Jews called elder; while *pastor* indicated the same person, as one to whom God had committed the oversight and guidance of the flock. This view has now the sanction of nearly all biblical scholars, English and German, Episcopal and non-Episcopal, and must be regarded as definitely settled.

2. *The duties of pastors are the preaching of the gospel, the administration of the ordinances, and the government and spiritual oversight of the church.*

(*a.*) *Preaching the gospel.* In Paul's address to the elders of Ephesus, he plainly implies that their work was substantially identical with his own teaching "publicly and from house to house;" for he proposed to them his own example of labor. "Apt to teach" is made an essential qualification in the pastor, and he is required to be "able by sound doctrine to exhort and convince the gainsayers." The highest work of the ministry, as presented in Scripture, is to act as "ambassadors for Christ" in proclaiming God's message to man.

(*b.*) *The administration of the ordinances.* In the commission Christ makes it the duty of the ministry not only to "teach," but also to baptize, thus including the administration of ordinances in their work. Philip the evangelist, acting under this commission, having made the Ethiopian eunuch a disciple, baptized him. No clear example is found of the administration of ordinances by any person not a minister of the gospel. Indeed, the ordinary discharge of this duty by the pastors may be inferred not only from its inclusion in the ministerial commission and from the example of Scripture, but also from the nature of the case. For it was a constant and public duty, which must have been committed to some persons, and the officers of the church were the natural administrators. In the absence of precept, therefore, committing it to others, we should infer that it devolved on them. But as there is no express command, nor absolutely decisive example, restricting the administration of ordinances to the ministry, we may conceive that under exceptional circumstances, when an ordained minister cannot be obtained, this service might, under the direction of the church, be performed by others.

(c.) *The government and spiritual oversight of the church.* These functions are indicated in the designations of the office. *Elder*, derived from Jewish usage, denotes a spiritual ruler. *Bishop*, from the Greek, designates one who has the oversight of others. *Pastor*, or *shepherd*, signifies one who guides, feeds, and protects the flock. Nearly all allusions to pastors refer to them as leaders, guides, overseers of the church, presiding over it and administering its government. Thus, they preside in the assemblies of the church: Paul exhorts the Thessalonians, "We beseech you to know them that labor among you and are over" (preside over) "you in the Lord and admonish you." They inspire and lead the action of the church, and administer its rebukes and discipline: the Hebrew Christians are exhorted, "Obey them that have the rule over you and submit yourselves: for they watch for your souls as they that must give account" (Heb. xiii. 17). They instruct the church by word and example, in doctrine and duty; as Peter, in his striking charge to the elders says, " Feed"—act as shepherds over—" the flock of God, which is among you, taking the oversight thereof, not by constraint, but willingly, not for filthy lucre, but of a ready mind; neither as being lords over God's heritage, but being ensamples to the flock. And when the Chief Shepherd shall appear, ye shall receive a crown of glory that fadeth not away " (1 Pet. v. 1–4). Thus divinely appointed as the guides and overseers of the church, they are invested with authority as the executive officers, through whom the power of the body is exercised; and, while they teach and rule according to God's word, the members are required to submit to them, as the flock follow the voice of their shepherds.

The powers and duties of pastors, therefore, briefly stated, are as follows: 1. To direct and supervise the public religious instruction of the congregation in the pulpit and in all other departments of church work: they are the spiritual guides of the church, and may not permit the inculcation of false doctrine. 2. To administer the ordinances within the church. 3. To preside in all meetings of the church, whether for devotion or business. 4. To watch over the personal experience and life of the members, exhorting, admonishing, reproving, rebuking, as those entrusted with the care of souls and expecting to give account. These powers and duties belong to the pastoral office, and within this sphere pastors act with rightful authority, as exercising functions devolved on them by God. But this authority is not absolute and final; for, as they receive their office through the church, so, if these powers are abused, the church may take the office from them.

3. *Pastors do not constitute a priesthood with mediating, sacrificial, and absolving powers.*

Sacerdotalism, the offspring of clerical ambition, developed itself early in the third century and ultimately triumphed in the patristic church. The three orders of the clergy, then beginning to appear, assumed to be a priesthood, and the church was modelled after Judaism. The bishop became *summus sacerdos*, high priest; the presbyter was *sacerdos*, priest; and the deacon was *Levita*, a Levite. A hierarchy arose with the power of mediating between God and man, of offering sacrifice to God, and of pronouncing absolution from sin. The significant and beautiful ordinances of the gospel were transmuted into sacraments, possessing, when ministered by priestly hands, a magical efficacy to remove sins and impart eternal life. The priesthood, in which were strangely-blended characteristics from both heathenism and Judaism, arrogated to itself the exclusive power of opening and closing the door of heaven. And sacerdotalism, alike in the Papal and the Episcopal Church, has in all ages since asserted these as the true characteristics and functions of the Christian ministry.

Two facts, however, suffice to destroy this assumption: 1. Ministers, in the New Testament, are never designated as priests. All believers are, indeed, "made kings and priests unto God," and constitute a "royal priesthood," since, through the blood of Christ, they all have access through the veil into the immediate presence of God to offer spiritual sacrifices to him. But the ministry are never called priests, nor in any way indicated as a priestly caste distinct from and above the people. On the contrary, all the titles given them utterly preclude the idea of a priesthood or of priestly functions; for these titles pertain to the synagogue, not to the temple. 2. Since the

Patriarchal age only two orders of priesthood have existed—that of Melchizedek and that of Aaron. The latter, without question, has been done away. The former still exists. But of this Christ is the one and final Priest, and his priestly work is performed, not on earth, but in the holiest of all, even heaven itself, where, "appearing in the presence of God," "he ever liveth to make intercession for us." The sacrifice he offered of himself was "once for all" complete and final, never to be repeated (Heb. ix. and x.). And it is the completeness of this one, final sacrifice, as at once and for ever putting away sin, which constitutes the message of the Christian ministry. There is, therefore, and in the nature of things there can be, no mediating, sacrificing, and absolving priesthood in the church. Christ is the one ETERNAL PRIEST: the ministry simply point the people to him. The assumption of priestly functions by man, therefore, is an invasion of the prerogatives of Jesus Christ.

4. *The number of pastors in each church is not fixed by Scripture, but it is probable, alike from apostolic example and from history, that in the Apostolic age there were ordinarily several who together constituted the presbytery of the church.*

(a.) *The testimony of Scripture.* We read of "the *elders* of the church" at Jerusalem, at Ephesus, and at Philippi. Paul and Barnabas "ordained *elders* in every church." Titus was left in Crete that he might ordain "*elders* in every city." In the catholic Epistles, James enjoins, in the case of the sick, that they "call for the *elders* of the church," and Peter exhorts "the *elders* which are among you;" in both which, as these apostles were addressing a large body of churches, the inference seems a necessary one that, as a common fact, a plurality of elders existed in each church. No clear example is found of a church organized under a single pastor. Our Lord, in addressing the "seven churches of Asia," directs each epistle to "the angel of the church;" and it has been hence inferred that each of these churches was organized under a single pastor, called "the angel of the church." But this expression is confessedly obscure; there is no certainty that it designates a pastor at all, and standing alone it is wholly inadequate to offset the otherwise uniform example of Scripture. And even were it certain that "the angel of the church" designated the pastor, it would by no means follow that there was no church presbytery; for, in that case, the only legitimate inference would be that in the latter part of the Apostolic age, when the book of Revelation was written, the presiding officer of the church presbytery had already assumed, as he naturally would, a certain degree of prominence, which made him the proper medium through which to address the church.

(*b.*) *The testimony of history.* This is equally explicit in regard to a plurality in the eldership. Neander, speaking of the apostolic churches, says: "The guidance of the communities was everywhere entrusted to a Council of elders."* The earlier Fathers uniformly speak of them in the plural. Clement of Rome (A. D. 96) speaks of the first-fruits of the apostles' labors as having been "appointed to be bishops and deacons." Polycarp (A. D. 140) exhorts the Philippian church to "subject themselves to their presbyters and deacons." Tertullian, speaking of the public worship of the church, says: "Certain approved elders preside." In no instance do the Fathers of the second century speak of a single bishop in a church, except when referring to the president of the church presbytery, who among his fellow-presbyters was only first among equals. The bishop of the second century was simply the presiding officer among the presbyters of a

* *History of the Christian Religion and Church*, Am. ed., vol. i., p. 184.

church, and was the pastor over a single congregation. Jerome states that at Alexandria, "until the middle of the third century, the presbyters always chose one of their own number as president, and gave him the title of bishop." But an extended citation of authorities is needless, for the existence of a presbytery in each church, composed of elders equal in authority, is attested by all the reliable records of the Post-apostolic age.

The question whether such a presbytery remains a part of the permanent constitution of the church, obligatory in all ages, has received different answers. The earlier Baptist confessions of faith—those of 1643 and 1689—recognize the plural eldership. The discipline adopted by the Philadelphia Association in 1743 presents it in the modified form of a ruling eldership, in which form, also, it still exists in some of the English churches. Among our churches the plural eldership is commonly regarded as a feature peculiar to the Apostolic age, rendered necessary by the absence of a class of men specially trained for the pastoral office, and by the special circumstances of the churches in that period of persecution, when they were often compelled to meet in small companies at separate houses, and their members were scattered in prisons and placed in positions of peril and suffering, thus requiring a larger number of instructors and far greater and more varied labors in the pastoral care. It is also urged that most churches do not possess several men adapted to such an office, and that the leadership of a single man would be more efficient than that of several men. With this view, in which there is much weight, our churches are generally organized under a single pastor, and many of the duties of the ancient presbytery, in the spiritual watch-care of the church, are transferred to the deacon's office. It is supposed that, in the changed circumstances of our age, this arrangement is not only lawful, but more expedient, especially as under it the pastor and deacons practically constitute a presbytery, and, so far as concerns the spiritual oversight, are often effectively doing its work.

On the other hand, it is said: There is serious reason to doubt whether an institution which rests on what seems the uniform example of the apostles can rightfully be set aside; as also whether, in the absence of such a guiding and conserving body within it, our church organization is not essentially weakened, alike in the purity and power of its church-life and in the wisdom and steadiness of its evangelizing efforts. Certainly, a permanent presbytery within the church, embodying its best experience and intelligence, and specially set apart to conserve its spiritual interests, would seem adapted both to give steadiness to its operations and maintain uninterrupted its worship and ordinances amidst pastoral changes, and to accomplish, far more perfectly than is possible under a single pastor, the spiritual oversight in visitation from house to house and the prompt, intelligent, and effective administration of discipline.

5. *A ruling eldership, as it exists under the Presbyterian constitution, has neither precept nor example in Scripture.*

The "ruling elders" in the Presbyterian Church are a body of laymen, presided over by the pastor, to whom are committed the admission and discipline of members and the spiritual oversight of the church. They have no authority to preach or administer ordinances. Two passages are quoted as authority for this office, which, however, evidently do not refer to permanent offices in the church, but to the gifts exercised in the incipiency of Christianity, several of which might be exercised by the same person. Thus, "Having then gifts differing according to the grace given unto us, whether prophecy, let us prophesy according to the proportion of faith; or ministry, let us wait on our ministering; or he that teacheth, on teaching; or he that exhorteth, on exhortation; ... he that ruleth, with diligence; he that showeth mercy, with cheerfulness" (Rom. xii. 6-8). And: "God hath set some in the church, first apostles, secondarily prophets, thirdly teachers, after that miracles, then gifts of healing, helps, governments, diversities of tongue" (1 Cor. xii. 28). Now, in this enumeration of gifts and functions "he that ruleth" and "governments" are mentioned, and it is inferred that these designate the ruling eldership. But it is plain that the reasoning which would interpret these as designations of a permanent office in the church would require that "he that showeth mercy" and "helps," and all the other functions mentioned, be also interpreted as each the designation of a distinct permanent office; and the result would be at least eight permanent officers in the church. Certainly, such an interpretation must be false. Paul's direction to Timothy is also cited: "Let the elders that rule well be counted worthy of double honor" (compensation), "especially they who labor in word and doctrine;" in which, it is alleged, a distinction is made between the "elders that rule" and the elders that "labor in word and doctrine." On this we remark: The apostolic churches, as already seen, had a plurality of elders; but all of these, though of equal authority and of like functions, did not possess in an equal degree the same gifts. While one would be eminent in preaching, another would excel in the pastoral care; and another still would be distinguished in both these departments, and, thus specially gifted, would devote his whole time to the office. It is of this class Paul here speaks—those who not only rule well, but also excel in public instruction, and consequently devote themselves wholly to the office. These, he says, should receive, not the ordinary compensation given to elders, but a double compensation, proportioned to the greater time and labor devoted to the work. The passage does not furnish the slightest evidence of a difference of office between the elders; on the contrary, the Greek adverb, here rendered "especially," in all ordinary usage implies that the persons emphasized after it constitute a part of the class mentioned before it. Besides, in Scripture an essential qualification for the eldership is that a man be "apt to teach"—a qualification certainly not necessary for ruling. In accordance with this, the biblical language habitually implies that teaching was combined with ruling in the functions of the elders, as in the following words of Paul: "Remember them which *have the rule over* you, who *have spoken* unto you the word of God" (Heb. xiii. 7, 17). Plainly, also, a ruling eldership, according to the Presbyterian conception, which assumes authority to admit and discipline and exclude members, is disproved by all those passages, heretofore cited, which show that these functions belong only to the church assembled as a congregation.

II. Deacons.

The word *diakonos* signifies, in general, one who serves, a servant employed in any capacity; but its special application in Scripture is to the second class of church officers. Of these we have probably the earliest record in the appointment of "the seven" (Acts vi. 1–6); for the work to which they were set apart—" to serve tables " or supervise the temporal affairs of the church—is one of universal and permanent necessity, while it is also recognized as distinct from that assigned to the ministry—" prayer and the ministry of the word "—and is designated by the verb *diakonein*, the appropriate term for the work of the deacon's office. The general sense of Christendom has, therefore, interpreted this as the institution of that office, and the subsequent references to the office in the New Testament confirm this view.

The following facts appear in Scripture: 1. The office is permanent in the church, for deacons are mentioned with bishops as ordinary officers, and their qualifications alone, besides those of bishops, are specifically stated (Phil. i. 1; 1 Tim. iii. 8–13). It is evident, also, that the need of such officers is permanent. 2. They are chosen by the whole congregation of believers, and are ordained by the ministry. The term of service, whether long or short, is not prescribed, and is doubtless to be decided by each church for itself. Experience has shown the desirableness of election for a limited period rather than for life, the body of deacons being so organized that a part go out of office at stated intervals, thus ensuring at all times a diaconate which shall possess alike the stability and wisdom which experience brings, and the energy and efficiency which may come from the occasional substitution of younger and more active men in place of the infirm or incompetent. The term of service, however, should not be so short as to require frequent changes. This takes from the dignity and moral power of the office, and introduces an undesirable element of instability. 3. The duty of the deacons is to administer the temporal affairs of the church, such as the relief of the poor, the support of public worship, the care of the church property, and the provision for the due administration of the ordinances. This is evident from their original appointment. They were to "serve tables"—that is, attend to the pecuniary arrangements for the temporal sustenance both of the poor and of the ministry, this being done from a common fund; and their work is thus placed in direct contrast with that of "the twelve," which was "prayer and the ministry of the word." While, therefore, the elders supervised the spiritual interests of the church, the deacons had supervision of its temporal interests. 4. The importance of the office is indicated by the special emphasis placed on the qualifications required. They are to be "men of honest report, full of the Holy Ghost and of wisdom; grave, not doubletongued, not given to much wine, not greedy of filthy lucre, holding the mystery of the faith in a pure conscience." They should "also first be proved," and "then use the office of a deacon, being found blameless" (Acts vi. 1-6; 1 Tim. iii. 8-10). Great care, therefore, is to be taken, in selecting the deacons, to secure men whose character shall command the respect and confidence of all men, and whose qualifications shall fit them for a wise and effective administration of the temporal affairs of the church.

In the hierarchical churches the deacons constitute the third order of spiritual officers, and are empowered to preach and baptize. They are not lay, but clerical, officers. As opposed to this view, however, it is significant that among the qualifications for the diaconate, Paul omits "apt to teach," and emphasizes those qualities which specially fit for secular duties, thus distinguishing the office from that of the preacher. The same distinction, separating the deacons to the temporal service, is seen in their original appointment. Philip, one of "the seven," it is true, preached and baptized; but it cannot be shown that he did this in his character as deacon, for he was also an evangelist (Acts viii. 26-40; xxi. 8.)

Deaconesses, it is evident, existed in some of the apostolic churches, for we read of Phebe, deaconess of the church in Cenchrea, and of certain women who at Philippi labored with Paul in the gospel, and who may be supposed to have had an official position (Phil. iv. 3). The injunction (1 Tim. iii 11) which in the English version refers to deacons' wives ought probably to be understood rather of deaconesses, as also the passage relating to widows (1 Tim. v. 9, 10). The existence of this office also in the post-apostolic churches is shown by the unanimous testimony of historians. But, as the Scripture evidence does not prove the custom universal, the question of the appointment of deaconesses is, doubtless, to be determined by each church for itself. The seclusion of females in the East, and the peculiar relations of the sexes in Greek cities in the Apostolic age, must often have made such female officers a necessity; and, so far as similar circumstances may now exist, it would seem the duty of the church to appoint them.

The organization of the church, as it respects its officers, is thus one of divine simplicity and effectiveness. The natural and obvious division of its work—committing the spiritual supervision to the pastors, and the temporal to the deacons—secures the highest efficiency, while it gives no stimulus to the clerical pride and ambition so manifest under hierarchical systems.

SECTION VIII.

THE CHURCH: ITS ORDINATION OF OFFICERS.

Ordination, or the public investiture of church officers with official authority, is clearly scriptural. It is not, however, the ultimate source of ministerial authority: this is found in the call of the Holy Spirit and the election by the church, of which ordination is the public recognition and the completing act.

This act, originally simple and beautiful as seen in Scripture, has been grossly perverted in the hierarchical systems which displaced the primitive church. In the Roman Catholic Church it is a sacrament, conferring the power of transmuting bread and wine into the body and blood of Christ, and of remitting or retaining sins; and even among Protestants the conception of a certain magical power conferred by it is often apparent, as if a special, invisible grace were thereby secured. No such thought is found in Scripture.

The word *ordain* in the New Testament never denotes the ecclesiastical ceremony of ordination. It is used six times in connection with a sacred office, and is in each instance the translation of a different Greek word. Thus, Mark iii. 14: "Jesus *ordained*" (*epoiēse*) "twelve to be with him;" Acts i. 22: "Must one be *ordained*" (*genesthai*) "to be a witness;" Acts xvii. 31: "By that man whom he hath *ordained*" (*horise*); 1 Tim. ii. 7: "Whereunto I am *ordained* a preacher" (*etethēn*). In all these the reference is clearly, not to a formal ceremony of ordination, but to the choice or appointment to a sacred office. Thus, also, Acts xiv. 23: "When they had *ordained*" (*cheirotonēsantes*) "them elders in every church and had prayed with fasting," where *ordained* denotes plainly the act of choice, while the "prayer with fasting" may refer to the formal act of setting apart to the office; Titus i. 5: "That thou shouldst *ordain*" (*katastēsēs*) "elders in every city," where the word signifies to *constitute, appoint*, and may possibly include the whole procedure, both the choice and the ordaining ceremony, but with evident emphasis on the former. The New Testament sense of *ordain*, therefore, is to choose or appoint, and does not necessarily or ordinarily refer to an ordaining ceremony.

Three instances of ordination, or the public setting apart to church office, are found in the New Testament—that of "the seven" (Acts vi. 6), "whom they set before the apostles, and when they had prayed they laid their hands on them;" that of Barnabas and Saul (Acts xiii. 1-3), respecting whom the Holy Ghost said to the ministry at Antioch, "Separate me Barnabas and Saul for the work whereunto I have called them. And when they had fasted and prayed and laid their hands on them they sent them away;" and that of Timothy, to whom Paul said (1 Tim. iv. 14), "Neglect not the gift that is in thee, which was given thee by prophecy, with the laying on of the hands of the presbytery." To these actual cases there is added the injunction given to Timothy (1 Tim. v. 22), "Lay hands suddenly on no man;" where the reference is clearly to ordination; and the natural inference is that the ceremony was customary in setting apart to the ministry. The following points are here to be noted: 1. The ministry alone confer ordination: in these examples, apostles, presbyters, and evangelists appear as officiating, but in no instance unordained persons. Special charge is given to the ministry in regard to the character and qualifications of candidates for the sacred office. Paul said to Timothy, "The things that thou hast heard of me among many witnesses, the same commit thou to faithful men, who shall be able to teach others also;" and he solemnly enjoins the utmost care in testing their fitness for the work by the charge, "Lay hands suddenly" (*hastily*) "on no man." Evidently, the ultimate responsibility of admitting to the ministerial office is here devolved on the ministry itself. They only, therefore, may act in setting apart to the sacred work. This is plainly the scriptural order, and only extreme necessity will justify a departure from it. In the apostolic churches, where each was organized with its own presbytery, there were always those competent to confer ordination. 2. In the ordination of a minister there is an evident propriety in inviting the co-operation of other churches; for it is desirable that he should be recognized as a minister, and should perform ministerial functions outside of his own church. Hence, it is customary to call an ordaining Council. This should be composed, not of select churches, but of all the neighboring churches, that it may properly represent the whole community of churches; no minister should consent to serve in a packed Council. And as ordination is conferred only by the presbytery, or ordained ministers, the Council should not proceed to ordain without the concurrence of a majority of the ministers composing it; otherwise, it is not the act of the presbytery, and the ordination is not scriptural. 3. The form of ordination is prayer and the laying on of hands, sometimes with fasting: these only are the ordaining acts. Other services may, indeed, be connected, such as a sermon, a charge, and the hand of fellowship to the candidate and a charge to the church, as is at present the custom; but these are not essential to ordination. The original form was singularly simple and striking. It consisted simply in the invocation of God's blessing on the person thus called to a sacred work, and a solemn consecration of him to it by the significant act of the laying on of hands. 4. Ordination confers no new grace or power; for the ordained person was chosen to the office because the church saw already in him the grace and power requisite for it. The presbytery, in the ordaining act, gives the solemn public sanction of the ministry to the call of the church, attesting the qualifications of the candidate for the office, and, invoking the divine blessing, consecrates him to it.

This view of ordination is opposed by the theory of an historic succession in the ministry by successive regular ordinations from the apostles. According to this, a twofold grace is conferred in ordination: 1. The power of consecrating, offering, and ministering the body and blood of Christ in the Eucharist, and 2. The power of absolution, or the remission of sins. The authority to confer this virtue in ordination is vested in the bishops, by whom it was received from the apostles, and has been transmitted through successive ordinations to the present day. As the result, ordination not received in this regular succession is invalid; and where there is no valid ordination there is no true ministry, no effectual preaching, no sacrament, no church, and no salvation.

To this theory I propose the following objections: 1. The sacerdotal powers, here said to be transmitted through apostolic succession, were never conferred on the apostles, much less have they been transmitted through the ages from them to us. 2. The Scriptures are silent as to any such succession and the necessity of it to a valid ministry; but surely, if this necessity existed, so momentous a fact would not only be stated, but emphasized. 3. Ordination did in fact confer no gift or power, for "the seven" were "full of the Holy Ghost and of wisdom" before their election, and were chosen on account of their fitness for the office. Barnabas and Saul were called of the Holy Ghost to the missionary work before their ordination, and that act only recognized this divine call, and dedicated them to their work. The ordination of Timothy was attended with exceptional circumstances; for, when he was ordained, a distinct prophetic utterance predicted his future eminence in the ministry, and Paul, as an apostle, united with the presbytery in the laying on of hands, so that Timothy received the supernatural gift or *charism* of the Holy Ghost (1 Tim. iv. 14; 2 Tim. i. 6). But neither prophets nor apostles are now present at ordinations, and the special *charisms* of the Spirit have ceased in the church. 4. If this theory of apostolic succession be admitted, there is no evidence that a valid ministry now exists on earth; for an historic succession of ordinations from the Apostolic age cannot be proved in any individual case. Even were such a succession promised, it would then be wholly uncertain in which of the several lines claiming it this succession has descended. Archbishop Whately justly said: "There is no Christian minister now existing that can trace up with complete certainty his own ordination, through perfectly regular steps, to the times of the apostles." 5. Finally, it is incredible that God has made the salvation of souls dependent upon this mysterious invisible virtue in the ministry—a condition as to which there is scarcely one chance in a thousand that it is met in any minister in Christendom; and if met, the proof of it cannot be made out. Such a supposition is repulsive, not only to the whole tenor of Scripture, but also to our most fundamental conceptions of God.

SECTION IX.

THE CHURCH: ITS DISCIPLINE.

Discipline includes all those processes by which a church, as entrusted with the care of souls, educates its members for heaven; such as their public and private instruction in the gospel, the maintenance of social meetings for their edification and comfort, and, in general, the cultivation of a spirit adapted to awaken and cherish the Christian life. In this lies the chief power of a church. A pure and healthful tone of religious life in the body, an all-pervasive spirit of love and loyalty to Christ and the church, are the most effective means of securing a pure life in the individual members; for the church is then a spiritual magnet to draw and hold souls to Christ and to itself.

But discipline, in a narrower sense, denotes the action of the church, whether as individuals or as a body, in reference to offences committed against the laws of Christ. In this sense it includes:

I. THE MUTUAL WATCH-CARE OF THE MEMBERS BY ENCOURAGEMENT, COUNSEL, ADMONITION, AND REBUKE. This is individual and private, and is a preventive of offences. Were this done, and done in the tender, loving, earnest spirit of religion, few instances of further discipline would be required. A true Christian watch-care, or mutual helpfulness in the members, is the highest development of church-life. David said: "Let the righteous smite me; it shall be a kindness: and let him reprove me; it shall be an excellent oil, which shall not break my head" (Ps. cxli. 5). And the gospel enjoins: "Brethren, if a man be overtaken in a fault, ye which are spiritual, restore such as are in the spirit of meekness; considering thyself, lest thou also be tempted" (Gal. vi. 1). "Put on, therefore, as the elect of God, holy and beloved, bowels of mercies, kindness, humbleness of mind, meekness, long-suffering, forbearing one another, and forgiving one another, if any man have a quarrel against any: even as Christ forgave you, so also do ye. And above all these things, put on charity, which is the bond of perfectness" (Col. iii. 12–14). Wherever the church-life approximates to this grand ideal the spiritual atmosphere is charged with such vitalizing forces that every soul within it is girt about with spiritual power, and is inspired to higher and holier living.

II. THE ADJUSTMENT OF PRIVATE PERSONAL GRIEVANCES. The following directions are here given by Christ: "If thy brother shall trespass against thee, go and tell him his fault between him and thee alone: if he shall hear thee, thou hast gained thy brother. But if he will not hear thee, then take with thee one or two more, that in the mouth of two or three witnesses every word may be established. And if he shall neglect to hear them, tell it unto the church; but if he neglect to hear the church, let him be unto thee as a heathen man and a publican" (Matt. xviii. 15-17). Here mark: 1. The aggrieved party, if the other does not, is to take the initiative in seeking an interview; the subject and the interview are to be strictly private; the object of it is, not altercation, but to gain an offending brother. 2. If this fails, and the offence is susceptible of proof, then one or two judicious fellow-members are to be chosen as witnesses and mediators, and the whole case is to be considered before them. 3. If this fails, the case, after due notification of the parties, is to be laid before the church, the proof adduced, and opportunity given for defence; and if the offence is proven, the offender is to be required to make reparation or be excluded.

Several further points are to be noted : 1. The aggrieved person has no discretion whether-to take this course or bear the wrong. It is obligatory, and he becomes an offender if he fails to do so. For this law is imperative, and even the Mosaic law enjoined: "Thou shalt in any wise rebuke thy neighbor, and not suffer sin upon him" (Lev. xix. 17). 2. If in the private interview the offence is denied, and there are no witnesses of the offence, the second step cannot be taken; for in that case the complaining party would become an offender, having published a charge which is without proof. In the absence of proof, he has no resource but in private admonition, and the patient committal of the matter to Providence. 3. If the "one or two more" before whom, in the second step, the case is laid regard the grievance as not real or as satisfactorily removed, the aggrieved party, though unsatisfied, cannot take the third step; for the offender has "heard them," and the accuser ought to be satisfied with the judgment of brethren selected by himself. 4. It is plain that if this great law of Christ were perfectly executed, there could be no personal feuds in the church; its simple provisions completely banish them, and wherever intestine strifes are found destroying the life of a church, they only attest the disastrous results of disregarding the words of the Head of the church.

III. THE ADJUSTMENT OF DIFFERENCES AFFECTING WORLDLY AFFAIRS. The Christian law, as given 1 Cor. vi. 1–11, enjoins that differences among members be not carried before worldly courts, but be referred to the judgment of judicious members of the church. It has been objected that this course was required in the midst of a heathen civilization, but cannot be regarded as obligatory in a Christian land, and under laws and courts formed by a Christian civilization. But the passage gives no intimation of the limitation of the rule to heathen countries; on the contrary, the reasons it assigns for the law are in their nature not transient and local, but permanent and universal. These are: 1. That Christians, who are ultimately to judge the world, and even angels, are better qualified to adjudicate these differences than worldly tribunals, and 2. That the appearance of members of the church as litigants before a worldly court is itself unseemly, and is inconsistent with their professed relations and hopes as members of Christ's body. These reasons are of permanent force. Differences among men are often decided, in human law, not according to equity, but by legal technicalities; this rule was intended to secure a judgment according to equity and the spirit of Christianity.

IV. PROCEDURE IN CASES OF PUBLIC OFFENCE, EMBRACING ALL OFFENCES AGAINST THE FAITH AND LIFE REQUIRED IN A CHURCH MEMBER, such as immoralities, heresy, covetousness, the making of divisions, habitual neglect of covenanted duties, and persistent violation of church order.

In the apostolic churches the elders, as overseers—rulers—of the flock, had the special responsibility of maintaining the discipline of the church. This is implied in Paul's address to the elders of Ephesus (Acts xx.), and in the qualification for the eldership stated 1 Tim. iii. 4, 5: "One that ruleth well his own house, having his children in subjection with all gravity: for if a man know not how to rule his own house, how shall he take care of the church of God?" The method of procedure indicated (Matt. xviii. 15-17), though there applied only to cases of personal grievance, is doubtless in spirit to be observed in all cases; for, in Tit. iii. 10, it is directed that the heretic be excluded only "after the first and second admonition." The process, then, would be substantially this: 1. The officers, becoming aware of reports implicating a member, would proceed privately to investigate them, and, if found true, would endeavor to reclaim. This is the most important step, since, if taken tenderly and privately, it is generally effectual. 2. The first effort failing, another would be made with every additional appliance which Christian fidelity and kindness could suggest. 3. This also failing, they would bring the case before the church with all the evidence; and if their statement of the case was controverted, the accused would have full opportunity for defence. The church would then decide, and, if adversely to the accused, they would require reparation or would proceed to exclusion.

The following points are here to be observed: 1. The rules of evidence which obtain in courts of law, since they are founded on essential justice, must govern in the reception of evidence in a trial before the church, except that the witnesses are not placed under oath; no evidence, therefore, which would be rejected in a legal trial can be accepted by a church. The application of this rule is specially important, since in cases of church scandal the popular gossip is so often mistaken for solid evidence. 2. In case of gross immorality, where the evidence is public and unmistakable, the exclusion is immediate and without formal trial, and the steps to bring the offender to repentance and restoration are taken afterward. This is evidently the course pursued in the case of the incestuous person described 1 Cor. v. and 2 Cor. ii. 1–11. The ground of this summary procedure is that the circumstances are such as to make confession worthless as evidence of penitence; only a subsequent life of purity can furnish this evidence. The church, however, is bound to use every effort afterward to save and restore those thus excluded. In this duty there is too often a lamentable failure, and the offender, whom persistent love and kindness might have reclaimed, is left by neglect to perish in his sin. 3. In our churches, as now organized without a plural eldership, the initiation of discipline commonly devolves on the pastors and deacons, who constitute practically, for this and other purposes, a church presbytery. In some churches there is a standing committee of discipline, on whom this responsibility rests. In others no definite arrangement exists, and it is left to any member to bring offences to the notice of the church; too often, from lack of early and private attention to offenders, the case has gone so far that the public discipline, when instituted, is almost necessarily unavailing to reclaim.

Exclusion is the final act of church power. It is the solemn withdrawal of fellowship from the offender, by which he ceases to be a member and is placed back in the world. Its effect on reputation, however, is modified by the nature of the offence requiring it. Hence, a distinction is sometimes made in the form of the act. In cases of vital error or immorality, involving the forfeiture of Christian character, the hand of *Christian* fellowship is withdrawn; while in cases of the violation of church order and of other offences, where the substance of Christian character may remain unimpeached, the hand of *church* fellowship is withdrawn. This, however, is a matter of mere custom; in any case, the formal relation of the excluded person as a member of the church is terminated.

The discipline of a minister is peculiar in two respects: 1. An accusation is to be received with unusual caution, both because his position creates a presumption in his favor, and because, as a minister, he is peculiarly exposed to malice. Paul enjoined: "Against an elder receive not an accusation but before two or three witnesses" (1 Tim. v. 19). 2. The action of a Council, as it was had to invest him with the ministerial office, should also be had to divest him of it. When, therefore, charges are preferred against a minister, it is the duty of the church so far to examine them as to determine whether the case is sufficiently serious to require an investigation; and, in the event of it so appearing, the church is then to summon a Council to investigate the charges. If the trial results in a conviction, the Council first proceeds to withdraw from him what the ordaining Council had imparted —that is, the fellowship, on the part of the ministry and churches, for him as a minister of the gospel, and the authority to exercise among them the functions of the sacred office; and it then advises the church to divest him of his pastoral office, his license, and his membership. These, as they were originally conferred by the church, can only be withdrawn by it; in reference to them, the action of the Council is only advisory.

A scriptural discipline, administered with tenderness and fidelity, is of the highest moment for the welfare of the church. It is an urgent necessity alike for the help of individual souls and for the purity, peace, and moral power of the body. Disorderly, inconsistent life in the church paralyzes the power of the pulpit; no other cause, probably, is so potent for evil in the churches as the general neglect of a true church discipline.

SECTION X.

THE CHURCH: VALID ONLY AS CONFORMED TO GOD'S WORD.

The principles relating to the church which have thus far been established may be concisely stated as follows: 1. A divine constitution of the church is given in the New Testament, and is the only form authorized by Christ; it is, therefore, of solemn and permanent obligation. 2. A church, being an institution within the kingdom of Christ, is properly composed only of subjects of that kingdom; its membership consists, therefore, only of credible believers in Christ, baptized on a personal profession of their faith in him. 3. All members of a church, as alike related to Christ, have equal rights; the vital powers of the body, therefore, are to be exercised by the whole congregation. 4. Each church is independent, and, while owing important duties to its sister-churches, is accountable, not to them nor to any outside body, but directly to Christ as Head of the church. 5. The officers of a church are bishops and deacons, the former supervising the spiritual, the latter the temporal, interests of the body.

The question remains to be considered: How may a true church of Christ be known? What constitutes a body of professing Christians a true church of Christ? We answer:

I. NOT MERE HISTORIC SUCCESSION FROM THE APOSTLES.

1. Were such an historic succession essential to the validity of a church, it would follow that the Scriptures are an insufficient guide in faith and practice, since the fact of such succession in the case of any church could not be ascertained from Scripture, but only from tradition. In this case, also, the great body of Christians could never certainly know the true church, as they could not make the historical investigation; and even if the investigation were made, their confidence must then rest on the testimony, not of God, but of man. 2. There might be an historic succession from the apostles, yet, in the lapse of ages, the whole form, doctrine, spirit, and life of the body be changed. The mere outward historic connection, therefore, might be no proof of identity of character.

It is possible, indeed, that there has been a continued succession of true churches from the Apostolic age to the present, although, in the present stage of historic investigation, such a succession is far from being clearly established. Every age of the Christian period has had a multitude of Christ's true confessors; and it is possible, perhaps probable, that churches essentially of the divine constitution have also existed. But we deny that an unbroken chain of succession is an essential mark of a true church. Such a doctrine is unprotestant, as it rests the validity of the Christian church on human tradition, and not on the divine word.

II. A CHURCH IS VALID ONLY BY VIRTUE OF CONFORMITY IN CHARACTER, DOCTRINE, AND ORGANIZATION TO THE CONSTITUTION GIVEN IN GOD'S WORD.

The divine constitution of the church has been given in the principles, precepts, and examples of the New Testament; it follows that any body of Christians conformed in its character, doctrine, and organization to that constitution is, by virtue of such conformity, a true church, invested with all the powers conferred on the church by Christ, and acting under his authority; for it is evident that Christ promised to the apostles inspired guidance in establishing the church, and that they, in directing their assistants, required them to organize churches modelled after apostolic example, and the apostolic church was thus indicated as the divine model for all the ages. The church constitution, as given in the New Testament, is thus of the nature of a general law of incorporation. In legislation, for example, we have the general banking law and the law for incorporating religious societies, and any body organized in conformity with that law is legal and becomes a body corporate, empowered by the State to do all the acts the law contemplates. In like manner, the constitution of the church has been framed by its only Lawgiver and Head, and is recorded and illustrated in the Bible. An association formed in conformity with that constitution is a divine church by virtue of such conformity, and acts under divine authority. It may have no formal connection with any previous church, but it is nevertheless apostolic and in the true succession. Conformity to the apostolic model makes it as true a church of Christ and invests it with as much divine authority as the original church of which the apostles themselves were members at Jerusalem.

A Christian man, therefore, is not compelled to trace a church through ages of superstition, in the mist and darkness of tradition, in order to know whether it is the true church of Christ. He need only open God's own word and study the model there delineated by God's own hand, and, following the infallible guidance of this, he shall know with assured confidence what is "the church of the living God, the pillar and ground of the truth."

SECTION XI.

THE CHURCH: HISTORICAL CONFIRMATION.

The constitution of the church, as here explained, is derived from the Scriptures, the only and sufficient authority in matters of faith and practice. The highest Patristic and historical authorities, however, confirm this view.

Mosheim says of the primitive churches: "Every church was composed of three constituent parts: 1. Teachers, who were also invested with the government of the community according to the laws; 2. Ministers of each sex (deacons and deaconesses); 3. The multitude or people. Of these parts the chief in point of authority was the people, for to them belonged the appointment of the bishop and presbyters, as well as of the inferior ministers; with them resided the power of enacting laws, as also of adopting or rejecting whatever might be proposed in the general assemblies, and of expelling, and receiving into communion, any depraved or unworthy members. In short, nothing whatever of any moment could be determined or carried into effect without their knowledge and concurrence." He adds: "With regard to government and internal economy, every individual church considered itself as an independent community, none of them ever looking, in these respects, beyond the circle of its own members for assistance, or recognizing any sort of external influence or authority." *

Neander, when speaking of the terms *episcopos* and *presbuteros*, says: "Originally both names related to the same office, and hence both names are frequently interchanged as perfectly synonymous. . . . Every church was governed by a union of the elders or overseers chosen from among themselves, and we find among them no individual distinguished above the rest who presided as *primus inter pares*, though probably, in the age immediately succeeding the apostolic, of which we have, unfortunately, so few authentic memorials, the practice was introduced to apply to such an one the name of *episcopos* by way of distinction. The government of the church was the peculiar office of such overseers. It was their business to watch over the general order, to maintain the purity of the Christian doctrine and the Christian practice, to guard against abuses, to admonish the faulty, and to guide the public deliberations, as appears from the passages in the New Testament where their functions are described. But their government by no means excluded the participation of the whole church in the management of their common

---

* *Commentaries on First Three Centuries*, pp. 179, 196 (Murdock's ed.).

concerns, as may be inferred from what we have already said respecting the nature of Christian communion, and is also evident from many individual examples in the apostolic church."*

Gibbon, who on this subject may surely be regarded as an impartial witness, says of the early churches: " The societies which were instituted in the cities of the Roman Empire were united only by the ties of faith and charity. Independence and equality formed the basis of their internal constitution. . . . The public functions of religion were solely entrusted to the established ministers of the church, the bishops and presbyters—two appellations which in their first origin appear to have distinguished the same office and the same order of persons. . . . In proportion to the respective numbers of the faithful, a larger or smaller number of these episcopal presbyters guided each infant congregation with equal authority and united counsels." After describing the subsequent appropriation of the term *bishop* to the presiding officer among the presbyters, and the powers committed to him, the historian continues: "These powers, during a short period, were exercised according to the advice of the presbyterial college, and with the consent and approbation of the assembly of Christians. The primitive bishops were considered only as the first among equals, and the honorable servants of a free people. Whenever the episcopal chair became vacant by death, a new president was chosen from among the presbyters by the suffrage of the whole congregation, every member of which supposed himself invested with a sacred and sacerdotal character. Such was the mild and equal constitution by which the Christians were governed more than a hundred years after the death of the apostles. Every society formed within itself

* *Planting and Training of the Church*, book iii., ch. 5.

a separate and independent republic; and although the most distant of these little states maintained a mutual as well as friendly intercourse of letters and deputations, the Christian world was not yet connected by any supreme authority or legislative assembly." *

Archbishop Whately, in his *Kingdom of Christ*, speaking of the early churches, says: "Though there was one Lord, one faith, and one baptism for all of these, yet they were each a distinct, independent community on earth, united by the common principles on which they were founded, by their mutual agreement, affection, and respect, but not having any one recognized head on earth or acknowledging any sovereignty of one of these societies over others. Each bishop originally presided over an entire church. A church and a diocese seem to have been for a considerable time coextensive and identical, and each church a diocese, and consequently each bishop or superintendent, though connected with the rest by the ties of faith, hope, and charity, seems to have been perfectly independent so far as regards any control, occasionally conferring with brethren in other churches, but owing no submission to any central authority."

The apostolic and Christian Fathers are full and distinct in their testimony respecting the primitive church organization. Clement of Rome, at the close of the first century, says: "The apostles, preaching in countries and cities, appointed the first-fruits of their labors bishops and deacons, having proved them by the Spirit." Polycarp, in the middle of the second century, exhorts the church at Philippi to "be subject to the elders and deacons," and makes no allusion to other officers. Jerome says: "A presbyter, therefore, is the same as a bishop; and before there were, by the devil's instigation, parties in re-

* *Decline and Fall of the Roman Empire,* ch. 15.

ITS POLITY.

ligion, and it was said among the people, I am of Paul, and I of Apollos, and I of Cephas, the churches were governed by the common council of presbyters."*

Respecting the election of officers, Clement of Rome cites as an apostolic rule in regard to church offices "that they should be filled according to the judgment of approved men, with the consent of the whole community." Cyprian, in the middle of the third century, required that the bishop be invested with his office "by the suffrage of the whole brotherhood and of the bishops present," and he urges the people to care in the selection of officers, for the reason that "they especially have the power either of electing worthy presbyters or of rejecting unworthy ones," and affirms that this right of choice by the people was observed in his day as resting on divine authority and apostolic usage.† Origen asserted that the presence of the people was required in the ordination of a presbyter to secure the election of the most worthy.‡ The Apostolical Constitutions, belonging probably toward the end of the third century, declare that the bishop is a "select person, chosen by the whole people." § The clearest proofs exist that many of the distinguished bishops of the Patristic period were chosen by the voice of the people, as Cyprian, of Carthage, Ambrose, of Milan, Martin, of Tours, Eustathius, of Antioch, Chrysostom, of Constantinople, and others. Even the Roman Pontifical, in the order for the ordination of a presbyter, recognizes the principle of popular suffrage, the bishop saying: "It was not without reason that the Fathers ordained that the advice of the people should be taken in the election of those persons who were to serve at the altar; to the end that, having given their assent to their ordination, they might the

---

* *Commentary on Titus.* † *Ep.* lxviii. 5. ‡ *Hom. vi.8 on Lev.*
§ Book viii. 8; 4 cf. 16.

more readily yield obedience to those who were so ordained."*

That the church, as a congregation, was the ultimate appeal in matters of discipline during the first three centuries rests upon equally clear testimony. Cyprian, speaking of the trial of certain offenders, declares that they "shall be tried, not only in the presence of his colleagues, but before the whole people;"† and he quotes an African synod as ordaining that, "except in danger of death or of sudden persecution, none should be received to the peace of the church without the knowledge and consent of the people."‡ Du Pin, an eminent Roman Catholic writer, after citing at great length the language of Cyprian addressed to Cornelius, Bishop of Rome, says: "From whence it is plain that both at Rome and at Carthage no one could be expelled from the church, or restored again, except with the consent of the people."§ Origen, at Cæsarea, and Chrysostom, at Constantinople, speak with equal distinctness on the right of the people to determine matters of discipline.

The fact is, moreover, everywhere obvious that the charge of a primitive bishop was, not over a diocese as now understood, but over a single church or congregation. This is shown by undoubted authorities. Campbell, an eminent Episcopalian historian, after quoting many Fathers of the second and third centuries, among others Ignatius, Justin Martyr, Irenæus, Tertullian, and Cyprian, concludes: "Now, from the writings of these Fathers it is evident that the whole flock assembled in the same place, *epi to auto*, with their bishop and presbyters, as on other

---

* *Pontific. Rom. in Ordinat. Presbyter*, fol. 38.
† *Ep.* xxxiv.   ‡ *Ep.* lix.
§ *De Antiqua Disciplina.*

occasions, so in particular every Lord's Day—or every Sunday, as it was commonly called—for the purpose of public worship, hearing the Scriptures read, and receiving spiritual exhortations. . . . Again, as there was but one place of meeting, so there was but one communion-table, an altar, as they sometimes metaphorically called it. 'There is but one altar,' said Ignatius, 'for there is but one bishop,' and accordingly but one place of worship." A further evidence that the primitive bishop presided over only a single congregation is seen in the fact that in the comparatively small territory of North Africa there were six hundred and ninety bishoprics, many of them known to embrace only a small town or village. Diocesan episcopacy did not become common till the fourth century, when the church was modelled after the empire. Ignatius is the only authority for the episcopacy during the first three centuries, and even he everywhere speaks of the bishop as over only one congregation, or parish. Of the fifteen epistles attributed to this Father, Archbishop Wake accepts seven as genuine, and Archbishop Usher only six; all the rest are unanimously rejected by Protestants as spurious. Of the seven accepted by Wake, the Chevalier Bunsen has proved four to be forgeries and the remaining three to be badly interpolated. The fair-minded Neander, the profoundest student of this Father, regards one only as having decided marks of genuineness. Bishop Stillingfleet, in his *Irenicum*, says: " Of all the thirty testimonials produced out of Ignatius in his epistle for episcopacy, I can meet with but one which is brought to prove the least semblance of an institution of Christ for episcopacy; and if I be not much deceived, the sense of *that* place is clearly mistaken."

A multitude of other authorities might be adduced;

but these, which are the highest in church history, suffice to show that the profoundest historical investigations confirm the view of the divine constitution of the church here derived from Scripture. And we close the subject with the words of Dr. Schaff: "The spirit and practice of the apostles thus favored a certain kind of popular self-government and the harmonious, fraternal co-operation of the different elements of the church. It countenanced no abstract distinction of clergy and laity. All believers are called to the prophetic, priestly, and kingly offices in Christ. The bearers of authority and discipline should, therefore, never forget that their great work is to train the governed to freedom and independence, and by the various spiritual offices to form gradually the whole body of believers to the unity of faith and knowledge, and to the perfect manhood of Christ."*

* *Church History*, vol. i. sect. 43.

PART II.

THE CHRISTIAN ORDINANCES.

SECTION I.

GENERAL VIEW.

RELIGION has in all ages found expression in symbolism. The sacrifice instituted at the Fall symbolized at once the confession of sin by the offerer, and the approach of a sinner to God only through the vicarious death of an innocent victim. The passover, in the blood of the slain lamb put on the lintel and door-posts of each house, signified the guilt and danger of the household, and their deliverance from God's judgment only through the blood of another slain for them. The Mosaic economy was one vast system of symbolism representing divine truth. The tabernacle, the sacrifices, the lustrations, the festivals, all the forms, were symbolic; they were significant acts expressive alike of the great truths of religion and of the profession of the worshipper's faith in them. The Christian religion, also, as instituted by Christ, has its symbolism—a symbolism far simpler indeed, but far more expressive and beautiful, than that of the Old Testament.

I. NUMBER OF THE ORDINANCES.

Baptism and the Lord's Supper are the permanent ordinances of the gospel. The Papal Church, as also the Greek, has seven sacraments, adding to the two named, Confirmation, Penance, Orders, Matrimony, and Extreme Unction. Protestants are unanimous in receiving only two. The Roman Catholic Church defines a sacrament as a "thing offered to the senses, which, by appointment of God, has the power at once of signifying and of effecting sanctification."* The Lutheran Church says: "We call rites, sacraments which have a command of God, and to which a promise of grace is added."† The Westminster Shorter Catechism defines a sacrament as "an holy ordinance instituted by Christ, wherein, by sensible signs, Christ and the benefits of the new covenant are represented, sealed, and applied to believers." ‡ The marks of an ordinance, as here conceived, are, 1. An outward symbol divinely appointed to represent a great fact or truth of the gospel and the personal relation of the recipient to that fact or truth. 2. A divine requirement, making its obligation universal and perpetual. These *criteria* are plainly present in Baptism and the Lord's Supper; they were instituted by divine authority and enjoined as of universal and perpetual obligation, and they not only symbolize great facts and truths of the gospel, but also constitute a personal profession of the recipient's relation to those facts and truths. For in them the significant action does not consist only in the acts of the administrator, in immersing in the name of the Trinity, and in consecrating the bread and wine, but also in the acts of the recipient, in his voluntary submission to baptism, and his eating and drinking

---
* *Rom. Catechism.* ii. 1, 11.   † *Apology for Aug. Conf.*, p. 200.
‡ Quest. 92.

at the Supper. These *criteria* are wanting in whole or part in the five added sacraments of the Roman Catholic Church.

II. Administrators of the Ordinances.

Ordained ministers of God's word are the proper administrators of the ordinances. There is, indeed, for this no positive divine precept, but it is the natural order, and it is fairly inferred alike from the fact that the duty of baptizing is enjoined by Christ in the ministerial commission, and that no clear example of the administration of ordinances by others is found in the New Testament. The validity of an ordinance, however, does not depend on the administrator, but on the character of the recipient and the nature of the act performed; for in respect to the administrator there is no positive law, while in respect to the character, both of the recipient and of the act, the law is explicit. Hence, the validity of baptism in the case of those immersed on a personal profession of faith is to be recognized, even when administered by men not themselves baptized; and hence, also, no church ought to neglect the ordinances when unable to obtain an ordained minister, but in such cases should appoint some proper person temporarily to administer them. Such a procedure rests, not on any right of a church to disregard a clearly-established divine order, but on the element of doubt, created by the absence of explicit precept or of extended example, whether this order is intended to be held as absolutely invariable, or may, under circumstances of necessity, be modified. The evidence shows it to have been the *usual* apostolic order; a departure from this order, therefore, can be justified only by unusual circumstances.

III. Obligation of the Ordinances.

The ordinances are *positive* institutions. The obligation to observe them, therefore, rests, not on our perception of their fitness, but wholly on the revealed will of God. Bishop Butler remarks: "*Moral* precepts are precepts the reasons of which we see; *positive* precepts are precepts the reasons of which we do not see. *Moral* duties arise out of the nature of the case itself, prior to external command; *positive* duties do not arise out of the nature of the case, but from external command. Moral and positive precepts are in some respects alike, in other respects different. So far as they are alike, we discern the reasons of both; so far as they are different, we discover the reasons of the former, but not of the latter."* It follows, as another has well said, that "as the obligation to obey a positive institution rests entirely on the revealed command of God, and not on our own perceptions of its appropriateness or of the general fitness of things, it requires *literal* as well as *sincere* obedience. No authority but that of the Supreme Lawgiver can change the form of an ordinance or positive institution of religion in the smallest particular. The power to change a positive institution involves the power to abrogate entirely. God only possesses this power. It has never been delegated to any of his creatures. Obedience to a positive institution of God, therefore, consists in two things: First, the *spirit* of sincere obedience, in which the understanding, the conscience, and the heart unite their full assent; . . . second, the *literal doing* of the *specific action* enjoined. Some other action than that commanded, or some other form observed as a substitute on the ground that no mere outward form can be in itself essential to salvation, is

---
* Butler's *Analogy*, part ii., ch. 1.

not, and from the nature of the case cannot be, obedience to a positive institution of Christ. Sincere obedience growing out of love, and the literal performance of the thing commanded, are both essential." *

The perpetual obligation of the ordinances is denied by the Quakers, who adduce such passages as the following: "I indeed baptize you with water unto repentance; but he that cometh after me is mightier than I, whose shoes I am not worthy to bear: he shall baptize you with the Holy Ghost, and with fire" (Matt. iii. 11). "If ye be dead with Christ from the rudiments of the world, why, as though living in the world, are ye subject to ordinances (touch not, taste not, handle not, which all are to perish with the using); after the commandments and doctrines of men?" (Col. ii. 20–22). From these passages it is inferred that the ordinances, though obligatory during the ministry of John, and used even during the ministry of Christ, ceased with the advent of the Holy Spirit, and are not now to be observed. Their perpetual obligation, however, is manifest from the following proofs: 1. Their design, as symbols representing the central, vital truths of the gospel, makes them of equal necessity in all ages. 2. The universal observance of them after the descent of the Holy Spirit, and during the age of the apostles, as is manifest in the Acts and in allusions in the Epistles. † 3. The explicit commands of the gospel requiring their observance till the second coming of Christ. Peter, on the conversion of Cornelius and other Gentiles, said: "Can any man forbid water, that these should not be baptized, which have received the Holy Ghost as well as we? And he commanded them to be baptized in the name of the

---

* Crowell's *Manual*, p. 149.

† See Acts ii. 38, 41, 42; viii. 36–40; xx. 7; Rom. vi. 3, 4; 1 Cor. xi. 23–26.

Lord" (Acts x. 47, 48). Ananias said to Saul: "And now, why tarriest thou? Arise and be baptized, and wash away thy sins, calling on the name of the Lord" (Acts xxii. 16) And Paul, when recording the institution of the Lord's Supper, said: "As often as ye eat this bread and drink this cup, ye do show the Lord's death till he come" (1 Cor. xi. 26). No intimation is anywhere found that these commands have ceased to be obligatory; and, without doubt, the outward ordinances were intended to be observed till the end of the world.

IV. Efficacy of the Ordinances.

Early in the history of the church the ordinances came to be regarded with superstitious veneration. In fact, they took, in the popular imagination, the place of the heathen mysteries. Extraordinary efficacy was attributed to them. Many of the Fathers spoke of them in the most extravagant language. Ignatius called the bread of the Lord's Supper "the medicine of immortality." The eloquent Chrysostom said: "They who approach the baptismal font are not only made clean from all wickedness, but also holy and just. Although a man should be foul with every human vice, the blackest that can be named, yet, should he fall into the baptismal pool, he ascends from the divine waters purer than the beams of the moon." Baptism and the Lord's Supper were on this account, as Neander observes, given to infant children because conceived "as absolutely necessary for salvation." Multitudes, misled by such teaching, pressed forward to receive the ordinances, supposing they conveyed a divine saving power.

This doctrine of sacramental grace was afterward developed more perfectly in the Romish Church. The Council of Trent, the recognized authority of Roman Catholics, declared: "A sacrament is something presented to the senses which has the power, by divine institution, not only of signifying, but also of efficiently conveying, grace." " If any shall say that the sacraments of the new dispensation do not contain the grace they signify, or that they do not confer the grace itself on those who oppose no obstacle, ... let him be anathema." The Reformers unhappily did not repudiate this fatal error. Luther taught that the grace signified actually resides as an inherent virtue in the ordinances, and this grace is conveyed to the recipients, but in the case of the adult only when he exercises faith. Hence, according to his view, baptism secures the salvation of all who die in infancy, and is in all cases essential to salvation; and the Supper communicates to the partaker the actual body and blood of Christ, by means of which, if the soul partake in faith, it receives eternal life. The English Church, in baptizing, say: "We yield thee hearty thanks, most merciful Father, that it hath pleased thee to regenerate this infant with thy Holy Spirit, to receive him for thine own child, and to incorporate him into thy holy church." Even the Westminster Confession of Faith declares: " By the right use of baptism the grace promised is not only offered, but really exhibited and conferred, by the Holy Ghost to such (whether of age or infants) to whom that grace belongs."

Now, this sacramentalism, which conceives of the ordinance as in itself containing divine grace, or as efficiently conveying it, we wholly reject. It conflicts with the whole current of Scripture teaching. For, 1. God always requires spiritual worship, and declares that, apart from this, the form is unacceptable to him: "God is a Spirit: and they that worship him must worship him in spirit and in truth" (John iv. 23, 24). 2. The one condition of salvation presented in the New Testament is personal faith in Christ—a spiritual, not a formal, condition. "Believe on the Lord Jesus Christ, and thou shalt be saved," is the word of God. Christ does, indeed, say: "He that believeth and is baptized shall be saved;" but he immediately adds—not he that is not baptized shall be damned, but—"he that *believeth not* shall be damned." He thus clearly shows that salvation is necessarily connected, not with baptism, but with faith. Baptism is, indeed, enjoined as an imperative duty, but not as containing or conveying salvation; it is only the outward, public expression of that inward faith by which salvation is obtained. Repentance and faith are constantly made prerequisite to the ordinances, but these are plainly exercises of a regenerated soul; and, as salvation thus precedes the ordinances, evidently it cannot be the effect of them. 3. The idea of acceptance with God by virtue of any outward rite is distinctly and strongly condemned in Scripture. Paul closes his great argument against the Jewish ritualists in these words: "For he is not a Jew, which is one outwardly; neither is that circumcision, which is outward in the flesh; but he is a Jew which is one inwardly; and circumcision is that of the heart, in the spirit, and not in the letter; whose praise is not of men, but of God" (Rom. ii. 28, 29). All ideas of divine favor as obtained by outward privilege or rite are here rejected, and a man's standing with God is plainly determined by inward, spiritual character. 4. Salvation based on outward forms, or conveyed through them, apart from spiritual condition, is repugnant to reason as well as Scripture. The conception of a mystic efficacy in the ordinances, as if there was something magical in a form or in a set of words, appeals, not to reason, but to superstition. The common sense of mankind instinctively feels that no outward rite can ever in itself confer spiritual grace.

What, then, is the efficacy of the ordinances? We answer: The Holy Spirit acts on the soul by means of the truth—truth whether set forth in language or in symbol. Thus, we are "born again, not of corruptible seed, but of incorruptible, by the word of God, which liveth and abideth for ever" (1 Pet. i. 23); and Jesus prayed for his disciples, "Sanctify them through thy truth" (John xvii. 11). Truth is the medium of the Holy Spirit's power in men. But as truth is more vividly set forth in symbol than in language, and as in the ordinances it is accompanied by a distinct act of the partaker—he being here not passively listening to it, but, with full assent of intellect, heart, and will, actively professing and obeying it—the truth is more clearly and affectingy apprehended in the ordinances, and becomes more effectually the medium of the Spirit's power within the soul. Their efficacy, then, may be conceived as twofold:

1. *They are symbols or visible representations of the vital, central truths of the gospel.* Augustine rightly defined *Sacramentum est verbum Dei visibile* "A sacrament is the word of God made visible." They represent in visible, unchanging forms the fundamental facts and doctrines of the gospel, thus setting them forth in a more distinct, impressive manner than is possible in words; for words address the ear—these symbols address the sight. Language, in the lapse of ages, undergoes changes in its structure and import, words alter in their meaning; but these expressive symbols remain unchanged, and their significance is unalterable. God has, therefore, set forth the two fundamental truths of the gospel, not in words only, but also in unchanging symbols. Regeneration, or the death to sin and entrance upon a new life in Christ, is expressed in the symbolic burial and resurrection in baptism. The atonement of Christ, as the only means of justification and the only support of this new life, is with

equal clearness symbolized in the Lord's Supper; and the ordinances, as the divinely-appointed witnesses of these vital truths, are to bear their impressive, unchanging testimony to the end of the world.

2. *They are symbolic acts in which a profession is made of personal faith in these truths.* They are a personal profession. When a man is baptized or partakes of the Lord's Supper, he does in these acts declare alike his belief of the truths these ordinances symbolize and his personal experience of them in his soul. It is the solemn public avowal that he has died to sin and risen to a new life in Christ, and that his hope now rests alone on the sacrifice of Christ, whose body was broken and blood shed for sin. It is the free, intelligent act of a redeemed soul, publicly declaring his personal experience of the new birth and his personal trust in the atonement of the Son of God. This voluntary profession, as the conscious, free, personal act of the recipient, was evidently and prominently present in every example of the celebration of the ordinances in the New Testament, and is, therefore, essential to their validity. For this reason, the ordinances cannot be administered to infants, because, in their case, it is not, and cannot be, the conscious, personal act of a free, intelligent, moral agent, but must be the unconscious, enforced act of a being not yet capable of intelligent, true worship. There is here neither an intellectual apprehension of the truths symbolized nor a voluntary exercise of faith in them; and the symbols, in such cases, can be only meaningless forms, representing no corresponding spiritual realities in the soul.

The ordinances, therefore, are not magical forms, conveying, *ex opere operato*, a secret, mysterious grace to those who receive them. The benefits they confer are these:

1. As vivid representations of the central facts and truths

of Christianity, they present them in a most distinct and affecting manner to the mind, and bring them in most direct contact with it. 2. As in receiving them the believer makes a personal profession of faith in Christ, his faith in them is expressed in a definite and most expressive act, and is thereby strengthened. They set before the soul a more vivid view of Christ, and awaken in it a deeper consciousness of union with him.

V. THE ORDINANCES, IN THEIR FORM AND ORDER, NOT TO BE CHANGED.

The ordinances being thus heaven-appointed symbols of vital truths, it results that, in their form and order, they may not be changed. In the symbolism of the Old Testament no man might alter the form. Here two laws were plainly fundamental: 1. That no symbol could be instituted except by God. He instituted sacrifices, circumcision, the passover, and all the ritual services; and in ordaining the tabernacle he charged Moses: "See thou make it according to the pattern showed thee in the mount." 2. No symbol, thus divinely instituted, might be changed by man; it was presumption. Nadab and Abihu presumed to offer incense kindled by other than the heaven-descended fire on the altar. Korah, Dathan, and Abiram ventured to assume the priest's office, which God assigned to Aaron; and the signal punishment with which they were visited stands out as a conspicuous vindication of the sanctity of the form and order of divine symbolism. Now, in the symbols of the New Testament these laws remain unchanged: they are in their nature universal. No man may alter or abrogate the symbols God has ordained.

Besides, the divine design in the ordinances is frustrated by altering their form. For God has two methods of setting forth his truth before men: one, by words or language; the other, by symbols or visible representations. The two symbols of the new dispensation represent the central, vital truths of the gospel. But the significance of a symbol, like that of a picture or portrait, depends on the distinctness and accuracy of the form. If the form is changed, it no longer conveys the truth designed. Who would not be indignant if a man should venture to alter the solemn words of Christ, "Ye must be born again"? But if it would be impious to alter the divine *words* which teach the necessity of regeneration, is it not equally impious to alter the divine *symbol* by which this great truth is visibly set forth before men? What finite mind can measure the injury done to the cause of vital religion and the souls of men by so altering this divine symbol as to destroy its power to set forth this momentous truth?

For more than three centuries the ripest scholarship has been engaged in biblical criticism, seeking to restore to the Hebrew and Greek text of God's word the very words in which the Holy Spirit spoke. With quenchless zeal and tireless industry, men like Griesbach, Lachmann, Tischendorf, and Tregelles have devoted their lives to the discovery and collation of ancient manuscripts, so as to ascertain with certainty the original words of Holy Writ. And we applaud their work: to find the very words in which God revealed eternal truth is an object worthy of heroic toil and sacrifice. But the ordinances, those great symbols in which God has also set forth his truth, and in which that truth was to be emphasized and made more impressive than was possible in words—is the maintenance of the original form and use of these an unimportant thing? Shall we be careful of the letter of God's word, and be careless as to the form of God's symbols?

The idea, therefore, that the form of the ordinance is non-essential is an utter misconception. For here the Holy Spirit is revealing truths by visible objects; and, as in all object-teaching, the whole value of the symbol lies in its form, its power to represent, to body forth, the truth symbolized. If this is destroyed, its whole purpose is lost. In insisting on the original God-given power of the ordinance we are not insisting on a non-essential point, but on the essence of the ordinance itself. We insist that man has no more right to alter a divine symbol than to alter the divine word; and in presuming to change the heaven-appointed symbol, he imperils the great truth that symbol was designed to represent.

The symbolism of the ordinances renders the *divine order* of them equally imperative. For baptism is the symbol of regeneration—it marks the entrance on a new spiritual life—while the Lord's Supper is the symbol of that faith in Christ's death by which this new life is sustained. The one symbolizes the new birth; the other, the bread of life by which the new-born are nourished. To administer the Lord's Supper to the unbaptized is to invert the natural order and destroy the divine symbolism. The apostles sacredly observed the divine order; it is never inverted in the Bible. Who, then, may presume to change the God-instituted order of these ordinances, and, by changing their relation, destroy their power to represent the truths he intended?

Baptism is the rite of admission to the church, the public act of separating from the world and uniting with God's people. It is the door of the house of God. The Supper, on the other hand, is an ordinance within the church, and is the highest expression of church-fellowship. The divine order distinctly symbolized the vital truth that regeneration is precedent to membership in the church. An inversion of the order of the ordinances, therefore, destroys their power to symbolize as God intended the distinction between the church and the world, and such an inversion necessarily tends to the actual obliteration of that distinction.

SECTION II.

THE FORM OF BAPTISM.

Bapto, the radical form, is never used to designate the rite of baptism, but is, as Professor Stuart rightfully says, "purposely, as well as habitually, excluded." Its meaning, as all parties concede, is: 1. *To immerse, to plunge;* 2. *To dye, to stain.* The latter is derived from the former, as dyeing was usually effected by dipping. The term, therefore, needs no examination here, especially as the concession is also universal that *baptizo*, while retaining the primary signification of *bapto, to immerse,* is not in all respects a synonym of it.

Baptizo, with its derivatives, is exclusively employed when the rite of baptism is designated; this term, therefore, demands our exclusive attention.

I. THE CLASSIC USAGE.

The classics never employ *baptizo*, or its derivatives, except when an immersion or a complete covering of the person or thing spoken of is indicated as the radical idea. Dr. Conant, after an elaborate examination of the word through the whole compass of Greek literature, says: "The grand idea expressed is to put into or under water (or other penetrable substance), so as entirely to immerse or submerge; this act is always expressed in the literal application of the word, and is the basis of its metaphorical uses. The idea of *emersion* is not included. Whether the object immersed sinks to the bottom, or floats in the liquid, or is immediately taken out, is determined, not by the word itself, but by the nature of the case, and by the design of the act in each particular case."* Dr. Anthon, the eminent classical editor, says: "The primary meaning of the word is *to dip* or *immerse;* and its secondary meanings, if it ever had any, all refer in some way or other to the same leading idea. Sprinkling, etc., are entirely out of the question." Professor Moses Stuart, of Andover, who carefully examined the subject, seeking a different conclusion, is constrained to admit that the only established classic senses of the word are: 1. *To dip, plunge, immerse* anything in liquid: 2. To *overwhelm*, literally or figuratively.† Liddell and Scott, the acknowledged lexical authority in classic Greek, define *baptizo* "*To dip in* or *under water;*" and they explain its figurative uses, such as to *soak*, to *drown*, to *sink*, as derived from this. The highest scholarship of this age, and of all preceding ages, sanctions the decision of these eminent linguists. The figurative usage of the word in the classics is rich and varied; but no example has been adduced in which the force of the figure does not depend, either directly or remotely, on this radical signification.

II. THE SEPTUAGINT USAGE.

Baptizo is used in the Septuagint four times: 2 Kings v. 14: Naaman "*dipped himself* seven times in the Jordan;" Isa. xxi. 4, which may be rendered literally "*Iniquity immerses*," "or overwhelms," *me;* Judith xii. 7;

* *Meaning and Use of Baptizein.*
† "Mode of Christian Baptism," *Bib. Rep.*, vol. iii., No. 2.

Sirach xxxiv. 25. The last two of these only require special examination; the others, without reasonable question, indicate immersion.

Judith xii. 6-9: And Judith "sent to Holofernes, saying, Let my lord now command to suffer his handmaid to go forth to prayer. And Holofernes enjoined his bodyguards not to hinder her. And she remained in the camp three days, and went forth nightly to the ravine of Bethulia and *dipped herself* in the camp at the fountain of water." It is objected in this case that an immersion was here impossible, and, if possible, it would have been indecorous. We reply: 1. The fountains of Bethulia must have been abundant, since, according to chapters vi. and vii., the entire supply of water for the city was derived from them. 2. The design of the ablution was the removal of ceremonial defilement contracted by contact in a heathen camp; for this the law required an entire ablution of the body. 3. The time was midnight; the lady was attended by her maid (chap. xiii. 3); the soldiers were specially charged not to molest her: all the circumstances forbid the idea of spectators. 4. If she required for the purification only sprinkling or pouring, there was no reason for leaving her tent at all to go to the fountain, for in this case a pitcher of water would have sufficed.

Sirach xxxiv. 25: "He who is *immersed* from a dead body and toucheth it again, what did he profit by his bathing?" It has been objected that *baptizo* here signifies sprinkling, since "the water of separation" was sprinkled on him who touched a dead body. But observe: The law (Num. xix. 2-9) required several acts of him who touched a dead body—to be sprinkled with the water of separation; to wash his clothes; "to bathe himself in water." Plainly, the last act in the process is here, by synecdoche, made to designate the whole, as, in Heb. ix. 13, the first act of the process is, by the same figure, used for the whole. Thus, in Acts xx. 7, *to break bread* designates the Lord's Supper in both acts, the breaking and the pouring—a part designating the whole, but the verb *to break* does not thereby come to signify *to pour:* the synecdoche does not in either case change the meaning of the word. Besides, in this passage, the word *loutron*, "bathing," itself suggests an immersion rather than a sprinkling.

III. THE NEW TESTAMENT USAGE.

Baptizo, in the New Testament, is always used with the fundamental idea of immersion, either literal or figurative. Of this we present the following distinct lines of proof:

First: The classic and Septuagint usage, already examined, requires this sense in the New Testament, unless plain indications show a departure from it.

The primary meaning of the word and its ordinary meaning elsewhere being confessedly "immersion," the presumption clearly is that such is its import in the New Testament. The burden of proof rests on him who affirms a different import. It will be observed also that the argument for another meaning is a labored attempt to make out from alleged exceptional uses that in the New Testament the word has not its natural and ordinary sense, and this against the whole current of philological and historical evidence. And if this were made out, it would show that, while the Greek language had in common use separate and definite words to express sprinkling and pouring, the Holy Spirit, neglecting these, strangely selected a word everywhere else signifying "immersion," to express these other and very different acts— a conclusion which must surely need the most weighty proofs, since it seems an impeachment of the divine wisdom.

Second: The lexicons of the New Testament, both earlier and later, almost without exception, restrict the meaning of *baptizo* to "*immersion.*"

It seems needless to quote the testimony of the earlier lexicographers and scholars, such as Scapula, Schleusner, Bretschneider, Passow, and the long array of other names distinguished in New Testament literature; for Professor Stuart, of Andover, in his work above quoted, affirms that "all lexicographers and critics of any note are agreed that *baptizo* means to *dip, plunge,* or *immerse* in any liquid." In this view have concurred not only all the Reformers— Luther, Melanchthon, and Calvin—but also the most eminent scholars since the Reformation alike on the Continent and in England. Of the most recent lexicographers, Cremer, in his *Biblico-Theological Lexicon of the New Testament Greek,* recently translated, defines *baptizo,* "*to immerse, submerge,*" and speaks of "the peculiar New Testament and Christian use of the word" as an "immersion, submersion for a religious purpose." He gives no other literal sense. Wilke's *Lexicon of the New Testament Greek,* edited by Grimm and lately issued in Germany, defines *baptizo:* 1. "*To immerse repeatedly, to submerge;* 2. *To wash or bathe* by immersing or submerging; 3. *To overwhelm.*" He affirms that baptism, in the New Testament, is "an immersion in water." Professor Sophocles, of Harvard University, a native Greek, in his *Lexicon of the Greek of the Roman and Byzantine Periods,* B. C. 140 to A. D. 1000, defines it in the same way, as signifying, 1. *To dip, immerse, sink,* with figurative uses derived from this; 2. Middle, *to perform ablution, to bathe;* 3. *To plunge* a knife; 4. *To baptize;* and he insists that "there is no evidence that Luke and Paul and the other writers of the New Testament put upon this verb meanings not recognized by the Greeks." The most eminent biblical scholars of the recent period, as Fritsche, Lange, and Meyer in Germany and Conybeare and Howson, Alford, Lightfoot, Ellicott, and Plumptre of the Anglican Church, are in full accord with these latest utterances in New Testament lexicography.

Third: The construction in which baptizo is found implies the sense of immersion.

It is construed with the word expressing the element of baptism as follows: 1. Once with *eis*, Mark i. 9: "*into* the Jordan." 2. Thirteen times with *en, in*, followed by a word denoting either water or the Holy Spirit. 3. Three times with the dative without a preposition, that case being here used, according to its common signification, to denote the sphere in which the action took place. Other examples of the verb construed with prepositions occur, but these are all in which the construction involves the element of baptism, and in which, therefore, the form of the act would be indicated; and, while in all these the construction suggests the idea of an immersion, in most of them that idea is absolutely required.

Fourth: The passages usually adduced as admitting a different sense do, in fact, require the sense of immersion.

Mark vii. 3, 4: "The Pharisees and all the Jews, except they wash (*nipsōntai*) their hands oft, eat not, holding the tradition of the elders. And when they come from the market, except they wash (*baptisōntai*), they eat not. And many other things there be, which they have received to hold, as the washing (*baptismous*) of cups, and pots, and brazen vessels, and of tables (*klinōn*)." Here the inconvenience of the acts referred to is supposed to forbid an immersion. But observe: 1. The marked contrast evidently intended between *nipsōntai*, "wash their hands" (v. 3), and *baptisōntai*, "wash" (v. 4), implies that the act expressed by the latter was far more onerous and difficult than that expressed in the former. The progress in the thought, as conceived by De Wette and Meyer, is this: "(*a*) Before every meal the washing of hands; but (*b*) after the return from the market, where there was so much danger of coming in contact with unclean men, the bath was used as a washing of the whole body." 2. It is not affirmed that these customs were required by the law, but they are adduced as instances of the superstitious, absurd excess to which the Pharisees went in ceremonial purifications. Sprinkling would certainly have been a much less obvious excess, and would hardly have called for so special a notice. It is the great inconvenience to which they put themselves which the passage specially emphasizes. 3. The law did require ablution of the entire person for ceremonial uncleanness (Lev. xi. 32; xv.), and that the traditionalists among the Jews actually required immersion in the cases here mentioned is attested by men of the highest authority in Jewish learning. Thus, Maimonides, the learned Hebrew theologian and expounder of their traditional law in the twelfth century, says: "If the Pharisees touched but the garments of the common people, they were defiled and needed immersion, and were obliged to it. Hence, when they walked the streets, they walked on the sides of the way, that they might not be defiled by touching the common people."* Grotius, one of the most profound students of rabbinic literature, comments on this passage: "They cleansed themselves very carefully by not only washing their hands, but even by washing their body." 4. The word *klinōn*, here rendered "tables," in the margin "couches," is not found in the oldest manuscripts, the Sinaitic and the Vatican, as also in others of high authority; and it is therefore omitted from the latest text of Tischendorf as in all probability not a part

* See Dr. Gill *in loco.*

of the inspired word. But if its genuineness be supposed, the alleged improbability of an immersion is purely imaginary. For, (1.) The *klinē* is not necessarily to be understood of a raised couch-frame; it commonly consisted then, as it does now, of a mere rug or cushion, which was spread down to recline on when eating. The same word is used to designate the bed on which the paralytic was brought to Christ, and which, when he was healed, the man carried back to his house (Matt. ix. 6). It was evidently nothing but the common rug on which Orientals recline either in eating or sleeping. But if a raised frame be supposed, the *klinē* would naturally designate, not the frame, but the rug that covered it, which alone would become unclean by contact, and which was easily removed and washed. (2.) The Jews' traditional law, or Mishna, contains some precepts which indicate that even the frames of the couches were required to be immersed by their superstitions. Maimonides says: "Their canon runs thus: A bed that is wholly defiled, if he dips it part by part, it is pure." Again: "If he dips the bed in it (the pool of water), although its feet are plunged into the thick clay (at the bottom of the pool), it is clean." Here, it is plain, even the frame was immersed, and was probably taken apart for the purpose. Dr. Gill, who was distinguished for his rabbinic learning, in commenting on this passage, has collected a large body of evidence from the Mishna of the absurd superstitious observances which the evangelist here condemns. Meyer says: "The expression in Mark vii. 4 is not to be understood of the washing of the hands, but of an immersion, which the word always means in the classics and in the New Testament—that is, according to the context, the taking of a bath." Thus also De Wette and others.

Luke xi. 37, 38: "And as he spoke, a certain Pharisee

besought him to dine with him; and he went in and sat down to meat. And when the Pharisee saw it, he marvelled that he had not first washed (*ebaptisthē*) before dinner." Here, also, the inconvenience of an immersion is supposed to require a different sense of the word—an objection which overlooks the difference between the dress and customs of Oriental life and those in the Western world. A bath would have required little time or trouble. Here Jesus had been in a crowd composed of all classes, and the possible defilement extended to the whole body. The washing of hands, therefore, would not have sufficed; but, as in the previous case (Mark vii. 3, 4), Jewish tradition required a complete immersion, for which, doubtless, the Pharisee's house furnished abundant means, as the better class of Oriental houses do now. Meyer comments on this incident: "They expected that he would first purify himself by an immersion—that is, by a bath (comp. on Mark vii. 3, 4)—before the meal." If the Pharisee himself would not eat after coming from a crowd without bathing (as is shown in Mark), it was certainly natural that he should expect so distinguished a rabbi as Jesus would not do so, and should express his surprise at the omission.

Acts ii. 41: "Then they that gladly received his word were baptized: and the same day there were added unto them about three thousand souls." It is here supposed that the immersion of three thousand at Jerusalem in one day is wholly improbable, if not impossible. But it should be observed the text does not affirm that three thousand were *baptized* on that day, but only that this number were "added to the church." How they were added is not stated. It is surely not impossible that many who had already been baptized by John the Baptist, and by the apostles during the ministry of our Lord, were among those who publicly united with the church on that day, and these needed no further baptism. But, not to insist on this, if we suppose the actual baptism of three thousand, there was no difficulty in immersion, as the following considerations show:

1. *As to administrators.* If we restrict the administration to such as had a ministerial commission, the twelve were certainly there; and of the "seventy" we know some were present, for one of them had just been chosen to the apostleship. These had all been commissioned by Christ himself to preach and baptize; and if all of them were present, it would be less than thirty-seven candidates to each administrator.

2. *As to time.* It is a mistake to suppose that immersion requires of necessity much more time than sprinkling or pouring; for in either method of administering the rite, the formula must be pronounced and the act performed in the case of each person separately. It must be remembered, also, that the dress and customs of Orientals require far less elaborate preparations for immersion than with us; especially would this be the case at the time of the Pentecost, occurring in the hot season of the year.

3. *As to water.* The supposition is certainly not necessary that all assembled at one time and place for baptism; it is, perhaps, hardly probable. But even were this necessary, an immersion would present no difficulty, for Jerusalem has in all ages been distinguished for its immense supply of water. Strabo's brief description of the city is: "Jerusalem, a rocky, well-enclosed fortress; within, well watered; without, wholly dry." It is a remarkable fact that in all the sieges through which the city has passed, though it has often been reduced to fearful straits from hunger, it has never suffered from lack of water. Dr. Robinson, after describing "the immense cis-

terns now and anciently existing within the area of the temple," says: "In addition to these, almost every private house in Jerusalem, of any size, is understood to have at least one or more cisterns, excavated in the soft limestone on which the city is built. The house of Mr. Lanneau, in which we resided, had no less than four cisterns; and as these are but a specimen of the manner in which all the better class of houses are supplied, I subjoin the dimensions:

	Length.	Breadth.	Depth.
	Feet.	Feet.	Feet.
I	15	8	12
II	8	4	15
III	10	10	15
IV	30	30	20

Most of these cisterns," he adds, "have undoubtedly come down from ancient times; and their immense extent furnishes a full solution of the question as to the supply of water for the city."

Besides these private tanks, there were at least six immense public pools accessible, any one of which was adequate for the immersion of three thousand. The dimensions of these pools are given by Dr. Robinson as follows:*

Pools.	Length.	Width.	Depth
	Feet.	Feet.	Feet.
Pool of Bethesda	360	130	75
Upper Gihon	316	200 to 218	18 at the ends.
Lower Gihon	592	245 to 275	35 to 42 at the ends
Pool of Hezekiah	240	144	
Pool of Siloam	53	18	19
The King's Pool	15	6	

* *Researches*, vol. i. pp. 323–348, ed. of 1856. See, also, *Sufficiency of Water for Baptizing in Jerusalem and elsewhere in Palestine*, by G. W. Samson, D D. American Baptist Publication Society.

Besides these, a reservoir of vast extent exists under the temple area, while within and around the city are the ruins of many others, not here named, which in the Apostolic age were in use. That these public pools are used for bathing, the visitor at Jerusalem may have ample ocular proof any day—and this was, without doubt, the custom anciently—while the gradually-descending sides of some of them, by successive platforms, afford convenience for bathing or baptism. Indeed, the Mosaic law required so much use of water for ceremonial ablutions, and the traditions of the elders so greatly increased the demand that the most extensive bathing accommodations must always have existed. Josephus affirms that from one to two hundred thousand stranger Jews, from all parts of the world, were wont to gather in and around the Holy City at the passover, crowding its sacred precincts and covering with their tents "the mountains round about Jerusalem." Most of these must have contracted ceremonial uncleanness on their journey, each of whom must needs "wash his clothes and bathe himself in water" before entering the temple. Surely, in the presence of such facts, the objection made to the immersion of the three thousand at the Pentecost, based on the lack of water, is simply absurd; it implies singular ignorance alike of the Holy City and of the Old Testament.

Bishop Ellicott's *Commentary on the New Testament*, edited in Acts by Professor E. H. Plumptre, D. D., says on Acts ii. 41: "The largeness of the number has been urged as rendering it probable that the baptism was by affusion, not immersion. On the other hand, (1.) Immersion had clearly been practised by John and was involved in the meaning of the word, and it is not likely that the rite should have been curtailed of its full proportions at the very outset. (2.) The symbolic meaning of the act requires immersion, in order that it might be clearly manifested, and Rom. vi. 4 and 1 Pet. iii. 21 seem almost of necessity to imply the more complete mode. The swimming-baths of Bethesda and Siloam, or the so-called Fountain of the Virgin, near the temple enclosure, or the bathing-places within the Tower of Antonia (Jos., *Wars*, v. 5, 8), may well have helped to make the process easy."

Heb. ix. 10: "Divers washings," *diaphorois baptismois*. These different baptisms are supposed by some to refer to different forms of ceremonial purification among the Jews, and thus to furnish ground for supposing that there were different forms of the Christian rite. But it is far more natural to refer it to the different occasions on which ablution was required than to a difference in the form of ablution. The different occasions on which the law required ablution are explained (Lev. xv. 16; xxvi. 28; Num. xix.). Professor Stuart comments: "Most evidently *baptismois* refers to the ceremonial ablutions of the Jews which were concerned with external purification." Thus all respectable commentators. Maimonides, the celebrated rabbi, speaking of Jewish ablutions, as quoted by Lightfoot, says: "Wheresover in the law washing of the garments or body is mentioned, it means nothing else than the washing of the whole body; for if any wash himself all over except the very tip of his little finger, he is still in his uncleanness."

Fifth: The baptisms of the New Testament, in the circumstances attending them, furnish proof that the ordinance was an immersion.

John baptized chiefly "in the Jordan," "in the river Jordan," a stream which, according to Lieutenant Lynch,* has a width varying from seventy-five to one hundred

---

* See Lynch's *Expedition to the Jordan and Dead Sea.*

and fifty feet and a depth varying from three to twelve feet. The exact position of Enon, where he also baptized (John iii. 23), is not determined. The name is Chaldee, and denotes *springs*. Two things only are known: the name denotes abundant waters, and it was selected by John as a place for baptizing "because there was much water there." *Hudata polla*, here rendered "much water," can hardly be restricted, as some affirm, to "many rivulets;" for the only other places in which it occurs present the image of mighty floods or of the sea (Rev. i. 15; xvii. 1; xix. 6). Olshausen comments: "When Jesus left the city, he bent his steps toward the Jordan, where he baptized, remaining, however, in the country of the Jews. John also was baptizing in the neighborhood, because the water there, being deep, afforded convenience for immersion." Now, if the rite did not require immersion, what need was there of resorting to rivers and to places where "there was much water"? In the vast crowds attending Christ's preaching, as at the Sermon on the Mount, no allusion is made to the need of water; it is mentioned only where baptizing is referred to. "Much water" certainly could not have been necessary for sprinkling or pouring, as it is not necessary for such purpose now.

Matt. iii. 16: "And Jesus, when he was baptized, went up straightway out of (*apo*) the water." Mark i. 9, 10: "Jesus came from Nazareth of Galilee, and was baptized of John in (*eis*) the Jordan. And straightway coming up out of (*ana-ek*) the water, he saw the heavens opened." The baptism of Christ, as described in these passages, is clearly indicated as an immersion. This is evident—
1. *From the meaning of baptizo.* Confessedly, the primary and usual sense of this word elsewhere is *immerse;* this, therefore, is its meaning here, unless the context requires a different one. 2. *From the construction and the necessary*

force of the words. In Matthew it is stated that the baptism took place "in the river Jordan," and that "when Jesus was baptized, he went up straightway out of the water," or rather, according to the best text, "*from* the water." Here, then, the verb requires immersion: the act was performed "in" the river, and after it "he went up from the water." Certainly the natural inference is that he was immersed, for there is no other conceivable reason for his entering the stream. But Mark is even more explicit as to the form of the act. Jesus "was baptized of John in (*eis, into*) the Jordan," where the preposition *eis, into*, is naturally construed as the exponent of the action of the verb. After the baptism Jesus is seen "straightway coming (*ana-ek*) *up out of* the water." Here the prepositions, *eis* and *ek*, are placed in contrasted relation, and must, therefore, as in Acts viii. 36–10, have their full force. Winer, in his *Grammar of the New Testament*, says: "*Ek* originally denotes issuing *from within* (the compass, sphere of) something (antithetic to *eis*)." The terms, therefore, the construction, and the circumstances here require immersion, as most commentators agree. Meyer comments: "*Eis ton Iordanēn*," into the Jordan—"a representation of the dipping into." Farrar says: "Jesus descended into the waters of the Jordan."* Thus Olshausen, Bloomfield, Campbell.

An immersion and emersion in this case is evident, also, from our Lord's words: "Thus it becometh us to fulfil all righteousness." For it is plain that, as he was not an actual sinner, he could receive this symbol of confession of sin and repentance only as indicating his voluntary assumption of the place of the sinful, the Sin-bearer for men, and his baptism was thus prefigurative of his death and resurrection for the putting away of sin. He,

* *The Life of Christ*, vol. i., *in loco*.

the Sinless One, therein freely took on him the position and responsibilities of the Sin-bearer by a symbolic act which symbolized at once the confession and renunciation of sin, and the death and resurrection he should accomplish for its removal. Thus Stier, on Matt. iii. 15, says of Christ's baptism: "It is truly and essentially the true *beginning-point* of that obedience the consummation of which, in the death of the cross in order to the resurrection, it pre-typifies. . . . As in this baptism, by prophetic figure, the righteous One places himself among sinners, so was he afterward baptized with the baptism of death, in which he as the Lamb of God bore our guilt, . . . and, as he finally spoke of his sufferings as a baptism, so does he now already contemplate in baptism his sufferings."*

Acts viii. 36–40: "And they went down both into the water, both Philip and the eunuch; and he baptized him. And when they were come up out of the water, the Spirit of the Lord caught away Philip." On the baptism of the eunuch, here recorded, I remark: 1. *The sufficiency of water for an immersion.* Three roads lead, and probably always have led, from Jerusalem to Gaza. Two of these present rival claims as the location of this transaction. That which passes through Bethlehem and Hebron has a large number of streams and pools ample for immersion, but ancient tradition fixes on the great fountain at Bethzur, twenty miles from Jerusalem, as the true place. The other road, west of this, passes through Beit Jibrin, the ancient Eleutheropolis, and is in some parts "desert." Dr. Robinson, describing this, says: "When we were at Tell el-Hazy, and saw *the water standing along* the bottom of the adjacent wady, we could not but remark the coincidence of several circumstances with the account of the eunuch's baptism. This water is on the most direct route

* *Words of the Lord Jesus*, vol. i.

from Beit Jibrin to Gaza, on the most southern road from Jerusalem, and in the midst of the country now 'desert' —that is, without villages or fixed habitations. The thought struck us that this might not improbably be the place of water described. There is at present no other similar water on this road; and various circumstances— the way to Gaza, the chariot, and the subsequent finding of Philip at Azotus—all go to show that the transaction took place near the plain."* 2. *The language suggests an immersion.* Before the act of baptism, "both went down into the water;" after the act of baptism, they "came up out of the water." Why go "down into the water"? If the act were sprinkling or pouring, it could not require then, as it does not require now, any such procedure.

It is objected in this, as in some other passages, that the prepositions *eis* and *ek*, here rendered *into* and *out of*, may be translated *to* and *from*, and consequently there is no need of supposing that the parties entered the water at all. We reply: 1. Such a deviation from the ordinary meaning of these prepositions is never found when, as here, they stand together and express contrasted action. When in an antithesis, they necessarily express *into* and *out of*. 2. The laws of interpretation require us to take words in their ordinary signification, unless the nature of the subject or the context forbids. A departure from this principle would unsettle the meaning of all language and destroy all certainty as to the most vital truths. Thus Christ said of the wicked: "These shall go away into (*eis*) everlasting punishment, but the righteous into (*eis*) life eternal" (Matt. xxv. 26). But if the objection here made be valid, there is no proof that either the righteous will go into heaven or the wicked into hell; they will go *to* or *toward* the abodes

* See *Researches*, vol. ii., note 32; also, Dr. Samson's *Sufficiency of Water*.

of bliss or of misery, but will never enter. Plainly, such exegesis deprives language of all definite meaning. It is said also that in such an expression as "He went up (*eis*) *into* the mountain" (Matt. v. 1), the preposition cannot mean *into*, since he did not penetrate the bowels of the mountain, but only went up on it. Here, however, the English idiom corresponds with the Greek, and requires the preposition *into;* for if it read *to, toward, up to*, it would not indicate the fact that he ascended it. "Into the mountain," in Greek as in English, indicates that he left the limits of the plain and entered within the limits of the mountain, just as one is said to go *into* a city or go *into* a field.

Acts xvi. 29-34: And the keeper of the prison "brought them out and said, Sirs, what must I do to be saved? And they said, Believe on the Lord Jesus Christ, and thou shalt be saved, and thy house. And they spake unto him the word of the Lord, and to all that were in his house. And he took them the same hour of the night, and washed their stripes, and was baptized, he and all his, straightway. And when he had brought them into his house, he set meat before them, and rejoiced, believing in God with all his house." Note here the order of the events: 1. The jailer brought the apostles out of the prison into his house, and they preached the gospel to him and to all there. 2. He conducted the apostles forth to a place where there was water, washed their stripes, and was baptized, he and all his. 3. After baptism he brought them up into his house, set meat before them, and rejoiced, believing in God with all his house. If, now, baptism was administered by sprinkling, why take them out of the house to perform it? In regard to water for immersion, it is an obvious remark that the river beside which they had been wont to meet for prayer was not distant, and the jailer's confidence in the apostles might have left him free to take them there. Lange says: "The rite was unquestionably administered in the court within the enclosure of the prison, at a well or tank." Such tanks or pools, often of large size, as already seen, were common in the courts of Oriental and Greek houses, and would be highly probable in a prison. Thus Conybeare and Howson, Meyer and De Wette.

In all the instances cited above the circumstances, so far as indicated, require us to understand baptism as an immersion; any other interpretation is inconsistent with the sacred record.

Sixth: The figurative usage of baptizo also requires immersion as the fundamental idea.

Luke xii. 50: "I have a baptism to be baptized with, and how am I straitened till it be accomplished!" Matt. xx. 22, 23: "Are ye able . . . to be baptized with the baptism that I am baptized with?" Baptism is here used to set forth the sufferings of Christ, but the image is wholly incongruous if the rite were sprinkling or pouring; it would belittle the whole subject. But the soul of Christ overwhelmed in sufferings, imaged by the body overwhelmed in water, is a figure striking and significant, and it is in strict analogy with Hebraistic usage. Thus, Ps. xlii. 7: "All thy waves and thy billows are gone over me." Lange comments: "*A baptism to be baptized with:* Over against the heavenly fire which he sends stands the earthly water of the sufferings which previously to that must roll over him. *To be baptized:* An image of the depth and intensity of this suffering, like a baptism performed by immersion." Olshausen says: "The figurative expression *baptism* involves at once the idea of a painful submersion (a dying to that which is old), and also a joyful rising (a resurrection in that which is new), as Rom.

vi. 3 shows. Such a path of suffering, in order to his being made perfect, our Lord declared stood yet before him." Alford also: "The symbolic nature of baptism is here to be borne in mind. Baptism = death. The figure in the sacrament is the *drowning*, the *burial* in the water, of the *old man*, and the *resurrection* of the *new man*. *The Lord's baptism was his death*, in which the body inherited from the first Adam was buried, and the new body raised again."

Acts i. 5: "John truly baptized with water, but ye shall be baptized with the Holy Ghost not many days hence." A common figure represents the Holy Spirit as *poured out*, and the same act, it is alleged, is here called baptism; it is, therefore, inferred that pouring is one form of baptism. Let us, however, test this principle of interpretation. When the apostles were baptized in the Holy Spirit at the Pentecost, it is said that they were " all *filled* with the Holy Ghost." The act of *filling*, then, according to this principle, must also be one form of baptism. Plainly, such a method of interpretation can only lead to the grossest absurdities. The true explanation is simple and obvious. The Greek *pneuma* literally signifies wind, or air in motion, and the figurative usage conformed to this radical idea. Hence, John is said to be "in the Spirit;" Christians are to "walk in the Spirit"—that is, the soul surrounded, pervaded, by the presence of the Holy Spirit, as the body is surrounded, pervaded, by the air. No figure could more perfectly set forth the fulness and richness of the Spirit's presence than the image of the soul immersed in it. Lange comments: "The gift of the Spirit is here termed a baptism, and is thus characterized as one of most abundant fulness, and as a submersion in a purifying and life-giving element." Meyer, on the parallel passage—Matt. iii. 11. "He shall baptize you with (*en*) the Holy Ghost and with fire"—says: "*En* (*in*) is, in accordance with the meaning of *baptizo* (immerse), not to be understood instrumentally, but, on the contrary, *in*— in the element wherein the immersion takes place."

Rom. vi. 3, 4: "Know ye not that so many of us as were baptized into Jesus Christ were baptized into his death? Therefore we are buried with him by baptism into death; that like as Christ was raised from the dead by the glory of the Father, even so we also should walk in newness of life." Paul is showing that a Christian, in the nature of things, cannot continue in sin, because he has died to sin and has risen to a new life in Christ. This death to sin and the new life in Christ, he says, are set forth in the very act by which we profess our faith to Christ. The points of comparison are: 1. Christ, in that nature on which sin was laid, died and was buried; believers, as also with him dead to sin, are in baptism symbolically buried with him. 2. Christ was raised from the dead and entered upon a new and glorious life in heaven; believers, as risen with him, are also in baptism symbolically raised from the dead to enter into a new and endless life. This great spiritual fact in the believer's experience—his death to sin and resurrection to new life is thus symbolized in the immersion and emersion of baptism. The apostle reasons, therefore, that the initial symbol of the Christian religion, in its very form, shows the impossibility that a Christian should live in sin, since such a return to a life of sin would be as if one who had died and entered into the new and glorious resurrection life should return to an earthly life of sin, and as if Christ himself, who once died here to put away sin, and then rose to his eternal glory in heaven, should return as the Sin-bearer and reassume his humiliation on earth. The argument of the passage is thus based on the form of the rite as an immersion and emersion.

Here observe: 1. The allusion in this passage to immersion as the form of baptism has been almost universally recognized by the church in all ages, embracing all the ancient commentators and nearly all the modern. Dr. Schaff, in Lange, *in loco*, says: "All commentators of note (except Stuart and Hodge) expressly admit, or take it for granted, that in this verse . . . the ancient, prevailing mode of baptism by immersion and emersion is implied, as giving additional force to the going down of the old and the rising up of the new man." Conybeare and Howson remark: "This passage cannot be understood unless it be understood that the primitive baptism was by immersion." Canon Lightfoot, of St. Paul's, commenting on this passage, says: "The sacrament of baptism, as administered in the Apostolic age, involved a two-fold symbolism—a death or burial, and a resurrection; these were represented by two distinct acts—the disappearance beneath the water, and the emergence from the water." 2. If the allusion here is to immersion, it necessarily follows that there was but *one* primitive form of the rite, and all Christians were immersed. For "*as many as were baptized*" were baptized into Christ's death, and were "*buried with him in baptism unto death*." 3. Burial, in Paul's day, was commonly in the earth, as is plain from Luke xi. 44: "Graves which appear not, and the men that walk over them are not aware of them;" although sometimes, among the wealthy, it was in the rock-hewn sepulchre; but it was in all cases a complete covering of the body, so that immersion was then, as now, a proper symbol of burial.

1 Cor. x. 1, 2: "All our fathers were under the cloud, and all passed through the sea, and were all baptized unto

Moses in the cloud and in the sea." Here the exact position of Israel, when the apostle contemplated them as baptized to Moses, was when they were *under the cloud* and *passing through the sea*. This was their position, in the writer's conception, when said to be baptized. No image of immersion could be more distinct. As Israel, covered by the cloud, entered the open sea, which "stood as a wall unto them on their right and on their left," and then emerged on the other side, it strikingly represented an immersion. Meyer comments: "*En te nephalē: en* is local, as in *baptizo en hudati* (Matt. iii. 11, *āl*), indicating the element in which, by immersion and emergence, the baptism was effected. Just as the convert was baptized *in water* with reference to Christ, so also that Old Testament analogue of baptism which presents itself in the people of Israel at the Red Sea, with reference to Moses, was effected in the *cloud* under which they were, and in the *sea* through which they passed." Alford says: They "entered by the act of such immersion into a solemn covenant with God, and became his church under the law as given by Moses, God's servant—just as we Christians by our baptism are bound in a solemn covenant with God, and enter his church under the gospel as brought by Christ, God's eternal Son." He adds: "The allegory is obviously not to be pressed minutely, for neither did they *enter* the cloud nor were they *wetted* by the waters of the sea; but they *passed under* both, as the baptized passes under the water, and it was said of them (Ex. xiv. 31), 'Then the people feared the Lord, and believed the Lord and his servant Moses.'"

1 Pet. iii. 21: "The like figure whereunto even baptism doth also now save us (not the putting away of the filth of the flesh, but the answer of a good conscience toward God), by the resurrection of Jesus Christ." This passage

shows—1. That Noah was saved by water—that is, he was delivered from destruction in the corruption of the old world, and borne into the new and renovated world by means of water. 2. That this salvation of Noah by means of water was a type of our salvation by water—that is, by baptism, by which in symbol we pass from the corrupt world of sin into the new world of holiness. 3. That we are saved by baptism, not because salvation is secured by the outward act (by which only the filth of the body could be removed), but by a conscience made right toward God through the resurrection of Christ; of which resurrection baptism is a symbol. Plainly, the passage thus analyzed was not designed to teach the form, but the relation, of baptism; but, so far as the form is indicated, immersion only meets its conditions. For the waters of baptism are compared to the Flood. Baptism, as an outward act, is "the putting away of the filth of the flesh," and as the symbol of an inward act it represents a conscience made right toward God by the resurrection of Christ.

Thus, in all instances of the figurative use of *baptizo*, the radical idea or basis of the figure is an immersion.

Seventh: The design of baptism, as an ordinance, indicates, with equal clearness, immersion as the only form of administration. As a symbol, it sets forth:

1. *Regeneration, or the new birth.* Jesus said: "Except a man be born of *water* and of the Spirit, he cannot enter into the kingdom of God" (John iii. 5), where "water" evidently refers to baptism as the outward symbol in which the inward work of the Spirit finds expression. The outward act is first mentioned, because, though not preceding in order of time, it is, as outward, the more obvious; as is also done Rom. x. 9 and Tit. iii. 5. Now, a change so radical and comprehensive as regeneration,

the entrance of the soul on a new spiritual existence, could not be symbolized in sprinkling or pouring; but in a solemn immersion it finds fitting expression.

2. *A death to sin and a resurrection to a new life in Christ.* Paul addresses believers in Christ as "buried with him by baptism, wherein also ye are risen with him through the faith of the operation of God, who hath raised him from the dead" (Col. ii. 12). Baptism is here a symbolic burial and resurrection; and the immersion of the body in water and emersion from it clearly and strikingly symbolize the inward, spiritual facts. The force and beauty of this symbolism has the recognition of all the ages. But how can sprinkling or pouring set forth a burial and resurrection? The symbol and the facts symbolized are incongruous.

3. *The complete surrender of the whole being, body, soul, and spirit, to the triune God, in full and eternal allegiance to Christ.* Believers are baptized "into the name of the Father, and of the Son, and of the Holy Ghost," to indicate the entire yielding of themselves to God. They "put on Christ," are "baptized into Christ," to show their entrance into all the new relations and privileges—righteousness, sonship, heirship—arising from their union with Christ and their full identification with Christ; so that whatever Christ is and has, they are and have by virtue of being one with him. Here, also, the utter inadequacy of sprinkling and pouring as symbols of the facts intended is evident; while the immersion of a believer to signify his voluntary death to all the conditions and relations of the old sinful life, and the emersion to signify entrance on all the conditions and relations of the new life in Christ, constitute a symbolism appropriate and impressive.

It seems evident, therefore, that the design of baptism as a symbol imperatively requires an immersion and an emersion as the only adequate expression of the things intended to be symbolized.

IV. PATRISTIC USAGE.

The form of the baptismal act during the Patristic period is clearly defined by the following things:

1. *The words and circumstances found in connection with the rite.* Justin Martyr calls baptism "*the water-bath* for the forgiveness of sins," and "*the bath* of conversion and the knowledge of God." Tertullian says of baptism: "With so great simplicity, without display, without any novelty of preparation, finally without expense, a man is let down into the water, and while a few words are spoken is immersed." Chrysostom says: "As he who is baptized in water rises again with great ease, not at all hindered by the nature of the waters, so also he (Christ), having gone down into death, with greater ease comes up; for this cause he calls it a baptism." In these and many other patristic passages the attending words and circumstances clearly necessitate an immersion and emersion.

2. *Those passages in which the force of a comparison or of an argument depends on an immersion.* Hermas, A. D. 150, says: "This seal is water, into which men descend appointed to death, but from which they ascend appointed to life." Tertullian, A. D. 200: "Know ye not that so many of us as were baptized into Christ Jesus were baptized into his death? . . . For by an image we die in baptism, but we truly rise in the flesh, as did also Christ." Basil, A. D. 320: "Imitating the burial of Christ by the baptism; for the bodies of those immersed are, as it were, buried in the water." "The water presents the image of death, receiving the body as in a tomb." Chrysostom, A. D. 320: "Divine symbols are therein celebrated—burial and deadness, and resurrection and life; and all these

take place together; for when we sink our heads down in the water, as in a kind of tomb, the old man is buried, and, sinking down beneath, is all concealed at once; then, when we emerge. the new man comes up." Ambrose, A. D. 400: "We discoursed respecting the font, whose appearance is, as it were, a form of sepulchre into which, believing in the Father, and the Son, and the Holy Spirit, we are received and submerged and rise—that is, are restored to life."* In these passages, which are cited only as examples of a multitude that occur, the whole force of the argument or of the figure depends on *the form of the rite as symbolizing a burial and rising;* apart from this, the language is meaningless.

3. *The general opposition to clinic baptism, given to such as were near death,* which was performed at first by *perfusion* (*perichusis*), or pouring water on and around the sick person, and at a later period probably by sprinkling. The first recorded instance of this is the case of Novatian, at Rome, who, being, as was supposed, in mortal sickness, was perfused (*perichutheis*), but recovered, and whose ordination as a presbyter was opposed on account of this baptism. Eusebius, quoting the language of Cornelius in regard to the ordination, says: "All the clergy and many of the laity resisted it, since it was not lawful that one who had been baptized on his sick-bed *by aspersion,* as he was, should be promoted to the clergy." This widespread disrepute of clinic baptism, grounded, in part at least, on the imperfection in its form, is one of the plainest facts of patristic history, and can only be accounted for by the common practice of immersion.

4. *The testimony of all reputable church historians.* Here

---

* Most of the patristic citations here and elsewhere are from Conant's *Meaning of Baptizein,* where the original is also given. See, also, *The Act of Baptism,* by Burrage, Am. Bap. Pub. Society.

all authorities concur. Neander, writing of the first three centuries, says: "In respect to the form of baptism, it was, in conformity with the original institution and the original import, performed by immersion, as a sign of entire baptism into the Holy Spirit, being entirely penetrated by the same."* Schaff, on the same period, says: "The usual form of the act was immersion, as is plain from the original meaning of the Greek *baptizein, baptismos;* from the analogy of John's baptism in the Jordan; from the apostle's comparison of the rite with the miraculous passage of the Red Sea, with the escape of the ark from the flood, with a cleansing and refreshing bath, and with burial and resurrection; finally, from the custom of the early church, which prevails in the East to this day."† Coleman declares: "In the primitive church, immediately subsequent to the age of the apostles, immersion, or dipping, was undeniably the common mode of baptism. The utmost that can be said of *sprinkling* in that early period is that it was, in case of necessity, permitted as an exception to a general rule. This fact is so well established that it were needless to adduce authorities in proof of it."‡ Smith's *Dictionary of Christian Antiquities*, in its elaborate article on baptism, says: "Passages already quoted in this article will have sufficed to show that the ordinary mode of baptism in primitive times, at least in the case of adults, was that the catechumen should descend into a font of water (whether natural or artificial), and while standing therein dip the head thrice under the water."§ Such also in substance is the testimony of Mosheim and Geisler, of Bingham and Hagenbach, of Guerike and Hase. Indeed, this part

---

* *Church History*, vol. i., p 310, Torrey's ed.
† *Schaff's Ch. Hist.*, p. 128. ‡ *Ancient Christianity*, p. 395.
§ Vol. i., p. 168.

of the investigation may well close in the words of Professor Stuart, of Andover, who, after citing many authorities, says: "But enough: 'it is a thing made out,' says Augusti—viz., the ancient practice of immersion. So, indeed, all the writers who have thoroughly investigated this subject conclude. I know of no one usage of ancient times which seems to be more clearly and more certainly made out. I cannot see how it is possible for any candid man who examines the subject to deny this."

V. Subsequent Usage of Christendom.

1. The Greek churches, which extend over Greece, Russia, Egypt, Abyssinia, Arabia, Palestine, and the whole of Western Asia, and in some of which the Greek language is, and ever has been, the vernacular, have always practised immersion and insisted on this as the true import of the word. Throughout the vast Christian communions of the Orient they have in all ages steadily refused to recognize sprinkling or pouring as baptism. Coleman says: "The Eastern Church has uniformly retained the form of *immersion* as indispensable to the validity of the ordinance, and they repeat the rite whenever they have received to their communion persons who have been baptized in another manner."* Dean Stanley says: "There can be no question that the original form of baptism—the very meaning of the word—was complete immersion in the deep baptismal waters, and that for at least four centuries any other form was either unknown, or regarded, unless in the case of dangerous illness, as an exceptional, almost a monstrous, case. To this form the Eastern Church still rigidly adheres, and the most illustrious and venerable portion of it—that of the Byzantine Empire—absolutely repudiates and ignores any

* *Ancient Christianity*, ch. xix.

other mode of administration as essentially invalid."* All the authorized rituals for baptism in the Greek churches require immersion. Alexander de Stourdza, Russian state councillor, of the orthodox Greek Church, says: "The distinctive characteristic of the institution of baptism is *immersion, baptisma,* which cannot be omitted without destroying the mysterious sense of the sacrament and contradicting at the same time the etymological signification of the word which serves to designate it. The church of the West has, then, departed from the example of Jesus Christ; she has obliterated the whole sublimity of the exterior sign; in short, she commits an abuse of words and of ideas in practising baptism by *aspersion,* this very term being in itself a derisive contradiction. The verb *baptizo, immergo,* has in fact but one sole acceptation. It signifies, literally and always, *to plunge.* Baptism and immersion are, therefore, identical; and to say *baptism by aspersion* is as if one should say *immersion by aspersion,* or any other absurdity of the same nature."† But further citation of authorities is here needless, as all church historians unite in affirming immersion as the theory and practice of the Greek churches.

Now, as it cannot be supposed that the Greek churches, consisting largely of Greek-speaking populations, have through all the ages mistaken the meaning of their own language, the inference, from their uniform doctrine and practice from the Patristic period to the present, would seem to be irresistible that *baptizo* signifies—and has always signified—*to immerse* when used of the Christian ordinance.

2. In the Roman Catholic Church the form of baptism continued to be immersion until the thirteenth century,

History of the Eastern Church, p. 117.
† Quoted in Conant's *Baptizein,* p. 150. Ed. 1864.

as all authorities show. Thomas Aquinas, who flourished in the middle of that century, although defending sprinkling, says: "The symbol of Christ's burial is more expressively represented by immersion, and for that reason this mode of baptizing is *more common* and commendable." . . . "It is safer to baptize by immersion, because *this is the more common* use."* The Council of Nismes, in 1284, while requiring immersion, made this exception in case of danger or immediate death: "If a sufficient quantity of water cannot be had for wholly immersing the infant, let a certain quantity of water be poured upon the infant." The Council of Ravenna, in 1311, was the first to make baptism allowable by sprinkling in all cases. It decreed: "Baptism is to be administered by trine aspersion or immersion [*sub trine aspersione, vel immersione*]."† Bossuet says of immersion: "We are able to make it appear by acts of Councils and ancient rituals that for thirteen hundred years baptism was thus administered." Hagenbach says: "From the thirteenth century sprinkling came into more general use in the West. The Greek Church, however, and the church of Milano still retained the practice of immersion."‡ Brenner, an eminent Roman Catholic, after an elaborate investigation, closed his work entitled *Historical Exhibition of the Administration of Baptism from Christ to our Times* with the following statement: "Thirteen hundred years was baptism generally and regularly an immersion of the person under the water, and only in extraordinary cases a sprinkling or pouring with water; the latter was, moreover, disputed as a mode of baptism, nay, even forbidden." The change thus made in the practice of the Roman Church from immersion to sprinkling was,

---

* *Summa Theologiæ*, part iii., Quest. 66.
† See Burrage's *Act of Baptism* for full citations.
‡ *Hist. of Doctrines*, vol. ii. p. 81.

however, not based on any change of conviction as to the original form of the rite. Roman Catholic theologians hold, and have ever held, that this was immersion, and they rest the validity of the change solely on the authority of the church to alter rites and ceremonies.

3. Among the Reformers, Luther and Calvin, with all scholars of that age, unitedly affirmed, in emphatic language, that immersion was the original form of the ordinance; as, indeed, do all continental scholars of the present age. Luther, in his work *De Sacramento Baptismi*, said: "The name baptism is Greek; in Latin it may be rendered 'immersion,' as when we immerse anything in water that it may be all covered with water. And although that custom has now grown out of use with most persons (nor do they wholly submerge children, but only pour on a little water), yet they ought to be entirely immersed and immediately drawn out, for this the etymology of the name seems to demand." His *Order of Baptism*, A. D. 1523, says: "Then let him take the child and dip it into the baptism." Calvin, in his *Institutes*, says: "The word *baptizo* itself signifies *to immerse*, and it is certain that immersion was observed by the ancient church."* But in establishing the Lutheran and Reformed churches these eminent men disregarded the form as not essential, and permitted the continuance of sprinkling, which in the sixteenth century had become the common practice on the Continent. And this form of the rite has remained in those churches, notwithstanding the universal admission that it is not apostolic.

4. In the English Church, however, immersion had remained; and at the Reformation it was continued in the Establishment. Lingard, in his *History and Antiquities of the Anglo-Saxon Church*, describing the canonical regula-

* Liber iv. 15–19.

tions for baptism in the ante-Reformation period, says of the adult candidate: "He then descended into the font; the priest depressed his head three times below the surface, saying, 'I baptize thee in the name of the Father, and of the Son, and of the Holy Ghost.'" And of the child: The priest "plunged it thrice into the water, pronounced the mysterious words, and then restored it to the sponsors." No change was made in this until the reign of Edward VI., when, in 1549, it was ordained: "If the child be weak, it shall suffice to pour water on it." The rubric of the English Church, as finally settled in 1662, reads as follows: "Then the priest shall take the child into his hands, and shall say to the godfathers and godmothers: 'Name this child;' and then, naming it after them (if they certify him that the child may well endure it), he shall dip it in the water discreetly and warily, saying, 'I baptize thee in the name of the Father, and of the Son, and of the Holy Ghost.' But if they shall certify that the child is weak, it shall suffice to pour water on it, saying the foresaid words." In the rubric of the Protestant Episcopal Church of the United States this is modified as follows: "And then, naming it after them, he shall dip it in the water discreetly, or shall pour water upon it." The above law of the English Church has remained unchanged; but in practice sprinkling, instead of being the exception, has become the rule. In the Scotch Kirk, John Knox, following Calvin, established sprinkling. Among the English Puritans, however, there was an earnest party favoring the original form. In the Westminster Assembly, 1644, as reported by Lightfoot, who was present, when it was proposed that the Directory of Public Worship relating to baptism should read, "The minister shall take water and sprinkle or pour it with his hand upon the face or forehead of the child," after long dispute, "it was voted so indifferently that we were glad to count names twice; for so many were unwilling to have dipping excluded that the vote came to an equality within one; for the one side was twenty-four, the other twenty-five, the twenty-four for the reserving of dipping, and the twenty-five against it."*

The results of the above historic survey of the subject may be summed up in the following statements: 1. The patristic churches universally practised immersion except in extreme sickness, and based their practice on the meaning of the word and the import of the rite. 2. The orthodox Greek Church, ancient and modern, with all the Oriental churches not of the Roman faith, has always insisted on immersion as being the true meaning of the word, and as necessary to the validity of the ordinance. 3. The Latin Church for more than thirteen centuries continued to use immersion; and the change afterward made to sprinkling was based, and is still based, by Roman Catholic theologians, not on any altered view of the original form of the rite, but only on the authority of the church to alter rites and ceremonies. 4. The practice of sprinkling amongst most of those who use it is not defended as resting on the true meaning of *baptizo* or as being the original form of the rite (both of which positions they deny); but in the Roman Catholic and Anglican churches it rests on an alleged authority in the church to change ordinances, and in the Lutheran and Reformed churches on the doctrine that the form, though properly immersion, is not essential. 5. Immersion, as the proper significance of *baptizo* and the original form of the rite, has been affirmed through all the Christian ages, and is still affirmed by the highest scholarship of Christendom, Oriental, Roman Catholic, and Protestant; the reverse

* *Works*, vol. xiii., p. 300. London, 1824.

has found advocacy only among a portion of the scholars in a few Pædobaptist sects in Great Britain and America. The great body of Christians are, and ever have been, Baptists in theory on the form of baptism. Few facts connected with the Christian religion have received a sanction so earnest and united from the ripest scholarship and piety of the Church of God in all ages as the fact that baptism, alike in the form of the original command and in the practice of the apostolic churches, was an immersion in the name of the Father, and of the Son, and of the Holy Ghost.

VI. Baptism as Represented in Ancient Monuments and Art.—Baptisteries.

The ancient baptisteries, found in all parts of Christendom, East and West, are among the most prominent monuments of early baptism. Not less than sixty-six of these are found in Italy alone, of which seven belong to the fourth century, four to the fifth, eleven to the sixth, and fourteen probably to the seventh. They are often structures separate from the church, generally circular or octagonal, and sometimes elaborate in architecture and richly adorned with art. The pool, usually in the centre of the building, was called in Greek *kolumbēthra*, in Latin *piscina*, both words denoting a considerable body of water; more rarely it was called *lavacrum, a bath*. The pools differ in size, as described by Dr. Cote, from whose work on *Baptism and Baptisteries* the following statements are selected. St. John Lateran at Rome, fourth century: " In the centre of the building is a magnificent circular basin, three feet deep, lined and paved with marble. It occupies a large proportion of the building, being about twenty-five feet in diameter." The pool has now been partially filled up, reducing the depth. St. Maria Maggiore, at Nocera, fourth

THE CHRISTIAN ORDINANCES. 153

century: "In the centre is a large basin, circular in the interior and octagonal externally. A descent of three steps leads to the bottom of the basin, which bears a strong resemblance to that of the baths of Pompeii, and was evidently used for the administration of baptism by immersion." St. Giovanni in Fonte, at Ravenna, fifth century: "In the centre is a large bath of white Grecian marble, ten feet in diameter and three and a half feet deep, and provided with an outlet for the purpose of emptying it." Cittanova, sixth century: "A descent of three steps leads into the font, or basin, which is surrounded by six columns. The diameter of the building is about forty feet and that of the basin ten feet." Novara, sixth century: "The large basin is octagonal in form, with three steps inside, and an outlet for the escape of the water. It is about four feet deep and eight feet wide." Florence, seventh century: "On the pavement of the baptistery is a large circle of copper with numerical figures and signs of the zodiac upon it, and in the centre of this stood originally a very fine octangular basin of a diameter of twelve feet. This large font was destroyed by Francesco de Medici upon the occasion of the baptism of his son Philip, in 1576, greatly to the displeasure of the Florentines, who carried away as relics, the fragments of marble and mortar." Verona, twelfth century: "In the centre is a large octangular basin of marble, twenty-eight feet in circumference, hewn out of a single block of Venetian marble. By actual measurement, we found the depth of this font to be four feet and a half." Pisa, thirteenth century: "In the centre of the baptistery is a large octagonal basin, fourteen feet in diameter and four feet deep."

When the writer was at Tyre, in 1874, among the massive ruins of the ancient cathedral, built in the fourth century by Paulinus and described by Eusebius, he saw a remarkable baptistery, then just discovered by the Prussian excavators. It was originally a monolith of white marble, but had been fractured and repaired. It stood on the original floor of the church, and steps, which were part of the monolith, were at each end. Its interior dimensions were as follows: Length, five feet three inches; width, three feet seven and a half inches; depth, three feet eight and a half inches. The candidate evidently entered the pool at one end, then knelt down in the water, and, according to ancient usage, his head was bowed forward into the water by the minister, who stood outside, and after being thus immersed he passed out by the steps on the other end. The baptistery was evidently used for adult baptism, as otherwise there is no explanation of the steps, and, found as it is on the lowest floor, there can be no doubt that it belonged to the original church. It is, therefore, an interesting monument attesting the form of baptism in the fourth century.

Now, baptisteries such as above described are found in all parts of ancient Christendom, and their presence makes it impossible to doubt the form of baptism in the patristic and mediæval churches. Such structures were plainly intended for immersion; their size, form, and arrangement wholly preclude the idea of their use for pouring or sprinkling.

The objection is made that, in some instances, these baptisteries are too small for adult immersion, especially two in Palestine—at Gophna and Tekoa. The dimensions of these are given by Dr. Robinson, as follows: That at Gophna "measured five feet in diameter, three and a half feet high, and two feet nine inches deep within; the inside being excavated in the form of a cross, with the corners rounded."* That at Tekoa "is octagonal, five feet in

---

* *Researches*, vol. ii., p. 263.

diameter on the outside, four feet on the inside, and three feet nine inches deep."* Here it will be observed that these fonts are not too small for adult immersion in the manner usual among the ancients, as described above at Tyre; that they belong to Greek churches, which, as above shown, have always practised immersion; that there is no evidence that either of these goes back beyond the crusades, when infant baptism had become nearly universal and fonts were often reduced in size, adapting them to infant immersion; and that for sprinkling or pouring such baptisteries would be utterly unadapted and preposterous. Singular mistakes arise from hasty observation. Thus, Mr. J. F. Wood describes as a baptistery a shallow excavation in stone at Ephesus, which Dr. Grant, of Cairo, an experienced archæologist, who accompanied the writer's party to Ephesus, pronounced only the nether stone of a large mill, such as he had often seen in Egypt. President Bartlett speaks of the well-known font in the Coptic chapel of Sitt. Miriam, at Old Cairo, as too small for immersion, in his haste failing to observe the large baptistery which stands at the entrance to the church, and overlooking the plain facts that the font in question is in no way adapted for sprinkling; that the Copts have never practised sprinkling, but always immersion; and that the chapel Sitt. Miriam, being the traditional refuge of the infant Jesus in Egypt, naturally became, after the introduction of infant baptism, a sacred place for the immersion of infants, and the font was adapted in size for them. In the eager search for evidence to justify sprinkling, mistakes of this kind constantly occur. But the slightest reflection must show that there is no conceivable reason for the erection of such a structure as a baptistery for sprinkling or pouring; the presence, therefore, of these

* *Researches*, vol. i., p. 486.

structures everywhere in ancient Christendom clearly attests the common practice of immersion in the ancient church.

Mosaics and Frescoes.

Several of these are supposed to represent the act of baptism; and of these some examples are cited as showing that the ancient form was not immersion. Thus, in the cupola of the baptistery at Ravenna, there is a mosaic representing Christ standing up to the waist in the Jordan, while John is pouring water upon his head from a cup. This mosaic, however, is confessedly, in part, not original, but a restoration by a recent hand, and notably this is true of the head of Christ and of the right arm of the Baptist; the representation, therefore, reflects, probably, the ideas only of the modern restorer. A fresco is found in the catacomb of St. Calixtus, in which the nude figure of a youth stands on the margin of water, while another figure beside him is laying his hand on his head. But Father Garrucci, one of the highest authorities, in describing the original form of this, says: "The youth, entirely naked, is entirely immersed in a cloud of water;" and all archæologists, as De Rossi and Martigny, affirm that it is an allegorical painting representing an immersion. Other of these pictorial representations, however, plainly depict immersion. In the catacomb of St. Pontianus, at Rome, a picture of Christ's baptism is found, which Bottari thus describes: "Upon the wall over the arch the Redeemer is represented as up to his waist in the water, and upon his head rests the right hand of John the Baptist, who is standing upon the shore. It is by mistake that modern artists represent Christ in the Jordan up to the knees only, and John pouring water on his head." In the church of San Celso, at Milan, an ancient church-book, ascribed to the fifth or sixth century, contains a picture of Christ's baptism, of which Bugati says: "The Redeemer is represented immersed in the water, according to the ancient discipline of the church, observed for many centuries in the administration of baptism."*

Ancient mosaics and frescoes, however, are uncertain testimony, because, while even their original date is in dispute, most of them, in their present form, are confessedly restorations, into which the restorer has introduced later ideas, and because, as is now generally agreed, they were intended, not as literal, but as allegorical, representations of the subject. That they did not in their ancient form represent baptism as sprinkling or pouring is evident from the following considerations: 1. The literature and monuments of the early Christian ages testify, with absolute unanimity, to immersion as the common form of the rite, and contemporary art cannot be conceived as contradicting their testimony. 2. These representations are found, for the most part, in baptisteries, the only use of which was for immersion; it would be absurd, therefore, to suppose pictorial representations of the rite in such places at utter variance with the purpose and use of them. 3. There is absolutely no high archæological authority for an interpretation of any of these pictorial representations of baptism otherwise than of an immersion; and all recent investigation, as conducted by those who devote their lives to Christian archæology, tends to show that Christian art, in the ancient period, was in full harmony with Christian literature, invariably testifying to immersion as the primitive baptism.

An interpretation of these pictures, however, has recently been given which may be worthy of consideration. The late Wharton B. Marriott, of Oxford, in his

* See full quotations in Burrage's *Act of Baptism*.

article on baptism in Smith's *Dictionary of Christian Antiquities*, affirms that, in the later Patristic age, both immersion and pouring were connected with the baptismal service; the former was the proper act of baptism, representing the burial and the resurrection with Christ; the latter, which followed the immersion, was the symbol of the descent of the Holy Spirit on the baptized person as he rose from the water. He adds: "This hypothesis of a double use explains some difficulties in ancient authors, more particularly in the treatise *De Sacramentis*, attributed to St. Ambrose, and in the Egyptian ritual. And its probability is confirmed by the fact that in the Armenian order of baptism, even to this day, the double usage of immersion and affusion is maintained. There the actual administration is described as follows: The priest asks the child's name, and on hearing it lets the child down into the water, saying, 'This, N., servant of God, who is come from the state of childhood (or from the state of a catechumen) to baptism, is baptized in the name of the Father, and of the Son, and of the Holy Ghost.'... While saying this the priest *buries the child* (or catechumen) three times in the water, as a figure of Christ's three days' burial. Then, taking the child out of the water, *he thrice pours a handful of water on its head*, saying, 'As many of you as have been baptized into Christ have put on Christ, hallelujah. As many of you as have been enlightened by the Father, the Holy Spirit is put into you, hallelujah.'" The usage of the Greek Church conforms to this, except that this second act occurs seven days after the immersion. The Greek ritual reads: "After seven days the child is again brought to the church for the ablution. After three short prayers the priest loosens the child's girdle and raiment, and, uniting the end of them, wets them with clean water and sprinkles the child, saying, 'Thou hast been justified, thou hast been enlightened, thou hast been sanctified, thou hast been washed, in the name of the Father, and of the Son, and of the Holy Ghost, now and ever, world without end, Amen.'" This view of a double use—immersion as the proper act of baptism, and affusion as the subsequent act, symbolizing the descent of the Holy Spirit on the baptized—is adopted also by Mr. Alexander Nesbitt, in his article on *Baptisteries*, in the volume above quoted, who, in accounting for the size of baptisteries, says: "As, during the earlier centuries, immersion, either alone *or accompanied by aspersion*, and not merely sprinkling, was deemed to be the proper mode of administering the rite, a large receptacle for water was required."

According to this interpretation, the pouring ceremony depicted in some of these mosaics and frescoes is not the act of baptism, but an act which followed baptism as a symbol of the outpouring of the Spirit on him who had emerged from the baptismal waters. The latter act, doubtless, often assumed an importance higher even than baptism, and thus found occasional representation in art; and in the eager quest for evidence in favor of sprinkling as baptism, the true purport of these pictorial representations has been misapprehended.

THE CATACOMBS.

These vast receptacles of the Christian dead, which extend under much of ancient Rome, had many representations, in sculpture, mosaic, *bas-relief*, and fresco, illustrating the ideas and customs of the early church. Many have devoted their lives to the investigation of what remains of these. "Bosio spent thirty years, Boldetti and Marangoni thirty years, Seroux d'Agincourt fifty years, and, in the present century, Garrucci and the brothers

De Rossi have spent over thirty years in absorbing study of these enigmatic remains." The work has many perplexities; for after the close of the fourth century, when burials ceased in the catacombs, a superstitious zeal arose for the discovery of the tombs of the martyrs, and for adorning them by restoring defaced pictures and adding a multitude of others. In the elaborate article on the *Catacombs* in Smith's *Dictionary of Christian Antiquities*, by Rev. Edward Venables, of Lincoln cathedral, it is said: "The fatal zeal displayed by successive pontiffs in the restoration and decoration of these consecrated shrines is the cause of much perplexity to the investigator who desires to discover their original form and arrangements. Nothing but long experience and an intimate acquaintance with the character of the construction and ornamentation of different periods can enable us to distinguish with any accuracy between the genuine structure of the catacombs and the paintings with which they were originally adorned and the works of later times. Many of the conclusions drawn by Roman Catholic writers from the paintings and ritual arrangements of the catacombs as we now find them, and the evidence supposed to be furnished by them as to the primitive character of their dogmas and traditions, prove little worth when a more searching investigation shows their comparatively recent date." In respect to frescoes, he adds:* "It must always be borne in mind, in examining the frescoes of the catacombs, that we are in all probability looking at the work of the eighth, or even a later, century, which only partially reproduces the original painting, and that any arguments founded on such uncertain data must be precarious." Rev. James Chrystal, of the Protestant Episcopal Church, who has devoted much time to the study of the catacombs in ex-

* Vol. i., p. 696.

posing what he calls "the very strange blunders which have been made as to the paintings in the catacombs," says: "Most noteworthy is one made by Bishop Kip, of California, in his work on the *Catacombs of Rome*. He adduces a picture of the baptism of Christ in the Jordan which is found in the catacomb of St. Pontian, as it is called, as being an instance of sprinkling or pouring. But as Aringhi in his representation of it shows, and as Perret in his picture of it, as well as in his text, expressly sets forth, it is an instance of immersion. Indeed, Bishop Kip's own picture of it shows it to be a dipping, and it seems strange how he could have failed to see this if he had used his eyes."

But, while mosaics and frescoes are thus of doubtful interpretation, there are unmistakable monuments of ancient baptism in the catacombs. Baptisteries are there which even in their ruins furnish the clearest evidence of immersion. "The most remarkable of these is that in the catacomb of St. Pontianus, the purpose of which is put beyond doubt by its pictorial decorations. The wall above the cistern retains a fresco of the baptism of our Lord." Northcote, in his *Roman Catacombs*, describes this baptistery: "A small stream of water runs through the cemetery, and at this one place the channel has been deepened so as to form a kind of reservoir, in which a certain quantity of water is retained. We descend into it by a flight of steps, and the depth of water always varies with the height of the Tiber. When that river is swollen so as to block up the exit by which the stream usually empties itself, the waters are sometimes so dammed back as to inundate the adjacent galleries of the catacombs; at other times there are not above three or four feet of water." Another of these baptisteries is found in the lowest tier of galleries in the catacomb of St. Agnes.

"It is a well-preserved chamber, with rude columns cut in the tufa rock at the corners. A spring of water runs through it. The paintings have entirely perished."* In periods of persecution, when Christian worship could be maintained only in these subterranean chambers of the dead, the sacred rite of baptism was here administered by a solemn immersion as the symbol of death to sin and of resurrection to holiness.

The testimony of ancient monuments and art, therefore, does not contradict, but is in perfect accordance with, the uniform testimony of patristic and mediæval literature. Both unmistakably point to immersion as the usage of the early ages of the church.

VII. Objections Considered.

The preceding argument amply shows that the scriptural form of baptism is immersion. There are, however, several objections and opposing theories which it is proper here to consider.

First: Immersion always inconvenient, often dangerous, and sometimes impossible. It is said: Immersion is always inconvenient; it is prejudicial to health, and in the case of the sick and dying it is impossible; it cannot, therefore, be the only divinely-appointed form of the rite. To this we reply: 1. It is not certain that our convenience in observing the ordinances was a primary consideration with God in directing their form. On the other hand, it is quite conceivable that in a positive institution intended, in some aspects of it, as a test of obedience to him, he might have studied our inconvenience as thus presenting a more decided test of our submission to him. But, not to insist on this, it is sufficient to answer that those who practise immersion do not, as a general fact, find it spe-

---

* Smith's *Dict. Christ. Antiq.*, vol. i., p. 313.

cially inconvenient, nor is there usually any possible necessity for making it inconvenient. 2. The objection as to health proceeds from false views of the effect of water on the body; in most cases even the most infirm are benefited physically from it. Those who practise immersion do, as a matter of fact, experience no ill-results from it, nor is there the liability to any in the proper administration of it. 3. The sick and dying have no need of baptism. If Providence, by sending ill-health, prevent obedience, plainly the obligation to baptism is removed. Certainly any attempt to perform it by changing its form, and thereby destroying its significance, can only be offensive to God. Besides, of what use is the ordinance to the dying — the rite of initiation into the earthly church to those who are just entering the church triumphant? Superstition only can find in such a case utility in the rite.

SECOND: IMMERSION, THOUGH THE SCRIPTURAL FORM, IS NOT ESSENTIAL. Many excellent men rest their practice of a different form on this non-essential theory. Admitting that immersion was the original form, they insist that, as it is only an outward ordinance, the church has the right to alter the form. On this we remark: 1. Man has never been granted the right to alter an ordinance instituted by God. Under the older dispensation such an alteration was deemed impious, as an invasion of the divine prerogatives. For this sin Nadab and Abihu were destroyed by the fire of God (Lev. x. 1-7); Korah, Dathan, and Abiram were swallowed up in the earth, which opened under their feet (Num. xvi.); Saul was rejected as the king of Israel (1 Sam. xiii. 8-14); and Uzzah perished by the stroke of God (2 Sam. vi. 1-10). The ordinances of the New Testament, though fewer in number, are not of less solemnity and authority, nor is there any evidence that they may be altered by man. 2. Baptism is, by means of its form, a symbol of divine truth; the distinctness, therefore, with which it represents that truth depends on the accuracy of the form. If that be altered, the truth God intended to present is not taught. To alter the divinely-instituted *symbol* by which the momentous truth of regeneration is set forth before the world is not less impious than to alter the divinely given *words* in which that truth is taught. The non-essential theory, applied to the form of a divine ordinance, does in fact disown the exclusive authority of God's word, and does so far impiously exalt man in the place of God.

THIRD: DR. DALE'S THEORY: BAPTISM NEVER AN IMMERSION. The four octavo volumes in which this theory is advanced by Rev. James W. Dale, D.D., of Pennsylvania, are entitled respectively, *Classic Baptism, Judaic Baptism, Johannic Baptism,* and *Christic and Patristic Baptism,* and contain a very full investigation of the form of baptism, with copious citations from classic, Jewish, biblical, and patristic writings. They give ample evidence of the industry, patience, and learning of the author, and it is claimed for them that they have conclusively proved that Christian baptism is never an immersion. The results supposed to have been reached may be best stated in the author's own words. At the close of the last volume he says:

"1. The baptism of inspiration is a thoroughly-changed spiritual condition of the soul, effected by the power of the Holy Ghost through the cleansing blood of the Lord Jesus Christ, and so making it meet for reconciliation, subjection, and assimilation to the one fully-revealed living and true God—Father, Son, and Holy Ghost.

"2. This one baptism of inspiration is, by divine appointment, ritually symbolized as to its soul-purification by pure water, poured or sprinkled, or otherwise suitably applied to the person, together with a verbal announcement of the spiritual baptism thus symbolized.

"3. Dipping the body into the water *is not, nor* (by reason of a double impossibility, found in the meaning of the word and in the divine requirement) *can it be*, Christian baptism. That Christian baptism is a water-dipping is a novelty unheard of in the church for fifteen hundred years. This idea is not merely an error in the mode of using the water (which would, comparatively, be a trifle), but it is an error which sweeps away the substance of baptism without leaving a vestige behind."

We propose here to examine the premises from which these remarkable conclusions are drawn. We shall not, however, investigate in detail the immense mass of matter gathered in these bulky volumes; such an investigation is wholly unnecessary for the determination of the truth or falsity of the theory advanced. The discussion will be restricted, therefore, to an examination of those fundamental positions of the author which, either as underlying assumptions or as formally-stated propositions, constitute the basis of his theory and are essential to its truth.

1. BAPTIZO, he affirms, *is derived, not from the primary, but from the secondary, meaning of* BAPTO. The latter has two meanings: (1.) To dip, to plunge; (2.) To dye, to stain, which was often, but not always, effected by dipping. *Baptizo*, the derivative, is derived, not from the primary sense, to dip, but from the secondary, to dye. It does not, however, take the signification to dye; but as *bapto*, when signifying to dye, indicates a thorough change in the condition of the subject as to color, so the derivative, *baptizo*, takes as its meaning "thoroughly to change the condition of an object by introducing it into some new condition." Consequently, *baptizo* never means to dip or

plunge as a physical act. This fundamental position of the author is very feebly supported. The chief argument offered is the alleged presumption that a derivative would not take the principal meaning of the parent word. He says: "That any language should give birth to a word which was but a bald repetition of one already in existence is a marvel that may be believed when proved." But in assuming this Dr. Dale is plainly in error; for, as a matter of fact, derivative words in Greek often take the main signification of the parent word, because the derivative has a stronger form, and is on that account preferred. Cremer's *Lexicon* will furnish any Greek scholar with numerous examples of this. Thus, *katharizo*, derived from *kathairo, to cleanse; rantizo*, from *raino, to sprinkle; methusko*, from *methuo, to be drunk*,—these are all derivatives which, in whole or in part, displaced the parent words, but which retained, as their most common meaning, precisely the signification of the radical form. These are only a few instances of many that might be adduced, and the Dale theory thus utterly fails, even in its initial proposition. Nor is he more successful in the passages cited in support of this novel definition, for none of them require the proposed sense of "a thoroughly-changed condition;" on the contrary, most of them imperatively demand the primary sense of *bapto* as the fundamental idea. Thus, a drunken man is described as "baptized in wine," where the man may indeed be conceived as placed in "a thoroughly-changed condition" by the wine; but it is far more natural to interpret the expression as a figure, in which he is represented as overborne, overwhelmed, under the influence of wine. A person "baptized in debts," "in sleep," "in night," "in grief," may possibly thereby come into "a thoroughly-changed condition," but this would be equally true if he were overwhelmed, immersed, enveloped, in these, yet no one would thence infer that the words overwhelm, immerse, envelop, signified simply "to thoroughly change the condition." Plainly, in all these cases the verb expresses not only a condition produced, but the form in which that condition is produced; and, indeed, Dr. Dale virtually admits this view when he affirms that the act by which this change of condition is effected usually involves an "intusposition," or the placing of the baptized within some element.

2. BAPTO and BAPTIZO, he further assumes, *belong to distinct classes of active transitive verbs, the one expressing action, the other condition.* *Bapto* belongs to the first class, always expressing the act by which a condition is produced; *baptizo* belongs to the second, always expressing a condition produced, and never the act or the form of the act producing it. *Baptizo*, therefore, always expressing condition only, never means to dip, to plunge, or any other definite form of an act; it always expresses the condition which results from an act, without reference to the form of the act effecting it. This distinction the author insists on with special emphasis, denying in the most positive manner that "*baptizo* expresses a definite act of any kind." The same distinction, he holds, exists in the Latin and the English. Thus, the English words *dip* and *plunge* represent the first class; but the words *whelm, soak, wet, bury*, belong to the second, and describe a result or a condition effected, but do not indicate the act by which the condition was effected. In this distinction, however, Dr. Dale is singularly unfortunate, for what he affirms of *bapto* is true of it only in the active voice, since in the passive it often expresses condition only; and what, on the other hand, he affirms of *baptizo* is true of it only in the passive, since in the active it commonly expresses action, and a definite form of action. Thus, *bapto*, in Rev. xix. 13

"clothed in a garment dipped (*bebammenon*) in blood," certainly does not express the act of dipping, but the condition or state, as having been dipped. On the other hand, when Plutarch says, "*Baptison seauton*, Plunge thyself into the sea,"* and Chrysostom praises David because "he did not (*baptisai*) plunge in the sword nor sever" the head of Saul,† both clearly indicate an act of definite form. To translate these passages, *Thoroughly change thyself into the sea; He did not thoroughly change the sword into Saul's head*, would make the veriest nonsense. A multitude of similar examples might be cited. The classification is equally untrue as applied to English words. Thus, it is said *plunge* belongs to the class always denoting action, and never condition. But the slightest attention to the English usage suffices to disprove this. Our author himself furnishes the needed examples. Thus:

> "Plunged in the deep for ever let me lie,
> Whelmed under seas,"

> "Or plunged in lakes of bitter marshes lie,
> Or wedged whole ages in a bodkin's eye."

We may also add the familiar couplet of Watts:

> "Plunged in a gulf of dark despair,
> We wretched sinners lay."

It is evident that in these examples, as in many others, the word *plunged* does not denote the act of plunging, but a condition, or state, as plunged. This fundamental position of the theory, therefore, utterly fails when tested by actual usage.

3. "BAPTIZO," according to Dr. Dale, "*in its primary use, expresses condition characterized by complete intusposition, without expressing, and with absolute indifference to, the form of the*

---

* *On Superstition*, iii.   † *Discourse*, iii., 7.

THE CHRISTIAN ORDINANCES. 169

act by which such intusposition may be effected, as also without other limitations—TO MERSE." It will be observed here the author admits, as he needs must, that *baptizo*, in its primary sense, expresses a condition which involves "a complete intusposition," or the putting the person baptized into some element; but he contends that the manner of the intusposition is not indicated. He further insists that, while an intusposition is implied, the taking out of the baptized from the element is not implied; so that, in the case of a human being, the intusposition implied in *baptizo* would involve drowning. Here, however, it must be noted that all we affirm of *baptizo* is—what the author here admits—that it involves an actual intusposition: the manner of effecting the intusposition is immaterial. And, in regard to the taking of the baptized out of the element, it is not necessary that the word should, in itself, express this part of the act of baptism, since the circumstances, in each instance of its use, sufficiently indicate the fact. Thus the word *immerse* does not, in itself, either in Latin or English, express the emersion of the person or thing immersed; nevertheless, it is used in numberless instances for a momentary immersion, wholly equivalent to *dip* or *plunge*. As a matter of fact, however, *baptizo* is often used to express a momentary immersion. Plutarch describes the soldiers of Alexander as dipping (*baptisontes*) with cups from large wine-jars and mixing-bowls, and drinking to one another; where Liddell and Scott define its meaning, "To draw wine from bowls in cups," and add, "of course by dipping them." Hippocrates, describing the respiration of a patient, says: "She breathed as persons breathe after having been immersed (*ek tou bebaptisthai*)."*
And Achilles Tatius, speaking of the manner in which the Egyptian boatman drinks water from the Nile, says: "He

* *Epidemics*, book v.

lets down his hand into the water, and dipping (*baptisas*) it hollowed, and filling it with water, he darts the draught toward his mouth and hits the mark."* In all these cases, as in a multitude of others, the word is plainly used, as the English word *dip*, to express an action which includes not only the putting of an object in or under some element, but also the immediate withdrawing of it. When, therefore, Dr. Dale concedes that an intusposition, or the putting within an element, is involved in the primary use of the word, he has conceded the main point insisted on by us: the manner of the intusposition, and the withdrawal of the baptized out of the enveloping element, are decided necessarily by the circumstances and the relations in which the word is used.

4. "BAPTIZO," the author adds, "in *secondary use, expresses condition, the result of complete influence, effected by any possible means, and in any conceivable way.*" By this he means, as he further explains, that no form of the act effecting the condition is implied, but that baptism expresses a condition resulting from complete influence, irrespective of the form in which that influence is exerted. Thus, a man under a sense of his sins says: "Iniquities baptize me"— that is, he is in a condition thoroughly under the influence of iniquities. A sleeping man is "baptized in sleep"— that is, he is in a condition thoroughly under the influence of sleep. *Baptizo*, the author insists, is not here used figuratively, but has its literal, natural sense: it simply expresses the condition of these men as under a complete influence, the one from iniquities; the other, from sleep. On this construction of the word the theory of Dr. Dale chiefly rests, but precisely here is one of his fatal mistakes. The figurative usage of *baptizo* he treats as a secondary literal usage; this word, however, has no secondary literal

* *Story of Clitophon and Leucippe*, book iii., chap. i.

meaning. No lexicographer gives it any literal signification which does not involve an immersion; nor do the passages quoted in this work sustain the author's position. *Baptizo* has a marked and rich range of figurative usage; but, unlike *bapto*, it has no secondary literal usage. A sleeping man is represented, by a beautiful figure, as "baptized"—that is, immersed, enveloped—in sleep. A man's iniquities " baptize "—that is, overwhelm—him, presenting an image of the multitude and greatness of them. To confound in this manner the figurative and the secondary use of words, and make the figurative a literal sense, is to confound all language and to destroy all certainty as to its meaning. There is hardly a word in any language which, if one may insist that its figurative uses must be treated as literal, will not be rendered wholly uncertain in import. Human speech, under such a process, would cease to be a reliable vehicle of thought. The author, it seems needless to add, here stands alone. All linguistic authority, German, English, and American, is arrayed against him.

The above propositions constitute the basis of Dr. Dale's theory of baptism. They appear and reappear throughout his work, either as formal statements or as underlying assumptions. With them the whole elaborate structure he has erected stands or falls.

We now proceed to consider his method in applying this theory to the use of the word in the New Testament. Here his fundamental position is that *baptizo*, "in religious usage, neither expresses dipping nor any physical baptism of any kind," but always denotes a thorough change of spiritual condition, and the receptive element after *baptizo* is never water or other material element, but is always the new spiritual conditions and relations into which the baptized pass. When ritual or outward baptism, therefore, is intended, it is not indicated in the word *baptizo*, nor in the words expressing the receptive element, but by accessory words, such as *en hudati*, "with water;" and these words, he affirms, express, not the receptive element, but simply the instrument, and in no instance imply that the ritual act was an immersion, but the contrary. Here three points are to be noted:

1. He insists that the prepositions and cases used with *baptizo* do not indicate that the ritual act was immersion. The preposition *en*, *in*, when used with water or with the Holy Spirit, is, in his view, not a proper Greek idiom, but is a Hebraism equivalent to the simple dative of instrument or means, to be translated *by* or *with*. Hence, the form of the act is not indicated; all that is indicated is that the water or the Spirit is the instrument by which the baptism is effected. But in this the author, while making a mere assumption as to the Hebraistic use of *en* in such cases, is again refuted by plain facts in the language. For, (*a*.) The preposition *en* is often used by Greek writers to indicate the element in or within which the action of *baptizo* takes place; when, therefore, it is used in the New Testament in such relations, it cannot be treated as a Hebraism or as expressing merely the instrument. For example, Polybius represents a body of soldiers, when attempting to cross a morass, as immersed (*baptizomenoi*) and sinking in (*en*) the pools."* Plotinus describes the corrupt and vicious soul as "yet immersed in (*en*) the body."† Basil speaks of steel as "immersed in (*en*) the fire."‡ Here *en* with the dative plainly does not denote merely the instrument, but, as often elsewhere, points to the element within which the act takes place. (*b*.) The simple dative, without a preposition, is also used where the instrumental sense cannot be supposed, and where it must denote, as the simple dative often does,

* *Hist.* lib. v.   † *Ennead* I., book viii.   ‡ *On Baptism*, book i., ch. 210.

the sphere within which the act is performed. Thus, an ancient medical writer, Alexander of Aphrodisius, speaks of the soul as "much immersed in the body (*baptisomenēn tō somati*)." Chrysostom, in expounding the seventh Psalm, describes Absalom as desiring "to plunge his right hand (the weapon it held) into his father's neck (*tō laimō baptisai tō patriko*)." Another writer says: "A mass of iron, drawn red hot from the furnace, is plunged in water (*hudati baptizetai*), and the fiery glow, by its own nature quenched with water, ceases."* Now, in these, as in frequent instances, the dative is used without a preposition where it clearly denotes the sphere within which the act is performed. To translate here as the instrumental dative would make nonsense. The author, therefore, entirely fails to show that the preposition or the case used after *baptizo* does not define the form of the act; the reverse is evidently the fact.

2. Dr. Dale affirms that *baptizo*, in its primary use as implying an intusposition, never is, nor can be, used of the ritual or outward act, because it makes no provision for the withdrawal of the intusposed from the enveloping element, and therefore, if applied to the ritual act, it would involve the drowning of the baptized. In its religious usage, therefore, the word implies intusposition only when used of the inward spiritual act, and in this case the receptive element—that is, the new spiritual condition into which the soul has passed—is put in the accusative with *eis*. Thus, John baptized (*eis*) into repentance; Christians are baptized (*eis*) into Christ—that is, they experience a thorough change of spiritual condition by passing into the new relations and conditions involved in being "in Christ," and this spiritual change is expressed in the word "baptized," which is here used, not

* *Homeric Allegories*, ch. 9.

figuratively, but literally. This position of the author, however, is fully refuted, not only by the arguments before adduced against this literalizing of figurative language, but also by the following considerations: (1.) If the spiritual act is, as he affirms, an intusposition, or the placing of the soul within the relations and conditions implied in being "in Christ," then evidently the ritual act, the outward symbol of the spiritual, must, in order to symbolize it, also be an intusposition; otherwise, the symbol does not set forth the thing symbolized. Submersion, if not emersion, would, according to the Dale theory, be essential to ritual baptism. (2.) According to Scripture, "as many as were baptized into Christ were baptized into his death," and were, "therefore, buried with him" by means of the baptism. But, though thus intusposed into Christ's death, they were not, as Dr. Dale's theory supposes, left intusposed there; for the apostle says: "Buried with him in baptism, wherein"—that is, *in baptism*—"ye are *risen* with him, through the faith of the operation of God, who hath raised him from the dead." Plainly, then, to be baptized into Christ, according to Paul, involves not simply an intusposition into his death, but also a rising with him, a resurrection; and the ritual act, as symbolizing the whole transaction, must needs be not a submersion only, but also an emersion. The author is here at utter variance with the apostle, for he represents the baptized as remaining for ever intusposed, whereas Paul represents the baptized as *in baptism* not only intusposed, but also raised out of that intusposition. It is evident, therefore, that this theory wholly misconceives baptism, alike as a spiritual and as a ritual act. (3.) The simple and natural view, however, which in all the ages linguistic authority and common sense have sanctioned, regards *baptizo* in such passages as figuratively used, the word denoting the outward symbol being employed figuratively to denote the inward act it symbolizes. Any other interpretation of necessity leads to some such absurdity as that just pointed out; for we are said to be "baptized into Christ," "baptized into his death," "risen with him," because baptism is the divinely-appointed symbol of union with Christ in his death and resurrection. This construction of *baptizo* as denoting primarily the outward, not the inward, act is required not only by its constant use for ritual baptism in the New Testament, but also by its common usage in Greek literature, where the element of it is ordinarily material, not ideal. Josephus says of Simon: "He plunged (*ebaptise*) the whole sword into (*eis*) his own neck." Plutarch speaks of Agamemnon as bravely "plunging himself (*baptizōn eis*) into the lake Copais." Chrysostom speaks of persons "exhorting to plunge (*baptisai*) the sword (*eis*) into the enemy's breast." Dr. Conant, to whose admirable work, *The Meaning of Baptizein*, we are indebted for many of these citations, gives no less than fifteen examples from Greek writers in which *baptizo* is thus followed by *eis* with an accusative, and in most of these the receptive element is material, not ideal. It is in accordance with this well-known Greek usage that Mark, in describing the baptism of our Lord (chap. i. 9), says: He "was baptized in (*eis*) the Jordan by John," where the preposition *eis* is the exponent of the action of *ebaptisthē*, the immediately preceding verb.

3. This theory also requires that *baptizo*, in religious usage, must always be understood of the inward, spiritual act; it is the context only which by some added expression can indicate that it was accompanied by the outward symbol. Hence, several of the New Testament baptisms, ordinarily accounted ritual, are in reality instances of the

spiritual act — the baptism, for example, of the three thousand at the Pentecost, and the baptism of Saul at Damascus; and, indeed, this baptism of the Holy Spirit, and not the ritual act, is that which is enjoined in the great commission. To this we submit the following reply: The assumption that *baptizo*, in religious usage, does not denote the outward act has already been shown to be false. When John "did baptize in the wilderness," the act affirmed in the verb is clearly defined as outward by other passages. To translate John "did change the spiritual condition in the wilderness" is to destroy the sense. When "the multitude" of Pharisees and Sadducees "came forth *to be baptized* of him," they certainly did not come to obtain "a thorough change of spiritual condition," for John calls them a "generation of vipers." When, in speaking of the baptisms under Christ's ministry, it is said, "Jesus himself baptized not, but his disciples," it is impossible to understand the word of other than outward baptism; for surely, if baptism was "a change in the spiritual condition," it must have been effected by Christ, and not by the apostles. When Paul, in writing to the Corinthians, declares that he was not sent to baptize, and thanks God that he baptized none of them except Crispus and Gaius and the household of Stephanus, he certainly does not intend, as this theory would make him say, that "a thorough spiritual change" in them was not the object of his ministry, and that he thanked God because this "thoroughly-changed spiritual condition" had been wrought through him only in the persons named. Such a supposition is utterly absurd. The theory thus hopelessly breaks down when tested by actual New Testament usage, where *baptizo* often stands in relations such as to compel its expression of the outward act.

It remains true, therefore, as all the ages have taught, that *baptizo*, in the New Testament as elsewhere, designates primarily the outward act of immersion. That this outward act symbolized a great change of spiritual condition and relation; and that the inward change thus symbolized is unspeakably more important than the outward symbol: all this is plain, and this we affirm with all emphasis. So potent is this conviction with us that we dare not administer the outward symbol, except in the presence of evidence that the higher spiritual reality it symbolizes already exists in the candidate, and that the outward sign is thus a real representation of the great inward fact signified. But surely this higher importance of the spiritual act is no ground for setting aside the ordinary force of language and restricting the word by which the Holy Spirit designates the symbol to the expression only of the thing symbolized.

Patristic baptism is the closing subject of these remarkable volumes. Here the main position of the author is that "Christian baptism is always represented by the patristic writers as a spiritual baptism." He admits—indeed, as he needs must—that in the ritual act "the bodies of the baptized, when in health, were momentarily covered in water in ancient times;" but he denies, with special emphasis, "that this momentary covering in water was believed to be Christian baptism, or, indeed, any baptism whatever." It was not this outward act at all, but the resulting spiritual effect only, which the Fathers called baptism.

Such a proposition, however, has not the slightest support in patristic literature; indeed, the reverse is palpably evident. For the Fathers everywhere designate the outward, ritual act as baptism, and often sharply distinguish between this and the spiritual change it represents.

Thus, Justin Martyr, in his *Dialogue with a Jew*, says: "For what is the benefit of that baptism (*baptismatos*) which makes bright the flesh and the body only? Be baptized (*baptisthēte*), as to the soul, from anger and from covetousness, from envy and from hatred, and behold, the body is clean." Cyril of Jerusalem, in his *Preface to Instructions*, speaking of Simon Magus, says: "Simon, also, the magian, once came to the bath; he was baptized (*ebaptisthē*), but he was not enlightened; and the body, indeed, he dipped (*ebapsen*) in water, but the heart he did not enlighten. And the body went down, indeed, but the soul was not buried with Christ, nor was raised with him." Certainly, Cyril here calls the outward act baptism and distinctly discriminates between it and "a thorough spiritual change;" for Simon "was baptized," but experienced no spiritual regeneration. The same writer, in his *Instruction VII.*, speaking of the baptism of the apostles by the Holy Spirit, says: "As he who sinks down in the waters and is baptized (*baptizomenos*) is surrounded on all sides by the waters, so, also, they were completely baptized by the Spirit." Chrysostom, in commenting on First Corinthians, says: "For to be baptized (*baptizesthai*) and to sink down, then to emerge, is a *symbol* of the descent to the underworld and of the ascent from thence. Therefore, Paul calls the baptism the tomb, saying, 'We were buried, therefore, with him by the baptism into death.'" Here the golden-mouthed Father calls the outward act baptism, and affirms of baptism, not that it is the inward experience, but that it is the *symbol* of it. Such citations might be multiplied indefinitely, but it is needless to adduce more, for these passages clearly show that the Fathers understood the outward act as a baptism, and distinguished between this and the inward change it symbolized. The main proposition of Dr.

Dale thus wholly fails when subjected to the test of actual patristic usage.

This singular proposition, however, even were it proved, would not affect the form of the ritual act; for as to this the author admits that, in the Patristic period, "the bodies of the baptized were momentarily covered in water"—that is, were immersed. He declares that he has "no purpose to deny or to question or to shadow this fact, but, on the contrary, to give it the most unhesitating acknowledgment." In this, then, he is in full agreement with us: the external form in that period was "a momentary covering of the body in water." Whatever weight, therefore, belongs to the authority and example of the earliest ages of the church, as to the form of ritual baptism, is thus freely conceded to the Baptist position. Dr. Dale insists, however, that the Fathers, in practising immersion, departed from the New Testament and from apostolic example.

But the supposition that immersion was a patristic perversion of the apostolic rite is forbidden not only by the considerations already adduced showing that immersion is the only form of baptism in the New Testament, but also by the utter silence of history in regard to such a change in the rite. For such an hypothesis, if adopted, requires us also to accept the following incredible things: 1. That this important change was made by the Fathers in the form and reason of the initial ordinance of the Christian religion, and no record, or even trace, of the time and manner of the change has come down to us; for, confessedly, the ritual act was immersion at the earliest point of which we have knowledge next to the Apostolic age, and neither history nor archæology furnishes the slightest hint that it was a change from the apostolic form. 2. That this great change was made, not in one church only, but in all the churches of Christendom; yet among the vast multitude of martyrs and confessors of that heroic age of the church, not one was found to resist this impious perversion of a divine institution and defend its Heaven-given form and purpose; for, in the immense literature of the Patristic period, much of which was written by men who suffered and died for their faith, there is not a single objection raised against immersion as the ritual form of baptism. 3. That notwithstanding most of these Fathers spoke the language of the New Testament as their vernacular, as did also the churches to whom they ministered, they either strangely mistook the meaning of this word *baptizo*, belonging to their own mother-tongue, or they with one consent wilfully perverted it; and the whole body of Christian people, throughout the wide extent of the churches, failed either in intelligence to perceive the mistake or in courage to rebuke the perversion. Now, it is plain that Dr. Dale's hypothesis of immersion as a patristic perversion of the apostolic rite necessarily involves these propositions, the mere statement of which reveals their utter absurdity: no careful student of the Patristic period, therefore, could admit the supposition.

The fundamental positions essential to the Dale theory of baptism are thus seen to be without foundation when subjected to the careful test of facts in language and history; and it is certainly a matter of regret that so much learning and industry should have been wasted in defending a proposition which, while in itself thus without basis, is also, as already shown, in direct opposition to the highest scholarship of the Christian ages and to the united and holiest convictions of the church of God, ancient and modern.

SECTION III.

THE ORDINANCES: THE SUBJECTS OF BAPTISM.

In baptism a Christian believer publicly makes profession of personal faith in Christ and assumes the obligations of Christian discipleship. The rite can be administered, therefore, only to those who are capable of making such a profession and of assuming such obligations. Pædobaptists, on the contrary, affirm that not only believers, but also their infant children, are to be baptized. The following facts, however, seem at the outset to create a presumption against infant baptism:

1. *The wholly contradictory grounds on which its validity is maintained.* Romanists deny its biblical authority and rest its validity on the authority of the church; and they justly insist, therefore, that Protestants, in practising the rite, abandon the great Protestant principle that the Bible is the only and sufficient rule of faith and revert to the authority of tradition. The German Reformers, with Luther, conceded its lack of New Testament authority; and yet, with strange inconsistency, in the Augsburg Confession it was made essential to infant salvation. The Anglican Church bases its validity on the faith of sponsors, who are supposed to represent the child before God till it comes of age. Most of the English, Scotch, and American churches rest it on the Abrahamic covenant, yet not a few of their ablest divines reject this as a foundation. The German theologians, with Neander, are emphatic in denying that it has either precept or example in Scripture; but they justify the rite as a legitimate outgrowth from germinal principles of the gospel, but of later development than the Apostolic age—a principle which, by denying the sufficiency of Scripture, in real-

ity subverts Protestantism. A still wider diversity exists in respect to the design of baptism in infancy and to the *status* of those thus baptized. Now, reasons so contradictory, after ages of investigation, certainly create a presumption that no solid scriptural basis for the rite exists; for if it were an ordinance of God, his will would be revealed in relation to an institution so important.

2. *Infant baptism has confessedly neither precept nor certain example in Scripture.* This is universally conceded; yet it is wholly incredible that the baptism of infants was required throughout the churches, Gentile as well as Jewish, and was commonly practised, and not one instance be recorded, or even alluded to, in the whole New Testament. So important and prominent a fact could not have been omitted. We might at least expect some intimation of duty respecting the rite; for even if it were admitted that the Jewish Christians received the rite in the place of circumcision, and therefore needed no command, certainly the Gentile Christians, who had no circumcision, would need instruction respecting it. What other reason can there be for the total omission of such a command, except that the rite was totally unknown to the apostles?

The above facts seem to us to make a presumption against the apostolic authority of infant baptism, and to place the burden of proof on him who ventures to practise a rite thus unknown to the New Testament.

FIRST: ARGUMENTS FOR INFANT BAPTISM EXAMINED.

I. THE ARGUMENT FROM THE COVENANT OF CIRCUMCISION.

This argument, as stated by its ablest advocate, the celebrated John M. Mason, D. D.,* may here be concisely expressed as follows: God's covenant with Abraham is perpetual; the new as well as the old dispensation is

* *Essays on the Church of God.*

founded on it. Under the old dispensation, the natural descendants of Abraham, with their natural offspring, were embraced in the covenant and were entitled to circumcision. It follows, therefore, that under the new dispensation, believers, who are the spiritual children of Abraham, with their natural offspring, are included in the covenant and are entitled to baptism, unless the New Testament forbids. But the New Testament does not forbid; the children of believers are, therefore, within the covenant and are entitled to baptism. On this we remark:

1. *The conclusion is not contained in the premises.* Truly stated, the argument is this: The Abrahamic covenant is perpetual. Under the old dispensation the natural children of Abraham, with their natural offspring, were in the covenant and were entitled to circumcision. Therefore, under the new dispensation, the spiritual children of Abraham, with their *spiritual* offspring—*i. e.*, partakers of their faith—are in the covenant and are entitled to baptism. For under the earlier dispensation it was the *natural* relation to Abraham which secured to the child a place in God's covenant and a right to circumcision, but under the later it is the *spiritual* relation to Abraham which secures a place in the covenant and a right to baptism. Plainly, even Dr. Mason's argument, when properly stated, shows that as of old carnal descent entitled to circumcision, so now spiritual descent—that is, participation of like faith—entitles to baptism; and baptism belongs, therefore, only to the children of Abraham by faith.

2. *The conclusion is disproved by an analysis of the Abrahamic covenant.* It is evident that this covenant had a double import, a literal and a typical. It pledged to Abraham three earthly blessings—viz., that his descend-

ants should be vast in number, that Jehovah would be their God, and that they should inherit the land of Canaan. These pledges were all literally fulfilled to Israel. But in its higher import it gave assurance that the children of Abraham by faith should be innumerable, that Jehovah would be their God through all the ages, and that they should inherit heaven, of which Palestine was the type.* These pledges God has been fulfilling to the children of Abraham by faith in all ages. Now, of this covenant, circumcision was the sign only of the literal import. For, (1.) Its prerequisite was only carnal descent from Abraham, and its effect was simply to entitle to the earthly privileges of Israel. (2.) The contrast drawn between the spirituality of the Christian and the carnality of the Jewish rite is further evidence (Matt. iii. 8, 10; Phil. iii. 3). (3.) The form itself of circumcision indicates its application only to carnal descent. (4.) The apostolic restriction of circumcision among Christians to Jews only confirms this view of its design as a sign of outward, national privileges. If, then, circumcision was administered to the natural children of Abraham as a sign of an interest in the temporal blessings of the covenant, it follows, by an obvious law of typology, that baptism, if its substitute, should be administered to the spiritual children of Abraham as a sign of an interest in the spiritual blessings of the covenant. If carnal descent entitles to the one, spiritual descent entitles to the other; and baptism is restricted, therefore, to "the children of Abraham by faith."

3. *Baptism is not the substitute of circumcision in any such sense as to render the terms of admission to the one, also the terms of admission to the other, and this is the only point in*

* See Gen. xii. 1-3; xiii. 14-18; xv. 1-7; xvii. 1-16; xxii. 15-18; Rom. iv. 9-12; Gal. iii. 6-16.

question. Circumcision was the rite of initiation into the old dispensation, baptism is the rite of initiation into the new; the two rites are plainly so far analogous, and in this sense the one is the substitute of the other. But as the two dispensations materially differ in the characters of their members, the old making no ritual distinction between the converted and the unconverted, so also the conditions of admission are essentially different. Indeed, the substitution of baptism for circumcision as the form of initiation itself creates a presumption that the design of the rite is different, and consequently the terms of admission to it different; otherwise, why make a change in the rite? But the most decisive reasons exist for denying that the terms of admission to the two rites are identical, and *this is the only point in question.* Thus, (1.) Circumcision was administered only to males; baptism is given to both sexes. (2.) It admitted all the circumcised into all the privileges of the nation; if, then, baptism be in all respects its substitute, baptized children should be admitted to all the privileges of the church. (3.) The covenant positively required the circumcising of servants as well as children, old or young; if baptism be its substitute, the parent is bound to have all his servants baptized. His whole household, godly or ungodly, willing or unwilling, must come with him at once into the bosom of the church. (4.) The apostles and Jewish Christians were both circumcised and baptized; but if one rite came in all respects in the place of the other, where was the need of this? Why not begin the new rite with infants, simply baptizing instead of circumcising them? But we know that in the case of infants the Jewish Christians continued strictly to practise circumcision, while we have no evidence that they administered both rites to their children; such a supposition is wholly improbable. Indeed, if they understood that the one rite was the divinely-ordained substitute for the other, how could they practise circumcision at all? (5.) In the bitter and widespread discussion respecting the obligation of circumcision on the Gentile Christians, no hint is given that baptism had taken its place; such a fact, had it been suggested, would have gone far to settle the question, and it is incredible that if it was a fact it should not have been stated. It seems plain, therefore, that the conditions of administration in the two rites are widely dissimilar, and the admission of infants to the one does in no way prove that they are to be admitted to the other.

4. *The Scripture passages commonly adduced for the Abrahamic covenant as a basis of infant baptism furnish a decisive argument against it.*

Col. ii. 11, 12: "In whom also ye are circumcised with the circumcision made without hands, in putting off the body of the sins of the flesh by the circumcision of Christ: buried with him in baptism, wherein also ye are risen with him, through the faith of the operation of God, who hath raised him from the dead." A careful analysis finds here asserted—(1.) That Christians are circumcised, not with the outward circumcision, but with a "circumcision not made with hands." (2.) That this Christian circumcision consists, not in the cutting of the flesh, but "in putting off the body of the sins of the flesh"—that is, in regeneration. (3.) That the outward symbol of this inward circumcision is baptism, in which they were buried with Christ as dead to sin and raised with him as alive to holiness. Here, then, circumcision of the heart, or the putting off the body of sin, is put in contrast with circumcision of the flesh; and it is affirmed of baptism, not that it takes the place of circumcision of the flesh, but that it is a symbol of the circumcision of Christ—that is, of regeneration. Plainly, therefore, if the passage can be supposed to suggest that, as circumcision was initiatory to the old dispensation, so baptism is initiatory to the new, it also indicates that, as the terms of admission to the one rite were carnal, so the terms of admission to the other are spiritual.

Rom. xi. 16-24: "For if the first-fruit *be* holy, the lump *is* also *holy:* and if the root *be* holy, so *are* the branches. And if some of the branches be broken off, and thou, being a wild olive tree, wert graffed in among them, and with them partakest of the root and fatness of the olive tree; boast not against the branches. But if thou boast, thou bearest not the root, but the root thee. Thou wilt say then, The branches were broken off, that I might be graffed in. Well; because of unbelief they were broken off, and thou standest by faith. Be not high-minded, but fear: for if God spared not the natural branches, *take heed* lest he also spare not thee. Behold, therefore, the goodness and severity of God: on them which fell, severity; but toward thee, goodness, if thou continue in *his* goodness: otherwise thou also shalt be cut off. And they also, if they abide not still in unbelief, shall be graffed in; for God is able to graff them in again. For if thou wert cut out of the olive tree which is wild by nature, and wert graffed contrary to nature into a good olive tree: how much more shall these, which be the natural *branches*, be graffed into their own olive tree?"

The figure of the olive tree here employed, when rightly analyzed, clearly disproves infant baptism. The "good olive" here is Abraham and his seed, considered as the external covenant people of God. Under the old dispensation external connection with this tree had been maintained by natural descent, but under the new dispensation, Paul affirms, it is conditioned on faith. Hence, after the coming of Christ, the unbelieving Jews, though natural descendants of Abraham, were by reason of their unbelief cut off as no longer true branches; but the believing Gentiles, though not natural descendants of Abraham, were by reason of their faith ingrafted as true branches of the good olive. Faith, not natural descent, being now the condition of a visible place among the covenant people of God, it resulted that the unbelieving Jew must be cut off, while the believing Gentile must be received; and the excision of the one must continue as long as he is unbelieving, while the grafted position of the other can also continue only as long as he is believing. The whole illustration, therefore, shows, (1.) That faith, not natural descent, entitles to a place among the visible people of God under the new dispensation; and, (2.) That none ought to be admitted to the church, the visible community of God's covenant people, except on condition of faith; natural descent cannot entitle to such admission.

It is difficult to see how infant baptism could have been more expressly excluded than it is by the two passages above considered, for in both the absolute necessity of a spiritual character, in order to entrance among God's covenant people, is distinctly presented and emphasized.

II. THE ARGUMENT FOR INFANT BAPTISM FROM SCRIPTURAL PASSAGES.

Matt. xix. 13-15: "Then were brought unto him little children, that he should put his hands on them, and pray: and the disciples rebuked them. But Jesus said, Suffer little children, and forbid them not, to come unto me: for of such is the kingdom of heaven. And he laid his hands on them, and departed thence." Here observe, (1.) They were brought that he might, not baptize, but "lay his hands on them, and pray;" and this was all he did. If infant baptism was a recognized institution, it is singular that the disciples should have objected to the bringing of the children, especially as this incident occurred in our Lord's journey through Perea, not long before his crucifixion; and if infant baptism had been instituted by him, the bringing of children to him to be baptized must long since have been a familiar fact and could not have called forth rebuke. (2.) Our Lord's words, "Of *such* is the kingdom of heaven," plainly refer, not to age, but to character, as is shown by his own exposition, Matt. xviii. 1-6—where, insisting on the necessity of the childlike spirit in order to entering the kingdom, he designates Christians as "these little ones which believe in me." Thus also, in the parallels, Mark x. 15; Luke xviii. 17, he explains his meaning in the words "Of *such* is the kingdom of heaven" by the added remark: "Verily I say unto you, Whosoever shall not receive the kingdom of God as a little child, he shall not enter therein." (3.) The incident clearly disproves the existence of infant baptism; for if that rite existed and would have benefited them, would Christ have sent these children away, as he did, unbaptized?

Acts ii. 38, 39: "Repent, and be baptized, every one of you, in the name of Jesus Christ, for the remission of sins, and ye shall receive the gift of the Holy Ghost. For the promise is unto you, and to your children, and to all that are afar off, even as many as the Lord our God shall call." Here it is to be noted: (1.) The apostle, in verse 38, places repentance before baptism—"Repent and be baptized"—thus indicating the essential prerequisite to the ordinance and excluding the idea of a baptism in the case of infants, who are incapable of repentance. Meyer comments: "The *metanoēsate* (repent) demands the *change of ethical* disposition as the moral condition of being baptized, which directly and necessarily brings with it faith." (2.) In referring to "children," verse 39, he is speaking, not of baptism, but of "the promise of the Holy Ghost," so that, if the word "children" here could be understood of infants, it would prove, not infant baptism, but infant regeneration and inspiration. The word "children," however, is clearly used here in the general sense of *posterity*, as in Acts xiii. 32, 33: "We declare unto you glad tidings, how that the promise which was made unto the fathers, God has fulfilled the same unto us, their children." Lange comments: "He specifies those for whom this promise of God was intended: (*a*) It concerns 'you,' the Israelites; (*b*) also 'your children'—*i. e.*, it is not restricted to the present moment, but extends to the future, and comprehends the generations in Israel that are still unborn. And yet the whole extent of the promise has not been presented to their view; it belongs, further, to (*c*) *pasi tois eis makran*, all nations—*i. e.*, heathens dwelling at a distance, as many as God shall summon." Thus also Barnes, Hackett, and most commentators.

1 Cor. vii. 14: "For the unbelieving husband is sanctified by the wife, and the unbelieving wife is sanctified by the husband; else were your children unclean, but now are they holy." Note here: (1.) The question before the apostle is, Shall a married couple, only one of whom is a believer, continue to live together? The answer is in the affirmative, and the reason urged is the religious influence of the believing over the unbelieving companion and over the children. (2.) If the allusion was, as alleged, to qualification for baptism, then not the children only, but also the unconverted husband or wife, are qualified for baptism; for in both cases such are "sanctified," made "holy," by the believing companion. (3.) If the reference be in any way to baptism, it proves that the children of such parents were not baptized; for if they had been, how could the

separation of the parents invalidate their baptism and render them in this sense "unclean"? Lange justly comments: "This whole argument militates against, rather than favors, the existence of infant baptism at this period. Had such a practice existed, it would be fair to presume that the apostle would have alluded to it specifically in confirmation of his position. Here, most of all, would have been the place to have mentioned it by name as furnishing ecclesiastical authority for the view he had taken. The fact that he does not mention it, therefore, affords some reason for concluding that the rite did not exist." Thus also Stuart, Barnes, Olshausen, Neander, Meyer, Alford, and nearly all exegetes of note.

Acts xvi. 15, 32-34; 1 Cor. i. 16. These passages record the baptism of three households, and the inference has been drawn that infants are to be baptized on the faith of the parent. Such an inference, however, is wholly unwarranted; for, (1.) There is no evidence of children in these families too young to exercise faith, or indeed of children at all; and even were there evidence of infants in them, the ordinary usage of language would forbid their inclusion in the term house or household, as here employed. We say: "Mr. A. and his family were at church to-day," but no one would for a moment suppose from that statement that his infant child was there. Only those capable of attending church would be included. The mention of households by no means necessitates the idea of infant children in them, for repeated instances occur in which entire households are spoken of as believing. This is affirmed of the household of the nobleman of Capernaum (John iv. 53), of Cornelius (Acts x. 2), and of Crispus (Acts xviii. 8). (2.) There is evidence that the three households mentioned as baptized were composed of believers. This may be inferred, in the case of Lydia, from ver. 40; it is directly affirmed in the case of the jailer, who "rejoiced, believing in God with all his house;" and it would seem plain as it respects the household of Stephanus, since they "addicted themselves to the ministry of the saints" (1 Cor. xvi. 15). (3.) The argument for household baptism on the mere faith of the parent or head proves far too much for those who use it; for, if valid, it requires the baptism of *all* the household, old and young, servants and children, willing or unwilling—a doctrine which is justly repudiated by all evangelical Christendom. Meyer, with whom concur the highest exegetical authorities in Germany and England, distinctly denies that the baptism of households is any evidence of infant baptism, and, commenting on Acts xvi. 15, he says: "On this question the following remarks are to be made: (1.) If in the Jewish and Gentile families which were converted to Christ there were children, their baptism was to be assumed in *those* cases when they were so far advanced that they could and did confess their faith in Jesus as the Messiah; for this was the universal, absolutely necessary qualification for the reception of baptism. Comp. also vs. 31, 32, 33; xviii. 8. (2.) If, on the other hand, there were children still incapable of confessing, baptism could not be administered to those to whom that, which was the necessary presupposition of baptism for Christian sanctification, was still wanting. (3.) Such young children, whose parents were Christians, rather fell under the point of view of 1 Cor. vii. 14, according to which, in conformity with the view of the apostolic church, the children of Christians were no longer regarded as *akathartoi* (unclean), but as *hagioi* (holy), and that not on the footing of having received the character of holiness by baptism, but as having part in the Christian *hagiotēs* (holiness) by their fellowship with their Christian parents. See on 1 Cor., *l. c.* Besides, the circumcision of children must have been retained for a considerable time among Jewish Christians, according to xxi. 21. Therefore, (4.) The baptism of the children of *Christians*, of which no trace is found in the New Testament (not even in Eph. vi. 1), is not to be held as an apostolic ordinance—as, indeed, it encountered early and long resistance—but it is an *institution of the church* which gradually arose in post-apostolic times in connection with the development of ecclesiastical life and of doctrinal teaching, not certainly attested before Tertullian, and by him still decidedly opposed, and, although already defended by Cyprian, only becoming general after the time of Augustine in virtue of that connection."

Scripture passages, it is evident, furnish no ground for infant baptism. Exegetical scholars, German and British, both earlier and later, concur with Professor Stuart, who admits: "Commands or plain and certain examples in the New Testament relative to it I do not find." Thus also Dr. Woods, who finds an argument for infant baptism in "the silence" of Scripture respecting it, thence arguing that the Bible does not forbid the rite, forgetting that such an argument is equally valid for the five spurious sacraments of Rome, and for all other rites which are assumed as having basis in the old dispensation and are not expressly forbidden in the new.

SECOND: ARGUMENTS AGAINST INFANT BAPTISM.

I. THE SCRIPTURES INVARIABLY REQUIRE PERSONAL FAITH IN CHRIST AS PREREQUISITE TO BAPTISM.

1. *The ministerial commission.* Matt. xxviii. 19: "Go ye therefore, and teach (disciple) all nations, baptizing them (those discipled) in the name of the Father, and of the

Son, and of the Holy Ghost." Mark xvi. 15, 16: "Go ye into all the world, and preach the gospel to every creature. He that believeth and is baptized shall be saved; but he that believeth not shall be damned." This fundamental law, under which the church and the ministry act, contains no warrant to baptize any except those who profess personal faith; but, on the other hand, it positively requires the ministry to baptize believers, and believers to be baptized. It is evident, however, that if the rite has been performed in infancy, neither the ministry nor the believer can perform the duty enjoined. It is objected to this interpretation that faith is here made prerequisite to salvation as well as to baptism; and if this interpretation be correct, infants, being incapable of faith, cannot be saved. We reply: This law, when it requires faith as prerequisite to salvation and baptism, does by that fact limit church and ministerial action to those capable of exercising faith. As to the salvation and baptism of infants the commission says nothing, and devolves no responsibility on the church or the ministry. The sphere of their duty is limited to such as are capable of hearing and believing the gospel. The salvation of infants God has reserved within his own power; the church has here no duty or responsibility; and the perversion of a divine ordinance to secure, by a mere physical act, the salvation of souls not yet capable of receiving instruction or of exercising personal faith, is an invasion of the divine prerogatives.

2. *Apostolic example and teaching.* In every instance in which baptism is recorded, a previous faith in Christ is either expressly stated or clearly implied. At the Pentecost it was those who "gladly received" the word who were baptized. In Samaria those who "believed" "were baptized, both men and women." The existence of faith

prior to baptism, and as a condition of receiving it, is equally clear in the case of the eunuch of Ethiopia, of Saul of Tarsus, of Cornelius, of Lydia, and of the jailer of Philippi. The apostolic example has absolute uniformity in this, nor is there the slightest hint that, apart from previous faith, the ordinance might be administered. On the contrary, the apostolic teaching everywhere regards baptism as implying a previous faith. Thus, Paul says to the Galatians: "Ye are all the children of God by faith in Jesus Christ: *for* as many of you as have been baptized into Christ have put on Christ" (Gal. iii. 26, 27), where, as is plain, their baptism is adduced as a proof of their faith.

II. THE CHARACTER AND SPIRIT OF THE NEW DISPENSATION REQUIRE A SPIRITUAL CHURCH MEMBERSHIP, AND THUS LIMIT THE RITE OF INITIATION TO SPIRITUAL PERSONS.

The old dispensation was predominantly external; the new is spiritual. The old was national, regarding men in the mass; the new is personal, dealing more with the individual soul. The old presented types and shadows, while the realities were yet future and unattained; the new presents realities, and its ordinances symbolize blessings not so much future as already possessed. The general aspects of the two dispensations are thus distinguished; and, in this view, it is evident that infant baptism belongs rather to the old than to the new economy. It is a sign without the thing signified, symbolizing no present fact in the experience of the child; while believers' baptism is the symbol of a present experience in the baptized—the living, blessed reality of spiritual regeneration.

Thus, in Jer. xxxi. 31-34, the Mosaic and Christian dispensations are placed in striking contrast: "Behold, the days come, saith the Lord, that I will make a new covenant with the house of Israel, and with the house of Judah: not according to the covenant that I made with their fathers in the day *that* I took them by the hand to bring them out of the land of Egypt; which my covenant they brake, although I was a husband unto them, saith the Lord: but this *shall be* the covenant that I will make with the house of Israel; After those days, saith the Lord, I will put my law in their inward parts, and write it in their hearts; and will be their God, and they shall be my people. And they shall teach no more every man his neighbor, and every man his brother, saying, Know the Lord: for they shall all know me, from the least of them unto the greatest of them, saith the Lord: for I will forgive their iniquity, and I will remember their sin no more." Here the Christian covenant is contrasted with the Mosaic, as to the character of its members, in four particulars: (1.) Instead of an external system of law, God will "put his law in their inward parts and write it in their hearts" (Jer. xxxi. 33)—that is, he will give them the spirit of true spiritual obedience. (2.) Instead of an outward relation to them as a nation, God will enter into a living union with them as individuals: he will be their God, and they shall be his people. (3.) Instead of being a mixed people, composed alike of saints and sinners, as Israel was, "they shall *all* know the Lord, from the least to the greatest." (4.) Instead of the temporary removal of sin by sacrifices that needed constant repetition, God "will forgive their iniquity, and will remember their sin no more." Plainly, the visible community of God's people, in the church of the new covenant, is here predicted as a body composed of regenerate souls, obedient, believing, and forgiven, and, in this respect, placed in contrast with the visible community of God's people in Israel under the old covenant, where the regenerate and unregenerate were intermingled without visible and ritual distinction. It is evident that the two dispensations are put in like contrast in Matt. iii. 7–12 and other passages, thus precluding the idea of an unregenerate church membership and the administration of an ordinance where no spiritual reality is represented.

III. Infant Baptism is Useless to those who Receive it.

When the rite was introduced, in the Patristic period, it served, as was supposed, an important purpose. The ground of its administration, as stated by Neander and other reliable historians, was "that none could be saved without outward baptism." The Papal Church affirms: "The proper effect of baptism is the remission of all sins, whether they were contracted from original corruption or our own fault."* The Reformers regarded it as securing salvation to those who die in infancy, and necessary to salvation in all cases. The Anglican Church makes it a means of regeneration.† The Westminster Confession declares it to be to the baptized "a sign and seal of the covenant of grace, of his ingrafting into Christ, of regeneration, of remission of sins, and of his giving up unto God through Jesus Christ, to walk in newness of life."‡ And Wesley said: "By baptism we, who are by nature the children of wrath, are made the children of God;" and, "In all ages the outward baptism is a means of the inward."

Now, with such conceptions of the effect of baptism, there is certainly some apparent utility in administering it to infants. But this notion of its saving efficacy is, at this day, generally repudiated by evangelical Christians. What utility, then, has the rite when administered to an

---
* *Catechism*, ii. 2, 44.   † *Baptismal Service*.   ‡ Ch. 23, sec. i.

infant? 1. Suppose the child dies in infancy; would it have been lost without baptism? No evangelical Christian will affirm this. 2. Suppose it lives to mature age; what aid does its baptism afford the child or its parent in forming a religious character? If any, then the children of Pædobaptists, who have received the rite, ought to present a contrast in character to the children of Baptists, who have not received it. Is this the fact? 3. Suppose baptism, as is alleged, places on the child the seal of the covenant, and thus renders its conversion more probable. If this be so, then it ought to follow that a larger proportion of the children of Pædobaptists are converted than of the children of Baptists. Is this the ordinary fact? Plainly, infant baptism, when subjected to these simple and obvious tests, proves to be a sign where nothing is signified: it is founded on neither precept nor promise from God, and results in no visible benefit to man.

IV. INFANT BAPTISM IS ITSELF WRONG, AND ITS ULTIMATE RESULTS ARE EVIL.

1. It rests on neither precept nor example in God's word, and it is, therefore, a form of will-worship—a rite of human institution, but claiming the authority of a divine ordinance. This intrusion of man upon the prerogatives of God is expressly condemned. Christ has said: "In vain do they worship me, teaching for doctrines the commandments of men" (Matt. xv. 9)—a passage which our Lord quotes freely from Isa. xxix. 13 in direct connection with the abuse of a divine command.*
2. It is the perversion of an ordinance of God. All the significance of baptism as a symbol of divine truth is destroyed when, instead of being the free personal act of a believing, redeemed soul, it is the compulsory act per-

* See Col. ii. 18-23.

formed on a child wholly incapable of moral action. The divine symbol is thus perverted, and the beneficent results it was designed to secure are prevented. Besides, so far as the rite prevails, it practically abolishes God's ordinance; for if the person thus baptized, on afterward attaining capacity for personal moral action, should become a true believer on Christ, he is debarred from the exalted privilege and duty of a personal confession of his Lord in this holy symbol; and the moral power of this significant act, in which a free, intelligent soul publicly devotes his whole redeemed being to God, is thus lost to the world. Who but the omniscient One can measure the far-reaching and disastrous results, alike to the individual thus debarred from a high privilege and duty and to the world thus deprived of the influence of such a confession? 3. The practical tendency of infant baptism is to a false and fatal dependence on a mere ceremony. The necessary effect of the doctrine that a child has thus been brought into covenant with God, or at least has been placed within the special promises of God, so far as it is believed in an unconverted soul, can only be to lull the conscience in carnal security, and thus imperil the soul's salvation. Probably few pastors of experience have failed to mark this tendency in the souls of the unconverted, silently but powerfully operating as a resisting force against all efforts to rouse them from indifference and to impel them to earnest effort for personal salvation. 4. The results of the institution, in its influence on the church and the cause of God, are plainly exhibited in history. No form of superstition has been more prolific of evil. Originating in the error that baptism has in it a saving efficacy, it has been the chief support of sacramentalism in all ages. Introducing, as it does, by a logical necessity, the children thus baptized as members of the church, it has filled the churches with an unconverted membership; and it has thus perpetually and necessarily tended to obliterate the distinction, in faith, spirit, and life, between the church and the world. Thus introducing the world into the church, it has led to the establishment of state-churches, with their formalism, corruption, and oppression. In the churches of the Old World it has been the chief agency in destroying spiritual vitality, and on this continent its influence is only too apparent in the advancing power of worldliness and sacramentalism in the churches which practise it. For all history has most impressively taught that a pure church is essential to a pure gospel; infant baptism, therefore, by precluding a regenerate church membership, is, and must ever be, destructive of a pure Christianity.

V. Infant Baptism Unknown in the First Two Christian Centuries.

The rite of infant baptism had an undoubted recognition in the North African church in the middle of the third century, although there is no adequate evidence of its practice elsewhere till a later period. In this investigation, therefore, we need only to examine the patristic writings of the first two centuries and a half to ascertain what evidence, if any, they furnish of its existence in that earlier period.

The Apostolic Fathers, A. D. 90–140.

Of these, Ignatius and Polycarp make no allusions to baptism. Clement, in his second epistle, when arguing that sins committed after baptism are unpardonable, makes distinct recognition of the engagements made at baptism as personal acts, and thus seems to exclude the idea of infants being baptized. Barnabas says: "Blessed are they who, having trusted to the cross, have gone down into the water, because they shall receive the reward in its time." "We descend," he says, "into the water laden with sins and corruption, and ascend bearing fruit, having in our hearts the fear (of God) and the hope which is in Jesus by the Spirit." Here there is a distinct recognition of the form as a burial and rising, and of the subjects as those capable of "the fear of God and the hope which is in Jesus." Hermas writes: "Before a man receives the name of the Son of God he is appointed to death, but when he receives that seal he is freed from death and appointed to life. That seal is the water into which men descend doomed to death, but they ascend appointed to life." Here also the form is indicated as a burial and a rising, and the subjects as capable of making a personal profession. These are all the references to the subjects of baptism in the apostolic Fathers, and they are not only silent as to infant baptism, but also plainly indicate the baptism only of believers.

THE EARLIER FATHERS, A. D. 140–250.

JUSTIN MARTYR, in his first *Apology*, addressed to the Roman emperor, probably about A. D. 138, says: "Many men and many women, sixty or seventy years old, who from children were disciples of Christ, preserve their continence." Here, "from children" (*ek paidōn*) has been supposed to teach that these persons had been disciples from *infancy*, but evidently the author intends only that from youth to age they had remained continent, using the word *paidōn* in its more common acceptation, denoting any age from five to twenty-five. Liddell and Scott define *pais*, a *child*, a *boy*, *youth*, *lad*. In the New Testament it is used of the children who greeted Christ in the temple, of Jesus when at the age of twelve, of the daughter of Jairus, and of Eutychus at Troas, and Justin himself uses it of Herodias' daughter, who danced before Herod. The word *mathēteuo*, ("were disciples") signifies discipleship by means of instruction, and forbids the idea of unintelligent infancy. Semisch, the learned Lutheran author of a monograph on Justin, says: "Whenever Justin refers to baptism, *adults* appear as the objects to whom the sacred rite is administered. Of infant baptism he knows nothing. The traces of it which some persons believe they have found in his writings are groundless fancies, artificially produced." And on the above passage he insists that *ek paidōn* denotes "the entrance of the period of youth," and quotes as a parallel Lucian's remark on the philosopher Demonax, "that he loved philosophy *ek paidōn*—from youth." Indeed, Justin's own words in this *Apology* show clearly that he knew only the baptism of believers. He writes: "As many as are persuaded and believe that these things are true which are taught and said by us, and engage to live accordingly, are instructed to pray and ask, with fasting, from God the forgiveness of the sins they have before committed, we also praying and fasting with them. Then they are led by us to a place where is water, and receive the new birth after the same manner of new birth in which we ourselves have been born again; for in the name of the Father of all, and Lord God, and our Saviour Jesus Christ, and of the Holy Spirit, they then receive the bath." Plainly, there is here reference only to the baptism of believers. But when it is remembered that Justin's *Apology* is a defence of Christians, formally setting forth before the emperor the institutions observed by Christians, the omission in it of any reference to infant baptism is presumptive evidence that the author knew of no such usage in the churches. This is confirmed also by Justin's words: "We were corporally born without our will, but we are not to remain children of necessity and ignorance, but in baptism are to *have choice, knowledge*, etc. This we learned from the apostles."*

IRENÆUS, in a work written probably A. D. 180, when speaking of Christ's purpose in becoming incarnate and living in human life, says: "Christ came to redeem all to himself—all who through him are regenerated to God (*renascuntur in Deum*)—infants, children, boys, young men and old. Hence he passed through every age: he became an infant, sanctifying the infants; among the children he became a child, sanctifying those who belong to this age, and at the same time presenting to them an example of piety, of well-doing, of obedience; among the young men he became a young man, that he might set them an example and sanctify them to the Lord." † On this passage, Hagenbach, in his *History of Christian Doctrines*, says: "It only expresses the beautiful idea that Jesus was Redeemer *in* every stage of life and *for* every stage of life; but it does not say that he redeemed children by the water of baptism, unless the term *renasci* be interpreted by the most arbitrary *petitio principii* to refer to baptism." ‡ With him concur Winer and most German scholars, who deny that *renascuntur* refers to the baptismal rite. This is confirmed by the fact that Irenæus never uses *renasci ad Deum* to denote baptism except with some expression denoting *water, bath,* etc.; elsewhere it always signifies salvation, as where he says that by Christ's coming Abraham "was regenerated to God."

The first two centuries, therefore, furnish no evidence of infant baptism. The New Testament, the apostolic

---
* Semler's *Ch. Hist.,* vol. i., p. 311.
† *Against Heresies,* book ii. chap. 22, sect. 4. ‡ Vol. i., p. 211.

Fathers, Justin and Irenæus, are utterly silent as to it; while, on the contrary, baptism is everywhere presented in their words as the act only of such as are capable of exercising and professing a personal faith in the Lord Jesus Christ. The late Chevalier Bunsen, an eminent Lutheran, in his learned work on *Hippolytus*, a Christian Father who suffered martyrdom A. D. 236, says of that period: "The church adhered rigidly to the principle, as constituting the true purport of the baptism ordained by Christ, that no one can be a member of the communion of saints but by his own solemn vow made in the presence of the church. It was with this understanding that the candidate was immersed in water and admitted as a brother upon his confession of the Father, the Son, and the Holy Ghost. Pædobaptism, in the more modern sense, meaning thereby the baptism of new-born infants, with the vicarious promises of parents or other sponsors, was utterly unknown to the early church, not only down to the end of the second, but indeed to the middle of the third, century."

TERTULLIAN, who died about A. D. 240, in his work *De Baptismo*, written not far from A. D. 200, opposes strongly the baptism of children; but it is wellnigh certain that he does not refer to the baptism of new-born infants, as his language more naturally applies to a later stage of childhood. The fact of his opposition is itself plain proof that in his day even childhood-baptism was not the universal, nor even the common, practice, and that it was not regarded as resting on apostolic authority. When, also, we remember that *De Baptismo* was specially addressed to Montanists, when Tertullian was the chief teacher of the orthodox church at Carthage, it remains wholly uncertain whether the premature baptism he opposes had any existence among the orthodox churches.

Neander, who made Tertullian a special study and wrote a life of him, says, in his *Church History:* " Tertullian evidently means that children should be led to Christ by instructing them in Christianity, but that they should not receive baptism until, after being sufficiently instructed, they are led, from personal conviction and by their own free choice, to seek for it with sincere longing of heart. . . . It seems, in fact, from the principles laid down by him, that he could not conceive of *any efficacy whatever* residing in baptism without the conscious participation and individual faith of the person baptized."* It is probable, therefore, from the writings of Tertullian, that a tendency already showed itself in North Africa, especially among the Montanists, to administer baptism to children too young to make a fully intelligent profession. This tendency he successfully resisted among the Montanists, for they rejected infant baptism ; but among the orthodox the rite developed itself, for we find, a little after the middle of the third century, Cyprian and sixty-six North African bishops decreeing, not only that it was right to baptize infants, but also that it was not necessary to wait even eight days from birth, the time anciently appointed for circumcision.

ORIGEN, who died at Tyre, A. D. 254, was a profound scholar and a voluminous writer; but his works unfortunately have come down to us in mutilated form, and largely in Latin translations badly interpolated. Much uncertainty, therefore, often exists respecting the genuineness of what is attributed to him. Several passages from his works are adduced as showing the existence of infant baptism; but none of these exist in the original Greek of Origen, and both their genuineness and the correctness of the interpretation put on them are doubtful. Thus,

* Vol. i., p. 312.

Origen, speaking on native depravity, says: "Since the baptism of the church is given for the remission of sins, baptism is given, according to the observance of the church, even to children." And again: "Because, through the sacrament of baptism, the pollution of nativity is removed, therefore children also are baptized." Elsewhere, commenting on the words of David, "In sin did my mother conceive me," he says: "For this also the church has received a tradition from the apostles to give baptism even to children; for they to whom the secrets of the divine mysteries were committed knew that in all persons there is the native pollution of sin, which must be done away by the water and the Spirit."

On these passages we remark: 1. As already seen, there is an uncertainty as to the genuineness of these passages, since it is confessedly true that Jerome and Rufinus, in whose translations they occur, often interpolate remarks of their own which represent, of course, the views and practice nearly two centuries later than Origen, when infant baptism was fully established. 2. The word *parvulus*, used in these passages, is not restricted to the designation of an infant, but is more commonly used for a child of greater age. Origen himself uses it to designate Christ when at the age of twelve he went up to the temple; in connection with which event, also, he designates Christ *infantulus*, *puer*, *infans*, clearly showing that these terms were applied to youth. There is no adequate evidence, therefore, that *parvuli* in these passages designates newborn infants; the probability is in favor of the reference to early youth. 3. Origen elsewhere clearly states who, and who only, were properly baptized. Thus, in his work against Celsus, the sceptic, he says: "We exhort sinners to come to the instruction that teaches them not to sin, and the unintelligent to come to that which produces in them understanding, and *little children* to rise in elevation of thought to the man, and the miserable to come to a fortunate state, or (what is more proper to say) a state of happiness. And when those of the exhorted that make progress *show they have been cleansed by the word*, and, as much as possible, *have lived a better life, then* we invite them to be initiated among us." Again, in his *Commentary on Romans*, he says: "If any one is *previously* dead to sin, he of course is buried with Christ; but if any one does not before die to sin, he cannot be buried with Christ, for no one while alive is buried. But if he is not buried with Christ, neither is he lawfully baptized." It seems evident, therefore, that Origen, like Tertullian, knew nothing of infant baptism as the baptism of new-born children, but only of the baptism of children, too young, indeed, to make a *credible* profession, but not to make a *voluntary* one. And the Chevalier Bunsen is clearly right when he says: "Tertullian's opposition is to the baptism of young, growing children; he does not say a word about new-born infants. Neither does Origen, when his words are accurately weighed."

Thus far we have reached the following results: 1. That in the first two centuries no trace of infant baptism is found; the rite was administered only to those who made a credible profession of faith. 2. That in the beginning of the third century tendencies appeared, especially in North Africa, to baptize at an earlier period, which, though resisted by Tertullian, ultimately resulted, under Cyprian, about the middle of that century, in establishing infant baptism in the North African orthodox churches, the opposition finding place chiefly in the ranks of the Montanists. 3. That no evidence is found of the existence of infant baptism, even at this time, elsewhere than in North Africa.

The foundation on which infant baptism based itself

was the doctrine of baptismal regeneration, and the consequent absolute necessity of the rite to salvation. The tendency to confound the thing symbolized and the symbol is seen, indeed, in the earliest Fathers. Justin Martyr speaks of baptism as "the water of life, which alone is able to cleanse those who have repented." Clement of Alexandria says: "Being baptized, we are enlightened; being enlightened, we are adopted; being adopted, we are made perfect; being perfected, we become immortal." Even Tertullian, in opening his work *De Baptismo*, apostrophizes "the blessed sacrament of water, by which, being washed from the faults committed in our former blindness, we are made free and heirs of eternal life." He declares that the Spirit "descends and broods over" the baptismal waters, "sanctifying them by his power; and when so sanctified, they acquire the power of sanctifying." Neander, in his *Church History*, says: "From the want of duly distinguishing between what is outward and what is inward in baptism (the baptism of water and the baptism of the Spirit), the error became more firmly established that without external baptism no one could be delivered from that inherent guilt, could be saved from the everlasting punishment that threatened him, or be raised to eternal life; and when the notion of a magical influence, a charm connected with the sacraments, continually gained ground, the theory was finally evolved of the *unconditional necessity of infant baptism*. About the middle of the third century this theory was already generally admitted in the North African church. The only question that remained was, whether the child ought to be baptized immediately after birth or not till eight days after, as in the case of the rite of circumcision."* The language of the later Fathers affirms in the strongest manner the efficacy and necessity of

* Vol. i., p. 313.

baptism. Thus, Ambrose says: "In the font there is a transition from the earthly to the heavenly;" and Jerome: "In the laver the old Adam altogether dies and the new one is raised up together with Christ; the earthly perishes, the super-celestial is born." Schaff, in his *Church History*, remarks: "Like Ambrose and other Fathers, Augustine taught the necessity of baptism for entrance on the kingdom of heaven, on the ground of John iii. 5, and deduced therefrom, in logical consistency, the terrible doctrine of the damnation of all unbaptized children, though he assigned them the mildest grade of perdition. The Council of Carthage, in 318, did the same."* Indeed, infant baptism and infant communion were based by the Fathers on precisely the same ground—that is, their necessity in order to salvation. Neander says: "As the church in North Africa was the first to bring prominently into notice the necessity of infant baptism, so, in connection with this, they introduced the communion of infants; for, as they neglected to distinguish clearly between the sign and the divine thing signified, and as they understood all that is said in the sixth chapter of John's Gospel concerning the eating of the flesh and drinking of the blood of Christ to refer to the outward participation of the Supper, they concluded that this, from the very first, was absolutely necessary to the attainment of salvation."† All historical testimony thus clearly points to this fontal error—the miraculous efficacy of the sacraments, and their consequent necessity in order to salvation as the one source of infant baptism.

This rite, however, though originating in a superstition already widely diffused in that age, only slowly spread in actual practice over Christendom. Of this the proofs are abundant.

* *Church History*, vol. ii., p. 482.   † *Church History*, vol. ii., p. 333.

1. *The catechumenical system*, in which, as is well known, great multitudes, both in youth and in adult age, were instructed preparatory to baptism. These preparatory schools belonged to every important church, and formed a prominent feature in church history from the second to the sixth century. They doubtless originated in the apostolic custom of brief instruction and examination before baptism, which gradually expanded into an elaborate course of training. Fully developed, these preparatory schools were graded in three classes—the *Auditores*, or hearers, who were admitted only to the reading of the Scriptures and the sermons; the *Prostrati*, who were allowed also to join with the church in the prayers; and the *Competentes*, who stood as formal applicants for baptism, and who, on completing the course became Perfectiones or Electi, accepted candidates for that ordinance. No careful student of history can doubt that this was the ordinary method of entering the church during that period. In the large cities the catechumens often numbered several thousand, and many of the most distinguished men thus entered the church. Schaff says of these schools: "They embraced people of all ranks, ages, and grades of culture, even philosophers, statesmen, and rhetoricians—Justin, Athenagoras, Clement of Alexandria, Tertullian, Cyprian, Annobius, Lactantius, who all embraced Christianity in adult years."* That the system embraced children of Christian parents, as well as others, is plain from the words of Basil, who, in his *Exhortatio ad Baptismum*, reproving the delay of baptism by catechumens, says: "Do you demur and loiter and put it off when you have been *from a child* catechised in the word? Are you not yet acquainted with the truth? A seeker all your life long, a considerer till you are old? When

* *Church History*, vol. i., p. 397.

will you become one of us?" Coleman, in his *Ancient Christianity*, says: "The rise of this order may be traced back to the latter part of the second century. The system was gradually developed in the third century, and reached its culminating point about the beginning of the fifth century, after which it fell by degrees into disuse."* He adds elsewhere: "The institutions of the church during the first five centuries concerning the requisite preparation for baptism, and all the laws and rules that existed during that period relating to the acceptance or rejection of candidates, necessarily fell into disuse when the baptism of infants began not only to be permitted, but enjoined as a duty, and almost universally observed. The old rule, which prescribed caution in the admission of candidates, and a careful preparation for the rite, was, after the sixth century, applicable for the most part only to Jewish, heathen, and other proselytes." In other words, the voluntary, intelligent profession of faith which during the first five centuries ordinarily preceded baptism was in the sixth century superseded by the involuntary, unintelligent act involved in infant baptism. In this statement of Coleman concur all the best historians. But it is evident that this wide prevalence of the catechumenical system during the first five centuries utterly precludes the general practice of infant baptism during that period.

2. *Many of the most distinguished men in the Patristic period were not baptized till adult age, although of Christian parentage.* Athanasius, Basil, Gregory Nazianzen, Chrysostom, Jerome, and Augustine were all baptized after they had reached adult life, yet they were all sons of parents one or both of whom were Christians. Some of them, as Gregory, were sons of Christian bishops; and of Basil,

* Page 118.

Gregory, and Augustine we have the record that they were specially dedicated to God in infancy by pious mothers, but not by baptism. Indeed, there is no clear proof of the baptism in infancy of any distinguished Father, although it is possible that Origen was baptized in early youth. Surely these facts, which cannot be set aside, are plain proof that infant baptism was not then the prevailing practice, however strongly insisted on in theory. Dr. Schaff justly remarks: "The cases of Gregory of Nazianzen, St. Chrysostom, and St. Augustine, who had mothers of exemplary piety, yet were not baptized before early manhood, show sufficiently that considerable freedom prevailed in this respect even in the Nicene and post-Nicene age."*

3. *The highest historical testimony leads to this result.* Neander, in his *Church History*, affirms of the period A. D. 312–590: "It was still very far from being the case, especially in the Greek Church, that infant baptism, although acknowledged to be necessary, was generally introduced into practice;" and he adds that it "entered rarely and with much difficulty into the church-life during the first half of this period."† Meyer, in his *Commentary on Acts*, after strongly denying its apostolic origin, says: "Concerning infant baptism, there is no witness before Tertullian, and it did not become general until after the time of Augustine." Schaff, also speaking of the post-Nicene age, says: "Notwithstanding the general admission of infant baptism, the practice of it was by no means universal."‡ But it is needless to multiply citations; for all reputable church historians, as Hagenbach, Gieseler, and Mosheim, concur in this statement.

The general results of this investigation, therefore, may

---

* *Church History* vol. i., p. 401. † Vol. ii., p. 319.
‡ *Church History*, vol. ii., p. 483.

be thus stated: 1. That infant baptism had no existence in the first two centuries, and no formal recognition in the church till the middle of the third century, and then only in North Africa. 2. That it was based, then and afterward, on a supposed magical power in baptism and its necessity in order to salvation. 3. That, notwithstanding this superstition, on which it was founded, was widely prevalent, the practice itself did not become general till the sixth century. 4. That the triumph of infant baptism was thus coincident with the triumph of the superstitions of the Papacy and with the beginning of the Dark Ages.

SECTION IV.

DOCTRINE OF THE LORD'S SUPPER.

This ordinance, which commemorates the dying love of Christ, has been for ages the centre of fierce theological conflict. In the Roman Church many a martyr perished for his temerity in opposing the papal dogma, and among the Reformers it proved the chief occasion of division and strife. These controversies relate chiefly to the question how, or in what manner, Christ is present in the Supper; in respect to which the Christian world is divided by four different theories.

I. TRANSUBSTANTIATION.

Many of the Fathers used language which implied a supernatural presence of Christ in the Supper, but none of them conceived of an actual change of the bread and wine into his flesh and blood. This was first taught, in formulated statement, by Paschasius Radbert, in the ninth century, who held that after the words of consecration are uttered there remains only the appearance of bread and wine: the actual substance is the body and blood of Christ. After three centuries of conflict this was proclaimed a dogma in the Roman Catholic Church by the Fourth Lateran Council, 1215, and in the sixteenth century it was reaffirmed with more ample statement and higher solemnity by the Council of Trent.

The doctrine, as thus stated, involves the following points: 1. That when the words of consecration are uttered by the priest, the bread and wine are instantly changed into the real body and real blood of Christ just as they actually existed on the cross. The properties of bread and wine, indeed, remain, such as color, form, and taste, but the substance is wholly changed. 2. That, as the body and spirit of Christ cannot be separated, it follows that not the body and blood only, but also the soul and divinity, the whole Christ is contained in the elements thus changed, and is contained in each separate particle of them. 3. That the Lord's Supper, or mass, is a true and proper sacrifice to God, the priest therein offering the real body, soul, and divinity—the whole Christ as he was offered up on the cross; it is, therefore, a real propitiation for sin and a means of securing God's favor. 4. That the elements, having thus become the true and real Christ, are to be worshipped and adored with the adoration and worship offered to God. 5. That, as the whole Christ is in each separate particle of the elements, the communicant receives in the bread or wafer, not the body only, but also the blood, of the Lord; and, as in the universal administration of the cup there is special danger of spilling the blood, the cup is to be withheld from the laity and given only to the clergy.

This miracle, which at the word of a mere man transmutes a wafer into God and makes the eucharist a perpetual repetition of the sacrifice of the cross, is affirmed chiefly from two passages.

1. The words of Christ (John vi. 53): "Except ye eat the flesh of the Son of man, and drink his blood, ye have no life in you." In this, however, a reference to the Lord's Supper is plainly inadmissible. For when Christ spoke these words, that ordinance had not been instituted. If they relate to it, the Old Testament saints and all who have died without the Supper have perished. The withholding of the ordinance from infants would be, in this case, fatal to their salvation. This literal interpretation of the passage, moreover, is condemned by Christ in verse 63: "The words that I speak unto you, they are spirit, and they are life." Whatever, therefore, be the meaning of these words, plainly they do not relate to the Supper.

2. The words used by Christ at the institution of the sacrament: "This is my body," "This is my blood." It is affirmed that these words are to be literally construed, and that with such construction they necessarily teach that the sacred elements are the true body and blood of Christ. But we deny the necessity of a literal construction. For the verb *to be* in all languages has a common meaning *to signify, to represent*, and in the New Testament this usage is frequent. Thus it is said: "I *am* the door;" "That rock *was* Christ;" "The seven candlesticks *are* the seven churches." In these passages, and in many others, the verb clearly means *to signify* or *represent;* and if in these, why not also in the words relating to the Supper? Indeed, the most imperative reasons require this interpretation. For, (1.) Christ, when he uttered these words, was sitting at the table with his disciples in his own proper body, and it is impossible that they could have understood

him literally. (2.) The bread, after the words of consecration, and at the time of eating, is still called bread,—1 Cor. x. 17: "We are all partakers of that one *bread*;" xi. 26, 27: ' As often as ye eat this *bread*,"—thus clearly showing that no such change had occurred. (3.) The literal construction is opposed to the plain testimony of the senses, which perceive in the elements only bread and wine; and if we reject the testimony of the senses, the foundation of all knowledge is destroyed, not on this subject alone, but on all subjects. (4.) It necessitates also the monstrous consequences that man has power to transmute bread and wine into God—a supposition not less impious than absurd; that the sacred elements or host, being thus the divine Christ, ought to be worshipped and adored, which is idolatry; and that the priest in every celebration of the mass offers a true and real sacrifice to God, whereas the Scriptures, in language emphatic and unmistakable, represent the one offering of Christ on the cross as complete and final. Finally, the withholding of the cup from the laity is opposed to the apostolic example and the uniform practice of the early churches; for the whole church, and not the clergy only, are represented as partaking of the wine. The apostles (1 Cor. x., xi.) never separated the elements as if the bread were common, but the wine appropriated to the clergy.

It is evident, therefore, that the dogma of transubstantiation has no basis either in Scripture or reason, and can be accepted only by those who place the so-called authority of the church above both.

II. Consubstantiation.

At the Reformation, Luther denied transubstantiation, but insisted on the real and corporeal presence of Christ in the Supper. He taught that "in, with, and under the consecrated bread and wine the true and essential body and blood of Christ are imparted to the communicant, and are received by him, though in a manner inexplicable by us and altogether mysterious." Zwingle, the Swiss Reformer, on the other hand, asserted that the sacred elements simply represent as symbols the body and blood of Christ. The struggle between the German and the Swiss theologians on this point was long and bitter, during which the moral power of the Reformation was seriously weakened. The Lutheran doctrine, as finally evolved, may be thus stated: 1. The bread and wine remain bread and wine after the words of consecration, but the real body and blood of Christ are mystically united with them; so that the communicant receives, in a corporeal sense, the actual body and blood of Christ in, under, and with the elements. 2. As a logical sequence, Christ's glorified body either is ubiquitous by the communication of divine omnipresence to it, or is, by divine power, specially present at each celebration of the sacrament; the former was Luther's view, the latter is the more common view of the Lutheran Church. 3. In partaking, the worthy and the unworthy alike receive the real body and blood of Christ, but with opposite effect. The worthy receive them unto salvation, the unworthy to condemnation

III. The Mystical Presence.

Calvin proposed a middle ground between the Lutheran and Zwinglian positions, hoping thus to reconcile the opposing parties. He denied the presence of Christ in the Supper in any corporeal sense, but insisted that he is *dynamically* present—that is, as the sun is in heaven, but its light and heat are on earth, so the glorified body of Christ is in heaven, but special divine influences radiate from it upon the believing soul while partaking of the sacrament. His words are: "Our souls are fed by the flesh and blood of Christ, just as our bodily life is nourished by bread and wine. The analogy of the signs would not hold unless our souls find their sustenance in Christ, which cannot be the case if Christ does not actually coalesce into one with us and support us through his flesh and blood. And although it seems incredible that, the places being so distant, the flesh of Christ should penetrate to us so as to be our food, let us remember how much the secret power of the Spirit transcends our senses, and how foolish it is to measure his immensity by our standard." And in his treatise on the Lord's Supper he adds: "We all, then, confess with one mouth that, on receiving the sacrament in faith according to the ordinance of the Lord, we are truly made partakers of the proper substance of the body and blood of Jesus Christ." His teaching plainly is that the believer, in partaking of the Supper, partakes, in a true and real sense, of the human nature of Christ.

Now, it is evident that the real presence in the Supper, whether conceived as corporeal or spiritual, must ultimately rest on a literal interpretation of the words of institution, the objections to which I have already stated. Here Luther and Calvin were less consistent than the Roman Catholics; for while the former accepts and the latter denies the literal construction, both, by labored refinements, explain away the simple, natural sense, and exhibit the vagueness and incoherence necessarily consequent on a forced construction of plain language. For when Christ says, "This is my body," he either means literally that it *is* his body, or figuratively that it *represents* his body; there is, and can be, no intermediate sense. If the body and blood of Christ are in any sense in the elements, they are there corporeally, because only thus do flesh and blood exist; and the bread and wine, therefore, which the senses perceive, must, on this hypothesis, be transmuted, as the Roman Catholic affirms, into the body and blood of Christ. If the literal construction be adopted, all attempts to evade transubstantiation are a violation of the plain laws of language.

IV. THE LORD'S SUPPER SYMBOLIC.

The bread and wine are symbols divinely appointed to represent the body and blood of Christ, through which symbols the sacrifice of Christ is vividly presented to the mind, and by partaking of which the believer expresses, in an outward and significant act, his faith in that sacrifice. The Supper is thus at once a symbol, setting forth this central, vital fact more distinctly than is possible in language, and a significant act, declaring the partaker's personal reliance on this fact as the ground of his salvation. Christ is present in the ordinance, as, according to his promise, he is always present in his truth; but, as truth finds its clearest and strongest expression in the symbol, he is present in the Supper in a more marked manner than in the word; for as, in the Supper, the believing soul more clearly apprehends Christ and more fully yields itself to him, so in it Christ more clearly manifests himself to the soul and more fully communicates to it of the fulness of his life.

No logical standpoint can be found between transubstantiation and this symbolic view. For, as we have seen, when Christ said, "This is my body," he either affirmed a literal, physical fact, as the Romanist claims or he affirmed a symbolic fact: "This represents my body." Any other than the symbolic interpretation involves not only an unnatural construction of the words, but also an element of mystery, if not of superstition, most injurious in its tendency.

If, then, we regard the Lord's Supper as symbolic, what is its significance?

1. *It symbolizes the death of Christ.* The bread broken and the wine poured forth represent the body and blood of Christ as offered up an atonement for sin. It is a vivid symbolization of the atoning sacrifice offered on the cross. "For, as often as ye eat this bread and drink this cup, ye do show the Lord's death till he come."

2. *It is a personal profession.* The partaker declares by eating of that bread and drinking of that cup his personal reliance on Christ's sacrifice as the only ground of his acceptance with God, and the only means of spiritual, eternal life. As the Hebrew, in partaking of the sacrifices offered on the altar, professed his faith in the truths those sacrifices symbolized, so the Christian, in partaking of the consecrated bread and wine, professes his faith in the truths symbolized by that sacrament. In this sense (as the apostle clearly shows, 1 Cor. x. 14–22) "the cup of blessing which we bless" is "the communion of the blood of Christ," and "the bread which we break" is "the communion of the body of Christ;" for it is the personal avowal by the partaker of reliance on him whose body was broken and blood shed for sin.

3. *It is an act of grateful commemoration*—a service done in remembrance of Christ's compassion in suffering and dying for us. He said: "This do in remembrance of me." As we look on the face of a departed friend which art has preserved, and handle afresh the tokens of affection he left behind, and recall in memory his words and acts of love, till it seems almost as if the dead were present and the familiar voice were sounding in the ear, so in the Supper the Saviour is "set forth evidently crucified among us;" and as we look on the symbols of his dying love we gratefully adore him as dying for us.

4. *It is a symbol of church-fellowship.* When a man eats of that "one bread" and drinks of that "one cup," he in this act professes himself a member of that "one body" in hearty, holy sympathy with its doctrines and life, and freely and fully subjecting himself to its watch-care and government (1 Cor. x. 17). Hence, in 1 Cor. v. 11, the church is forbidden to eat (in the Lord's Supper, as the context clearly shows) with immoral persons, thus distinctly making the ordinance a symbol of church-fellowship.

5. *The Supper is prophetic: it is a type of the marriage-supper of the Lamb in heaven.* Jesus said, when instituting it: "I will not drink hereafter of this fruit of the vine, until that day when I drink it new with you in my Father's kingdom" (Matt. xxvi. 29). His eye glanced down the ages of sorrow and oppression and blood through which his church should pass to the day of final triumph, when all his disciples, of every age and clime and people, shall gather in one body before his throne, exulting in his presence, to be for ever with their Lord. As we now gather at the table, therefore, not only do we look backward to the agony of his cross and the crown of thorns he once wore, but also forward to his throne of triumph and the "many crowns" which shall deck his brow there. And as we have fellowship with his sufferings and death here, we exultingly hope that we shall there be sharers of his blessedness and life.

Such is the import of the Lord's Supper. It is a striking and beautiful symbol of Christ's death for the soul, and is a solemn, personal profession, by the soul, of faith in his death as the ground of salvation. And through all the ages "till he comes" this ordinance is the Heaven-appointed symbol to express before men that divine fact and that high profession.

SECTION V.

QUALIFICATIONS FOR THE LORD'S SUPPER.

The Christian consciousness in all ages has recognized church membership as prerequisite to the Lord's Supper, including, of course, in this membership regeneration, baptism, and a consistent life in the church. Justin Martyr, in the second century, says: "This food is called with us the eucharist, of which none can partake but the believing and baptized, who live according to the commands of Christ." Bingham, in his *Antiquities of the Christian Church*, states: "None were permitted to partake of the symbols of Christ's body and blood but such as were first initiated by baptism." This was true of the patristic churches, alike of the East and of the West; of the Greek and of the Latin Church; of the Reformers in all divisions—Luther, Calvin, Knox, and Cranmer; of Churchman, Presbyterian, and Puritan. So clear and positive is this fact that Dr. Wall, in his *History of Pædobaptism*, says: "No church ever gave the communion to persons before they were baptized." "Among all the absurdities that ever were held, none ever maintained *that*—that any person should partake of the communion before he was baptized." This law of the Supper is still incorporated, in form or principle, in nearly all the church creeds, and is practically observed by almost all Christendom, Roman Catholic and Protestant, the only exceptions being a part of the English Baptists and some minor baptized sects in this country. The tendencies to "open communion," which have sprung from the sentimental liberalism of our age, are necessarily temporary, since they originate in no permanent, living biblical truths, and are in opposition to the grand currents of Christian thought and conviction flowing through the ages.

Now, this fact, that the Christian consciousness through all the centuries has recognized the restriction of the Lord's Supper to members of the church, creates a presumption in its favor as a divine law. It at least places the burden of proof on him who would depart from a principle thus enshrined in the deepest and holiest convictions of the Christian ages.

I. THE SCRIPTURAL LAW OF QUALIFICATION.

In the New Testament a credible profession of faith, in baptism, and a consistent membership in a Christian church are, both by precept and example, made precedent to participation in the Lord's Supper.

All the allusions to the ordinance imply these prerequisites in those who come to the Lord's table, as is evident from the following: 1. The apostles, who were present at the institution of the ordinance, were united as a special community with Christ and one another, for they had been specially chosen to "be with him," and had "left all and followed" him (Mark iii. 14; x. 28; Matt. xix. 27; Luke vi. 13). They were all baptized persons, for some of them are expressly said to have been baptized by John the Baptist, and all of them were administrators of baptism—a thing incredible if they themselves were not baptized (John i. 36–40; iv. 1, 2). The validity of John's baptism as a Christian ordinance has indeed been denied, but, so far as the Scriptures inform us, this was the only baptism received by Christ and his apostles—the very source and exemplars of the Christian ordinances—nor is there any instance in which those baptized by John were rebaptized after the Pentecost. The rebaptism of the twelve disciples at Ephesus, recorded in Acts xix. 1–7, cannot here be cited, for the ground of their rebaptism, as divinely stated, was not the invalidity of John's baptism as Christian baptism, but the radical defect in their knowledge of divine truth as taught by John. They did not know that John taught "the people that they should believe on him which should come after him—that is, on Jesus Christ"—nor had they "so much as heard whether there be any Holy Ghost." The repetition of baptism here, therefore, proves, not the invalidity of John's baptism, but the invalidity of any baptism without the prior knowledge of certain fundamental truths by the baptized. It is evident, then, that at the institution of the Supper all who partook were baptized, and were united in sacred covenant with one another and with Christ. 2. The commission by Christ to his disciples distinctly requires baptism on profession of faith prior to the reception of the Lord's Supper: "Go ye, therefore, and teach (disciple) all nations, baptizing them (those discipled) in the name of the Father, and of the Son, and of the Holy Ghost: teaching them to observe all things whatsoever I have commanded you" (Matt. xxviii. 19, 20). Here, first, they are to teach or make disciples; next, to baptize these disciples in the name of the Trinity; and then to teach them to observe the other commands of Christ, among which is that relating to the Supper. Now, as this commission is the foundation of authority for church and ministerial action, the *order* it prescribes is of solemn obligation. 3. The apostles, in exemplifying the commission, invariably administered the Supper only to the baptized. Baptism was the first symbolic act required after conversion; it stands everywhere as the rite of initiation into the Christian dispensation, and thus precedes the Lord's Supper. Thus, at the Pentecost the people first gladly received the gospel; next, they were baptized; and then, "continuing steadfast in the apostles' doctrine and fellowship," they joined in the breaking of bread or the Lord's Supper (Acts ii. 41, 42). At Troas, "upon the first day of the week, when the disciples [the best text has *we*] came together to break bread, Paul preached to *them*" (Acts xx. 7), plainly referring to the disciples at Troas, who had there been constituted as a church. Thus, also, Paul, in reprehending the disorderly celebration of the Supper at Corinth (1 Cor. xi.), makes no allusion to any but members of the church, thus indicating that only they partook. Such, in every recorded instance, was the exact obedience the apostles rendered to the plain order of the commission. 4. The relation of the two ordinances, in their import and position, requires the priority of baptism. Baptism is the symbol of regeneration, the entrance on a new spiritual life in Christ; the Lord's Supper is the symbol of that faith in Christ's atoning sacrifice by which this new life is sustained. The one symbolizes the new birth, the other the bread of life by which the new-born are nourished. The one is the rite of admission to the church, the door of the house of God; the other is an ordinance within the church, and is the highest formal expression of church fellowship. To administer the Supper, therefore, to the unbaptized is to invert the natural order and destroy the relation God has appointed. But such an inversion, by destroying the relation of the ordinances, destroys also the relation of the things symbolized; for the symbol of church membership is thereby placed before the symbol of regeneration, and thus the necessity of the new birth prior to entrance into the church is denied, and the door of the church is thrown open to the world.

These considerations clearly reveal the will of God respecting the qualifications for the Lord's Supper, and make plain the obligation resting on us.

II. This Law is Obligatory on the Church.

The church is responsible for the maintenance of this law of the Supper, and is the judge of the scriptural qualifications of those seeking admission to the table.

For, 1. The administration of the ordinances is entrusted to the church and the ministry, and in the Scriptures they are held accountable for their due observance. For in the commission and at the institution of the Supper the ordinances are committed to the ministry; and throughout the sacred records, as in 1 Cor. xi., the church is distinctly held responsible for their proper administration. The right of the church to judge of qualification for baptism is everywhere conceded—no one would allow the candidate to be the sole judge of his qualifications for that ordinance—but evidently equal reason exists for this rule in the Supper. 2. The Lord's Supper is the symbol not only of Christian, but also of church-fellowship; all the reasons, therefore, which require the church to decide in regard to church-fellowship also require it to decide in regard to admission to the symbol of church-fellowship. For Paul, in giving injunction to the Christian church concerning the exclusion of offenders, commands them "not to keep company, if any man that is called a brother be a fornicator, or covetous, or an idolater, or a railer, or a drunkard, or an extortioner: with such an one no not to eat" (1 Cor. v. 9–13), where the injunction "not to eat" seems clearly, from the whole connection, to refer to the Lord's Supper, which is thus made a symbol of church-fellowship. Thus, also, the apostle, in warning the same church against partaking in idol-feasts, declares that in so doing they would express fellowship with idols and idol-worshippers, and illustrates this fact in the Lord's Supper. He says: "The cup of blessing which we bless, is it not the communion of the blood of Christ? The bread which we break, is it not the communion of the body of Christ? For we being many are one bread, and one body; for we are all partakers of that one bread" (1. Cor. x. 16, 17). The last verse has been variously rendered. Calvin, Beza, and Bengel render it: "Because there is one bread, we being many are one body; for we are all partakers of that one bread." Alford: "Because we, the (assembled) many, are one bread, one body; for the whole of us partake of that one bread." Thus also Conant, Meyer, and others. However translated, the thought emphasized in the passage is that *because* all partake of the one bread the assembled *many* are symbolically presented as *one* body, and the Lord's Supper is thus plainly the symbol of church-fellowship. Now, as the duty of deciding on qualification for admission to church-fellowship belongs to the church, it seems evident that it must have also the duty of deciding on qualification for admission to this symbol of church-fellowship. 3. If the candidate were the sole judge of his qualification, it would follow that all who deem themselves qualified must be admitted, whatever their belief or character. But this would destroy the whole significance of the ordinance as a symbol of truth and a profession of faith. Plainly, a church might as consistently invite all to come without examination to its baptism and membership as to extend such an invitation to them to come to the Lord's Supper. This divine law of the Supper, therefore, a church may not disregard: it is bound to require the scriptural qualifications in those approaching the table. A candidate may have piety; but if, through error cherished, he is not in other respects qualified, the church may not set aside the law of God in deference to the error of the man. Loyalty to Christ and fidelity to the man in error alike require it to maintain the divinely-instituted rule for those who come to the Supper. For it is the LORD's Supper, not man's. An invitation, therefore, to those whom he has not invited is not catholicity or Christian liberality; it is presumption. It is the guest arrogantly presuming, in disregard of the express will of the Host, to call to the feast those whom he has not called.

III. RESTRICTION AT THE LORD'S TABLE ALMOST UNIVERSAL.

Restriction at the Lord's Table is not peculiar to the Baptist churches: it is the position of nearly all Christendom.

The Christian communities, as already seen, have in all ages been nearly unanimous in regarding this as an ordinance within the church, and in restricting its observance to those belonging to the church. Good men have, indeed, differed as to what is the proper comprehension of the term church—whether it shall include only the churches of their own denomination, or also those of some of the many other denominations claiming to be churches. They have differed, also, as to what is baptism, the rite initiatory to the church—whether it has only one form and its proper subjects are only personal believers, or whether it has three forms and children are also proper subjects of it. Within these limits there have been, and there are, differences; but in the restriction of the Lord's Supper to those regarded as baptized members of a church there has been, and there is, little difference. All the historic creeds of Christendom recognize this restriction either in formal statement or by plain implication, and all the historic churches have conformed to this in their practice. This was the doctrine of Luther and Calvin, of Knox and Cranmer. Doddridge, author of the *Rise and Progress*, remarks: "It is certain that, as far as our knowledge of primitive antiquity reaches, no unbaptized person received the Lord's Supper." President Dwight, in his *Theology*, says: "It is an indispensable qualification for this ordinance that the candidate for communion be a member of the visible church of Christ in good standing. By this I intend that he should be a person of piety, that he should have made a public profession of religion, and that he should have been baptized." The eloquent Dr. Griffin, in his *Letter on Communion*, said: "We ought not to commune with those who are not baptized, and of course are not church members, even if we regard them as Christians. Should a pious Quaker so far depart from his principles as to wish to commune with me at the Lord's Table I could not receive him, because there is such a relationship established between the two ordinances that I have no right to separate them; in other words, I have no right to send the sacred elements out of the church."

Nor is this testimony restricted to men of the past generation: equally explicit is the language of eminent Pædobaptists in this generation. Dr. A. A. Hodge, now professor of theology at Princeton, says: "The faith and practice of all the evangelical churches is that the communion is designed only for believers, and therefore that a credible profession of faith and obedience should be required of every applicant."* Dr. John Hall, of New York, as quoted approvingly by Rev. T. H. Beecher, of Elmira, said: "If I believed, with the Baptists, that none are baptized but those who are immersed on profession of faith, I should, with them, refuse to commune with any others." The General Assembly of the Presbyterian Church, at a recent session, resolved "that it is not in accordance with the spirit and usage of the church to invite

* *Outlines of Theology*, p. 514.

persons, believers, not members of any evangelical church, to partake of the Lord's Supper." In the Protestant Episcopal Church, the *Prayer Book*, under the head of *Confirmation*, says: "There shall none be admitted to the communion until such time as he be confirmed or be ready and desirous to be confirmed;" in practice, however, this rule is not enforced in the case of strangers who may be present. The Lutheran Church in this country has recently adopted a rule which is popularly stated: "Lutheran pulpits for Lutheran ministers only; Lutheran altars for Lutheran communicants only." The Reformed Presbyterian Church has always held to restriction of the Supper. Rev. John N. McLeod, D. D., in defining its views, says: "On the subject of sacramental communion, the principles of the church are that such communion is the most solemn, intimate, and perfect fellowship that Christians can enjoy with God and with one another; that when Christians are associated together in a church state, under a definite creed, communion in the sacraments involves an approbation of that creed; and that, as the church is invested with authority which she is bound to exercise to keep the ordinances pure and entire, sacramental communion is not to be extended to those who do not approve the principles of the particular church or submit themselves to her authority. . . . She does not feel at liberty to allow every man to be the judge of his own qualifications for sealing ordinances, or to dispense those ordinances to such as do not assent to her religious principles, or whom she could not submit to her discipline were they found violating their Christian obligations."

These examples, which might be greatly multiplied, clearly show that the restriction of the Lord's Supper to those regarded as baptized members of a church is recognized in principle and practice by the great body of

Christians; the deviations from it are exceptional. The difference between Baptists and other evangelical denominations, therefore, does not relate so much to the Lord's Supper as to baptism. No church believing scriptural baptism and consistent church membership divinely-instituted qualifications for the Supper, and also believing the responsibility of deciding upon the scriptural qualification of the candidate to be devolved upon itself, could conscientiously invite those it deems unbaptized to the Eucharist; for in so doing it would violate the divine order. A Pædobaptist church, however, may consistently invite those who, whether as infants or adults, have received immersion, or pouring, or sprinkling, for it believes any of these forms to be valid baptism. But a Baptist church can extend the invitation only to those who have been immersed upon an intelligent profession of faith; for in the Baptist view the immersion of a personal believer is the only real baptism, and sprinkling or pouring is not baptism. Baptism, then, is the grand point of difference as to the participation of the Lord's Supper. *Hibbard on Baptism*, a recognized theological text-book among Methodists, has the following just paragraph: "It is but just to remark that in one principle Baptist and Pædobaptist churches agree. They both agree in rejecting from communion at the table of the Lord, and in denying the right of church-fellowship to, all who have not been baptized; valid baptism they consider essential to constitute visible church membership. This also we hold. The only question, then, that here divides us is, What is essential to valid baptism?"

IV. OBJECTIONS CONSIDERED.

First: Some members of Pædobaptist churches have been immersed on profession of faith; as their baptism is confess-

edly valid, why should they not be invited to the Lord's table?

1. Because of the inconsistency of their church position. They have united with a church in which, according to their own belief, the ordinances are not scripturally administered, and their membership, so far from being a testimony against this perversion, is a public personal sanction of it. Their walk is, therefore, "disorderly." They wilfully sacrifice to taste, convenience, or worldly interest their serious convictions respecting an ordinance of God. 2. The Baptist churches, if they invited all immersed members of other churches to the table, would be involved in the inconsistency of inviting persons to that highest symbol of church-fellowship whom, if applicants for actual membership, they would be compelled to refuse; for the standards in most Pædobaptist churches do not, as with us, require evidence of conversion as a condition of church membership. In the Episcopal and Lutheran churches, if the candidate assents to the creed and is not scandalous in life, he is entitled to admission. Among Presbyterians, according to Dr. Hodge, "The visible church consists of all those who profess the true religion, together with their children;"* and if these children, on coming to years of understanding, do not repudiate their baptismal vow and are of moral life, they are to be admitted, according to the same writer, to all the privileges of membership. In the Methodist churches, according to their *Discipline*, "there is only one condition previously required of those who desire admission into these societies, and that is a desire to flee from the wrath to come and to be saved from their sins." In none of these churches, if we judge from their standards, is evidence of conversion prerequisite, as with us, to membership.

* *Theology*, vol. iii., p. 545.

Some of them, we rejoice to know, are better than their creeds, and have a thoroughly spiritual membership; but this is by no means true of all. Now, with such broad and vital difference in the terms of admission to the church, with what consistency could Baptist churches insist on evidence of conversion in applicants for membership if they invited to the Lord's Supper—the highest symbol of membership—members of churches in which no such evidence was required? 3. Besides, such an invitation would involve the inconsistency of inviting to the table those whom, if actual members, it would be the duty of the church to exclude. For example, a member in a Baptist church, in plain violation of its principles, adopts the practice of infant baptism, and, notwithstanding kindly labor, persists in the offence. Clearly, in such a case, the church ought to exclude the offender. But with what consistency could it exclude him from membership for that reason while inviting to the symbol of membership those who advocate and adopt the same practice? Besides, suppose such a person, after his exclusion, has united, as he naturally would, with a Pædobaptist church, and is a member there in good standing. In this case an invitation from the Baptist pulpit of all baptized members of other churches to the Lord's Supper necessarily includes him, and under it he could rightfully come and sit down at the very table from which he had just been excluded. Church discipline would thus be brought into utter contempt. It is evident, therefore, that no church, without gross inconsistency and confusion, can deal with members for such offences while inviting to this symbol of membership those who practise the same things.

Now, it seems plain that, as the Lord's Supper is a most solemn act of church-fellowship, none ought to partake except members of the church, or those who, from their doctrine and practice, could be consistently received to membership. An invitation of persons to this highest symbol of church membership whose principles or life would compel us to refuse them actual membership is hypocrisy.

Second: Pædobaptists are sincere in their view of the ordinances: ought not their sincere intention, therefore, to be accepted with us? As they have answered their own consciences, why not leave the subject of their baptism between them and God?

1. This is precisely where we do leave it. We do not impugn their sincerity. We do not censure—nay, we honor—them for celebrating the Lord's Supper according to their own views of duty. We simply claim for our consciences the same freedom which we accord to them. Believing, as we do, that the Lord of the Table has made baptism prerequisite, how can we, without a violation of conscience, disregard this law and invite those whom we believe to be unbaptized? For, however much we may honor men for their sincerity, certainly no one will pretend that a sincere intention creates the fact of baptism where the rite itself has not been performed. 2. In declining to invite to the Lord's Table, there is no necessary impeachment of the Christian character of the non-invited. For the law of the Supper does not require Christian character *only* as the condition of partaking: it demands also baptism and a consistent church membership. At the first celebration of the Supper, Christ did not invite the seventy, nor Lazarus, nor the Marys, nor even his own mother; but this was not an imputation on their Christian character. It was simply an exact observance of the law of the ordinance; for they were not yet, like the apostles, united with Christ in the peculiar fellowship of a church.

Third: All Christians expect to commune together in heaven; why should they not, then, commune together on earth?

1. If there is a wrong in separation at the Table, who are responsible for the wrong? Those who obey the law of the Supper? or those who disregard it? 2. The objection, however, implies a total misconception of communion at the Lord's Table. It confounds Christian and sacramental communion. There is no celebration of the Lord's Supper in heaven; but the communion of saints there, like the communion of saints here, consists in a holy fellowship of spirit, in sympathy, in spiritual intercourse, in worship. Such communion we enjoy freely with all Christians, whatever their name. But to confound this communion of Christian souls with the communion of the body and blood of Christ in the Eucharist is a strange confusing of very distinct things. For in the Supper there is no communion of Christians with one another, but each soul is silently communing with Christ in the symbolic communion (participation) of his body and blood.

Fourth: Restriction at the Lord's Table, as practised by the Baptists, is narrow and exclusive.

1. If there is exclusiveness it is not in the Baptist practice; for we require nothing of others which we do not also require of ourselves. The Lord's Table in our churches is open to all men on precisely the same conditions on which we approach it ourselves—that is, a simple compliance with the divine law of the Supper. We gladly welcome all those who in this are obedient to Christ. 2. The law of the Supper, as above defined, was not made by us, nor is it held only by us. It has been, and is, held by most evangelical Christians; they restrict the Supper to those whom they deem baptized and members of a church. The difference is not as to the law of the ordinance, but as to what is baptism and who are baptized.

They receive only those whom they deem baptized; we receive only those whom we deem baptized; but they have three forms of baptism, and we only one form. In neither case is the door to the Table wider than the baptism. If, then, there is any narrowness, it is in our baptism; but surely it is neither narrow nor exclusive to adhere firmly to what we believe to be God's law of the ordinances: this is simple fidelity to him. *The Interior*, the Presbyterian organ in Chicago, some time since uttered these just words: "The difference between our Baptist brethren and ourselves is an important difference. We agree with them, however, in saying that unbaptized persons should not partake of the Lord's Supper. Their views compel them to believe that we are not baptized and shut them up to close communion. Close communion, in our judgment, is a more defensible position than open communion, which is justified on the ground that baptism is not prerequisite to the partaking of the Lord's Supper. To chide Baptists with bigotry because they abide by the logical conseqences of their system is absurd."

V. UNRESTRICTED PARTICIPATION OF THE SUPPER INEXPEDIENT.

Union among different denominations at the Lord's Table has no real advantages, and is attended with manifold inconsistencies and evils.

For, 1. It supplies no deep and widefelt need. Each church celebrates the Lord's Supper as often as it deems expedient, ordinarily affording ample sacramental seasons for its members, and leaving neither desire nor opportunity for celebrating it with others. Indeed, Christians in general instinctively feel the impropriety of uniting in that symbol of church-fellowship in churches with which they could not conscientiously unite in membership. 2. It neither secures nor promotes Christian union. The truth is, the differences among Christians lie farther back than the Lord's Table; they originate in radically-opposed views of the constitution and ordinances of the church, and no mere sitting together in an outward ordinance can remove them. The labored and ostentatious attempts sometimes made to manifest Christian unity by a union in the celebration of the Supper have signally failed; for, while commonly attended by a gush of sentiment, they have neither lessened the rancor of theological and church antagonisms nor led to practical church union. Christian common sense instinctively perceives that there is, and can be, no union, except in the truth; true unity springs only from union in belief; no outward act can produce it. 3. It tends to the destruction of all church authority and discipline. In the widely-divergent views of Christian life among different churches, it renders consistent discipline impossible; for no church can discipline a member for an offence while inviting to the Table members of other churches guilty of the same offence. Thus the direct tendency of the practice is to lower the standard of Christian life, since no church adopting it can consistently require in its own members a style of Christian life higher than the very lowest type prevailing in any one of the churches which it invites to the Lord's Table. 4. Mingling of the baptized and the unbaptized at the Supper destroys the significance and value of both ordinances; for if baptism is not prerequisite to the Lord's Supper, it logically results that it is not prerequisite to church membership. Many of the "open-communion" churches of England have members, and even officers, who have never been baptized in any form, and in nearly all of these churches baptism, the divine symbol of regeneration, has ceased to have distinctive prominence and is administered in a corner. Besides, if this intermingling is practised, where shall the limit be placed? If all professing Christians are invited, then the church sits down with every man who chooses to call himself a Christian, however heretical, or even immoral, and thus all the significance of the ordinance is destroyed. If the invitation is restricted, as it usually is, to members of *evangelical* churches, then who shall determine what is an evangelical church?

Now, the restriction of participation at the Lord's Table within each denomination avoids all these evils. It is founded upon the obvious principle that the Lord's Supper, being an act of church-fellowship, should be administered only to members of the church, or to those who, from their views of doctrine and duty, might be consistently received as such. It implies no Christian disfellowship. It leaves ample scope for Christian charity, co-operation, and communion. It simply restricts the Lord's Supper, the highest symbol of church-fellowship, within each denomination. And, deeply as we must deplore the divisions existing among Christians, it is plain that while this diversity remains such as to require a separation into distinct denominations, it does equally require that all acts of church-fellowship be restricted within each denomination.

INDEX OF SUBJECTS.

ABRAHAMIC COVENANT, 181, 188.
Adjustment of differences in worldly affairs, 90.
Agamemnon, 175.
Agnes, St., catacomb of, 161, 162.
Alexander, 169.
   of Aphrodisius, 173.
Alford, 191, 227.
   on 1 Cor. x. 1, 2, 140.
   on Luke xii. 50, 137.
Ambrose, 209.
   chosen by the people, 42.
   on a font, 144.
Anglican Church, 181, 197.
   practised immersion until the sixteenth century, 150.
Annobius, 210.
Anthon, Dr., on baptizo, 119.
Apostles, qualifications and work, 67.
Apostolical Constitutions, 101.
Apostolic churches, not under a common government, 48, 49.
Apostolic Fathers, 200.
Aquinas, Thomas, on immersion, 148.
Aringhi, 161.
Armenian order of baptism, 158.
Associations, how composed, 56.
   purpose of, 57.
   voluntary nature of, 57.
Athanasius, 211.
   chosen by the people, 42.
Athenagoras, 210.
Augsburg Confession, 181.
Augustine, 193, 209, 211, 212.

BAPTISM, act of, during the Patristic period, 143.
   admitting to the church, 117.
   expressly appointed by Christ, 18.
   of Christ, 131–133.
   of the eunuch, 133.
   of jailer, 136.

Baptism, the form of, 118.
   language of Chrysostom on, 110.
   subjects of, 181.
   why given to infants, 110.
Baptismal regeneration, Anglican Church, 111.
   Luther, 111.
   Westminster Confession, 111.
Baptist confessions of faith in 1643 and 1689, 76.
Baptisteries, ancient, monuments of immersion, 152.
   at Cittanova, 153.
   at Florence, 153.
   at Gophna, 154.
   at Nocera, 152, 153.
   at Novara, 153.
   at Pisa, 153.
   at Ravenna, 153.
   at Tekoa, 154.
   at Verona, 153.
   of St. John Lateran at Rome, 152.
   recently discovered in Tyre, 153, 154.
   sixty-six in Italy, 152.
Baptists an illustration of unity, 50.
Baptizo, classic usage of, 118, 119.
   construction in which found, 123
   Cremer on, 122.
   Dr Anthon on, 119.
   Dr. Conant on, 118, 119.
   Liddell and Scott on, 119.
   New Testament usage of, 121–143.
   Patristic usage of, 143–146.
   Prof. Sophocles on, 122.
   Prof. Moses Stuart on, 119.
   Septuagint usage of, 119, 120, 121.
   Wilke, edited by Grimm, on, 122
Bapto, its meaning, 118.
   Prof. M. Stuart on, 118.

INDEX OF SUBJECTS.

Barnabas, 201.
Barnes, Dr. A., 190, 191.
Bartlett, President, error of, 155.
Basil, 172, 210, 211.
   on baptism, 143.
Beecher, Rev. T. H., 229.
Beit Jibrin, 133.
Bengel, 227.
Bethesda, 130.
Bethulia, fountains of, 120.
Bethzur, 133.
Beza, 227.
Bible the only authority on outward institutions of Christianity, 20.
Bingham, 222.
Bishops in the primitive churches, 102, 103.
   chosen by the people, 101.
   of second century, presiding officers among the presbyters, 75.
Bloomfield on baptism of Christ, 132.
Boldetti, 159.
Bosio, 159.
Bossuet, on immersion, 148.
Bottari on picture of baptism in catacomb of St. Pontianus, 156.
Brenner on immersion, 148.
Bugati on picture in San Celso, Milan, 156.
Bunsen, Chevalier, 204, 207.

CALIXTUS, catacomb of, fresco in, 156.
Calvin, 217, 222, 227.
   on immersion, 149.
Campbell, on baptism of Christ, 132.
   on the Fathers of the second and third centuries, 102, 103.
Catacombs, 159.
Catechumens, 210, 211.
Celsus, 206.
"Centennial Trustee Law," 65.
Charter of a church, 65.
Christ, reigns on the throne of the universe, 23.
   reigns in the invisible, spiritual church, 23.
Christian institutions a visible expression of divine truth, 16.
Christians, the great body of, Baptists in theory as regards the form of the ordinance, 152.
Church assembly at Jerusalem (Acts xv.) not a meeting of several churches, 49.

Church, a, composed of those associated to maintain the worship, truths ordinances, and discipline of the gospel, 35.
   composed of those baptized on a personal profession of faith, 34, 35.
   composed of believers in Christ, 29, 31.
   defined by Presbyterian standards, 31.
   definition of, 29.
   external relations of, 47–65.
   forms of incorporation in the United States, 64, 65.
   in things temporal subject to the state, 63, 64.
   in things spiritual independent, 64.
   officers of, 66–82.
   organization, 38.
   simplicity and effectiveness of organization, 82.
   relations to its members, 42–46.
   rights and duties of, 44.
   the, what it is, 24.
   true, not mere historic succession from the apostles, 95.
   uses of the word not found in the New Testament, 28, 29.
Churches, each accountable to Christ, 51.
   state, 31.
   subject to no external ecclesiastical control, 47.
Church members, rights and duties, 45, 46.
Church membership, Dr. Francis Wayland on rights of, 46.
   in Presbyterian Church, 31.
   in Protestant Episcopal, 32.
   in Roman Catholic Church, 31.
   regeneration as a condition of, 32–34.
Chrysostom, 168, 173, 178, 211.
   chosen by the people, 42.
   on baptism, 143, 144.
Chrystal, Rev. James, on catacombs 160, 161.
Clement of Alexandria, 208, 210.
Clement of Rome on election of church officers, 101.
Clinic baptism, opposition to, 144.
Coleman, 211.

INDEX OF SUBJECTS. 241

Coleman on the act of baptism in the early church, 145.
 on the form of baptism in the Eastern Church, 146.
Community of churches, their rights and duties, 54.
Conant, Dr. T. J., 175, 227.
 on baptizo, 119.
Congregational church organization, 39.
 its divine constitution, 39–43.
Consubstantiation, 216.
Conybeare and Howson on Rom. vi., 3, 4, 139.
Copais Lake, 175.
Copts, practise immersion, 155.
Cornelius, chosen Bishop of Rome through suffrages of people and pastors. 22.
Cote, Dr. W. N., his *Baptism and Baptisteries*, 152, 153.
Council, Fourth Lateran, 214.
 of Carthage, 209.
 of Nismes, allows pouring in case of danger, 148.
  requires immersion, 148.
 of Ravenna, decrees "aspersion or immersion," 148.
 of Trent, 214.
Councils, Baptist, how composed, 58.
 for the ordination of a minister, 59, 60.
 for recognition of a church, 58, 59.
 for settlement of difficulties in a church, 61, 62.
 for trial of a minister, 60, 61.
Covenant and articles of faith, written or printed, reasons for, 37.
Covenant of circumcision, 182–188.
Cranmer, 222, 228.
Cremer's lexicon, 166.
 on meaning of word *baptizo*, 122.
Cyprian, 193, 205, 207, 210.
 account of election of Cornelius, Bishop of Rome, 42.
 chosen bishop by the people, 101.
 on election of a bishop, 101.
Cyril of Jerusalem, 178.

Dale, Dr., his theory of baptism,164.
Deaconesses in some apostolic churches, 82.
Deacons, by whom chosen, 80.
 duties of, 80.

Deacons, earliest record of, 79.
 importance of their office, 81.
 powers of, in hierarchical churches, 81.
 recognized as distinct office, 79.
Demonax, 202.
De Rossi, the brothers, 160.
De Wette and Meyer on Mark vii. 3, 4, 124, 125.
Dialogue with a Jew, 178.
Dictionary of Christian Antiquities, on Catacombs, 160.
 on the mode of baptism in primitive times, 145.
Discipline, church, for offences against the laws of Christ, 88.
 Chrysostom of Constantinople, 102.
 Cyprian of Carthage, 102.
 Du Pin, 102.
 Origen of Cæsarea, 102.
 processes by which a church educates its members for heaven, 87.
Discipline of a minister, 93, 94.
"Divers washings," Prof. Stuart on Heb. ix. 10, 130.
Doddridge, 228.
Du Pin on church discipline in the early churches, 102.
Dwight, Pres., 229.

Egyptian boatman, 169.
Ekklesia, Christian usage of the word, 27–29.
 classic usage of the word, 25, 26.
 defined by Liddell and Scott, Cremer, and Trench, 25, 26.
 usage of the Septuagint, 26, 27.
 used in the New Testament 115 times, 27.
 used in the New Testament to designate a local assembly of Christians 92 times, 27.
 used to designate the whole body of Christ's redeemed in heaven and on earth, 27, 28.
Election of bishops in third and fourth centuries, 42.
Ellicott, Bishop, on Acts ii. 41, 129.
Enon, 131.
Ephesus, curious mistake of Mr. J. F. Wood at, 155.
Episcopal Church organization, 38.

Epistle of Ignatius, Stillingfleet on, 103.
Epistles of the Fathers, Bunsen on, 103
  genuineness of, 103.
  Neander on, 103.
  Usher on, 103.
  Wake on, 103.
Eusebius on the ordination of Novatian, 144.
Evangelists, their special work, 68.
Exclusion the final act of church power, 93.
Expediency, doctrine of, 15.

FARRAR on baptism of Christ, 132.
Flood, the, waters of baptism compared to, 141.
Font, Ambrose on its form, 144.
  destruction of, at Florence, by Francesco de Medici, 153.
Fountain of the Virgin, 130.
Fourth Lateran Council, 214.

GARUCCI, 159.
  on fresco in catacomb of St. Calixtus, 156.
General Assembly, 229.
German Reformers, 181, 197.
Gibbon on government of the early churches, 99.
Gieseler, 212.
Government of the early churches, 97.
Greek churches, immersion the practice of the, 146.
  act of sprinkling seven days after the immersion, 158, 159.
Gregory Nazianzen, 211, 212.
Griesbach, 116.
Griffin, Dr., 229.
Grotius on Mark vii. 3, 4, 124.

HACKETT, Dr. Horatio B., 190.
Hagenbach, 203, 212.
  on immersion, 148.
Hall, Dr. John, 229.
Hermas, 201.
  on baptism, 143.
Hibbard on baptism, 231.
Hippocrates, 169.
Hippolytus, 204.
Hodge, Dr. A. A., 229, 232.
"Homeric Allegories," 173.

IGNATIUS, 200.

Ignatius on episcopacy, 103.
Immersion of three thousand at Pentecost, 126–130.
Independency not isolation, 52.
  objections to, 47–51.
Infant baptism, 182.
Irenæus, 203, 204.

JEROME, 206, 209, 211.
  definition of a bishop, 100.
  on custom of the church in Alexandria, 76.
  on government of churches, 101.
Jerusalem, its supply of water, 127–129.
  three roads from, to Gaza, 133.
John the Baptist, 173.
Josephus, 175.
Justin Martyr, 178, 201, 202, 204, 208, 210, 222.
  on baptism, 143.

KIP, Bishop, strange blunder of, 161.
Knox, John, 222, 228.
  establishes sprinkling in the Scotch Kirk, 150.

LACHMANN, 116.
Lactantius, 210.
Lange, 190.
  on Acts i. 5, 137.
  on baptism of jailer, 136.
  on congregational election of officers, 41.
  on Luke xii. 50, 136.
Letters of dismission, 45.
Liddell and Scott, 169, 201.
Lightfoot, Canon, on Rom. vi. 3, 4, 139.
  report on discussion in Westminster Assembly, 150, 151.
Lingard on baptism in England before the Reformation, 149, 150.
Lord's Supper, the, 213.
  its first celebration, 234.
  obligatory on the church, 226.
  prophetic, 221.
  qualifications for, 222.
  restriction of, 228.
  symbolic, 219.
Lucian, 202.
Luther, 181, 218, 222, 228.
  his order of baptism, 149
  on immersion, 148.

INDEX OF SUBJECTS. 243

Lutheran Church, 230.
Lynch, Lieut., on width and depth of Jordan, 130, 131.

McLeod, Rev. J. N., 230.
Maimonides on Jewish ablutions, 130.
  on purification after defilement, 124, 125.
Marangoni, 159.
Marriott, Wharton B., on the double usage of immersion and affusion, 157, 158.
Mason, Dr. John M., 182, 183.
Meyer, 191, 192, 212, 227.
  on 1 Cor. x. 1, 2, 140.
  on Luke xi. 37, 38, 124.
  on Matt. iii. 11, 137, 138.
Ministers never called priests in the New Testament, 73.
Mishna, the, some of its precepts on immersion, 125.
Missionary enterprise in the Apostolic period, 53, 54.
  societies, 62, 63.
Montanists, 204, 205.
Mosaic at Ravenna in part a recent restoration, 156.
Mosaic institutions established after a divine model, 16.
Mosaics and frescoes, uncertain testimony of ancient, 157.
Mosheim, 212.
  on the constitution of the primitive churches, 97, 98.
Mystical presence, the, 217.

Neander, 181, 191, 197, 208, 209, 212.
  on elders in the apostolic churches, 75.
  on expediency, 15, 16.
  on Epistles of the Fathers, 103.
  on government of the primitive churches, 98.
  on original institution of baptism, 145.
Nesbitt, Alexander, on the double usage of immersion and affusion, 159.
  on the size of the early baptisteries, 159.
Nile, the, 169.
Noah, 141.
North Africa, six hundred and ninety bishoprics in, 103.

North African churches, 200, 207, 208, 209.
Northcote on Roman catacombs, 161.
Novatian, opposition to his ordination, 144.
  clinic baptism of, 144.

Officers in the church of divine constitution, 66.
  belonging only to the Apostolic period, 67, 68.
Olshausen, 191.
  on baptism of Christ, 132.
  on John iii. 23, 131.
  on Luke xii. 50, 136, 137.
"Open-communion" churches, 237.
Ordain, use and meaning of, in New Testament, 83.
"Ordained them elders," Acts xiv. 23, early English translation, 42.
Orders of clergy, in the Episcopal Church, 69.
  in the Papal Church, 69.
Ordinances, Christian, administrators of, 107.
  divine order of, 117.
  efficacy of, 110.
  not to be changed in form and order, 115, 118.
  number of, 106, 107.
  obligation of, denied by the Quakers, 109.
Ordinary officers in the church pastors and deacons, 69.
Ordination conferred by elders, 70.
  conferred by the ministry only, 84.
  confers no new grace or power, 85.
  form of, 85.
  historic succession maintained by some, 86.
  in Roman Catholic Church supposed to give divine powers, 83.
  perverted in hierarchical churches, 83.
  public investiture of church officers, 82.
  scriptural, 82.
  supposed twofold grace in, 86.
  three instances recorded in the New Testament, 84.
  of Timothy, exceptional circumstances of, 86, 87.
  supernatural gift or *charism* in, 87.

Ordination, Whately on regular succession, 87.
Origen, 205, 206, 207, 212.
　on choice and ordination of a presbyter, 101.

Pædobaptists, sincerity of, 234,
Papal Church, 197.
Pastors, duties of, 70-72.
　not priests, 73, 74.
　number in each church not fixed, 74.
Patristic authority, 13.
　no logical place among Protestants, 15.
Perret, 161.
Personal grievances, how to be adjusted, 89.
Phebe, deaconess of the church in Cenchrea, 82.
Plotinus, 172.
Plural eldership in the Apostolic age, 76.
　can it be set aside in the present age? 77.
Plutarch, 168, 169, 175.
Polybius, 172.
Polycarp, 200.
　exhortation to the Philippian church, 75, 100.
Pontianus, catacomb of, 156, 161.
Power of a church in things not divinely ordered, 42, 43.
　to elect its own officers, 40-42.
　to receive, discipline, and exclude members, 39, 40.
Presbyter, bishop, pastor, used interchangeably in New Testament, 69.
Presbyterian Church, distinction between presbyter and ruling elder in, 69.
　organization, 38, 39.
Priest, Christ the one eternal, 74.
Priesthood, blending characteristics of heathenism and Judaism, 73.
　two orders, Melchizedec and Aaron, 74.
Procedure in case of public offence, 91.
Prophets in the Apostolic period, their twofold function, 67, 68.
Protestant Episcopal Church, 38, 230.
Public pools in Jerusalem, 129.

Radbert Paschasius, 214.

Reformed Presbyterian Church, 230.
Robinson, Dr. Edward, on cisterns in Jerusalem, 127, 128.
　on dimensions of cisterns in Jerusalem, 128.
　on dimensions of pools in Jerusalem, 128.
　on road from Jerusalem to Gaza, 133, 134.
Roman Catholic Church, practised immersion until the thirteenth century, 147-149.
Roman pontifical on popular suffrage, 101, 102.
Royal priesthood all believers, 73.
Rufinus, 206.
Ruling elders in the Presbyterian Church, 77.
　in the New Testament, 77, 78.

Sacerdotalism appears early in the third century, 73.
Sacerdotal powers never conferred on the apostles, 86.
　never transmitted by them, 86.
Sacramentalism rejected by Baptists, 111, 112.
Sacraments, definition of by Augustine, 113.
　Council of Trent, 110, 111.
　Lutheran Church, 106.
　Roman Catholic Church, 106.
　Westminster Shorter Catechism, 106.
　number of, in Papal and Greek churches, 106.
　symbolic acts, as a profession of faith, 114.
　symbols of vital truths of the gospel, 113.
Samson, Dr. G. W., on sufficiency of water for baptizing in Jerusalem and elsewhere in Palestine, 128.
Schaff, Dr. Philip, 209, 210, 212.
　on Rom. vi. 3, 4, 139.
　on the act of baptism in the early church, 145.
　on the government of the early churches, 104.
Semisch, 202.
Seroux d'Agincourt, 159.
Siloam, 130.
Simon Magus, 178.
Sitt, Mariam, 155.

INDEX OF SUBJECTS. 245

Sophocles, Prof., meaning of word *baptizo*, 122.
Soul-liberty, maintained through ages of persecution by Baptists alone, 64.
 now fully recognized in the United States, 64.
Stanley, Dean, on the form of baptism in the Eastern Church, 146, 147.
Stier on Matt. iii. 15, 133.
Stillingfleet, 16.
Stourdza, Alexander de, on the distinctive characteristic of baptism, 147.
Strabo, description of Jerusalem, 127.
Stuart, Prof. Moses, 191, 193.
 on *baptizo*, 119, 122.
 on immersion, 146.
Synecdoche in Sirach xxxiv. 25 and in Heb. ix. 13, 120, 121.

TATIUS, Achilles, 169, 170.
Teachers and preachers, 68, 69.
Tell-el-Hazy, 133.
Tertullian, 193, 204, 205, 207, 208, 210.
 on baptism, 143.
 on the public worship of the church, 75.
"The Interior," its views on "close communion," 236.
Tischendorf, 116.

21 *

Tower of Antonia, its bathing-places 130.
Transubstantiation, 213.
Tregelles, 116.
Trench, definition of *ekklesia*, 26.
Tyre, baptistery recently discovered in, 153, 154.

UNITY a oneness of spirit, doctrine, and life, 50.

VENABLES, Rev. Edward, 160.
Vitringa, definition of *kahal*, 26.

WALL, Dr., 222.
Watch-care, Christian, enjoined in the gospel, 88.
Watts, 163.
Wayland, Dr. F., on rights of church members, 46.
Wesley, 197.
Westminster Assembly nearly equally divided on baptism, 150, 151.
Westminster Confession, 197.
Whately, Archbishop, 16.
 on apostolic succession, 87.
 on the government of the early churches, 100.
Wilke, meaning of word *baptizo*, 122
Winer, 203.
Woods, Dr., 193.

ZWINGLE, 217.

INDEX OF SCRIPTURES.

EXODUS.
14 : 31...........................140

LEVITICUS.
10 : 1–7.............................163
11 : 32...............................124
15 124
15 : 16...............................130
19 : 17.................................89
26 : 28...............................130

NUMBERS.
16 163
19 130
19 : 2–9.............................120

1st SAMUEL.
13 : 8–14..........................163

2d SAMUEL.
6 : 1–10............................163

2d KINGS.
5 : 14.................................119

PSALMS.
42 : 7.................................136

ISAIAH.
9 : 6, 7................................22
11 : 19.................................22
21 : 4.................................119
31 : 13...............................198

JEREMIAH.
31 : 31–34........................195

DANIEL.
7 : 13, 14............................22
9 : 23–27............................22

MICAH.
5 : 2.....................................22

JUDITH.
12 : 7.........................119, 120

SIRACH.
34 : 25......................120, 121

MATTHEW.
3 : 7–12.............................197
3 : 11............109, 137, 138, 140
3 : 15.................................131
3 : 16.................................131
5 : 1...................................135
15 : 9.................................198
17 : 24–27..........................64
18 : 1–6.............................189
18 : 15–17.....................89, 91
18 : 17..........................17, 39
18 : 18.................................18
18 : 20.................................47
19 : 13–15........................188
19 : 27...............................223
19 : 27, 28..........................67
20 : 22, 23........................136
22 : 21.................................64
25 : 26...............................134
26 : 29...............................221
28 : 19.........................34, 193
28 : 19, 20........................224

MARK.
1 : 9...................................175
1 : 9, 10.............................131
3 : 14..........................83, 223
7 : 3, 4........................123–126
10 : 15...............................189
10 : 28...............................223
16 : 15, 16........................194
16 : 16.................................24

LUKE.
6 : 13.................................223
11 : 37, 38.........................124
11 : 44...............................139
12 : 50...............................135
18 : 17...............................189

JOHN.
1 : 36–40...........................223
3 : 5......................24, 141, 209
3 : 23.................................131
4 : 1, 2...............................223
4 : 23, 24..........................111
4 : 53.................................191

6 : 53.................................215
6 : 63.................................215
17 : 11...............................113

ACTS.
1 : 5...................................137
1 : 15–26............................40
1 : 22...................................83
1 : 22, 23............................67
1 : 24...................................67
2 : 38, 39..........................189
2 : 38, 41, 42....................109
2 : 41..........................34, 126
2 : 41, 42..........................225
2 : 44, 46............................48
4 : 19, 20............................64
4 : 31, 32............................48
5 : 12, 13............................48
6 : 1–6....................40, 79, 81
6 : 2...................................41
6 : 2–5................................48
6 : 6.....................................84
8 : 12...................................35
8 : 14–17............................67
8 : 26, 40.....................24, 81
8 : 36–40.........109, 132, 133
8 : 38...................................27
9 : 31...................................28
10 : 2.................................191
10 : 47, 48........................110
11 : 15, 17..........................33
11 : 22.................................53
11 : 22–24..........................67
13 : 1–3........................64, 84
13 : 32, 33........................190
14 : 23...................18, 41, 83
15 : 1...................................48
15 : 22.................................48
16 : 15...............................191
16 : 15, 31–33..................192
16 : 29–34........................135
17 : 14.................................67
17 : 31.................................83
18 : 8.................................192
19 : 1–7.............................223
19 : 6...................................33
20 : 1...................................91
20 : 7..................109, 121, 225
20 : 17, 28..........................70
21 : 8...................................81
21 : 10, 11...........................67

21 : 21.................................193
21 : 22................................48
22 : 16..............................110
22 : 17-21..........................67

ROMANS.

6 : 1-14..............................35
6 : 3....................................18
6 : 3, 4.....................109, 138
6 : 4..................................130
6 : 17, 18...........................30
10 : 9................................141
11 : 16-24.......................187
12 : 6-8..............................78
14 : 17................................24
16 : 17................................40

1st CORINTHIANS.

1 : 16................................191
5..92
5 : 1-5................................39
5 : 9-13............................226
5 : 11................................221
6 : 1-11..............................90
7 : 14......................190, 192
9 : 1....................................67
10......................................216
10 : 12......................139, 140
10 : 14-22........................220
10 : 16, 17.......................227
10 : 17..............................216
11 ....43, 216, 225, 226
11 : 2, 20-34.....................18
11 : 23-26........................109
11 : 26..............................110
11 : 26, 27.......................216
12 : 28................................78
14..67
14 : 40................................43
16 : 3..................................41
16 : 15..............................192

2d CORINTHIANS.

2 : 1-11..............................92
2 : 4, 5...............................39

GALATIANS.

1 : 1....................................67
1 : 11-20............................67
3 : 2....................................33
3 : 26, 27.........................195
6 : 1....................................88
7 : 7-9................................67

EPHESIANS.

1 : 13, 14...........................33
1 : 20-23............................23
2 : 1....................................30
3 : 10, 21...........................28
4 : 8-13........................24, 66
5 : 25-27............................27
6 : 1..................................193

PHILIPPIANS.

1 : 1.....................18, 66, 80
4 : 3....................................82

COLOSSIANS.

1 : 18, 24...........................28
2 : 11, 12.........................186
2 : 12................................142
2 : 20-22..........................109
3 : 12-14............................88

2d THESSALONIANS.

3 : 6....................................40

1st TIMOTHY.

2 : 1, 2...............................64
2 : 7....................................83
3 : 1-5................................19
3 : 1-7................................70
2 : 1-13..............................66

3 : 1-15..............................18
3 : 4, 5...............................91
3 : 8-10..............................81
3 : 8-13..............................80
3 : 11..................................82
4 : 14...................70, 84, 87
5 : 9, 10.............................82
5 : 19..................................93
5 : 22..................................84

2d TIMOTHY.

1 : 6....................................87

TITUS.

1 : 5..............12, 19, 67, 70, 83
1 : 5-7................................70
3 : 1....................................64
3 : 5..................................141
3 : 10..................................91

HEBREWS.

2 : 12..................................27
9 : 10........................74, 130
9 : 13................................120
12 : 23................................28
13 : 7, 17............................79
13 : 17................................72

1st PETER.

1 : 23................................113
2 : 13-17............................64
3 : 21.................35, 130, 140
5 : 1, 2...............................70
5 : 1-4................................72

1st JOHN.

5 : 19..................................31

REVELATION.

1 : 15................................131
17 : 1................................131
19 : 3................................131
19 : 13..............................167

www.ingramcontent.com/pod-product-compliance
Lightning Source LLC
Chambersburg PA
CBHW031732230426
43669CB00007B/324